# CHATTANOOGA
## AN ILLUSTRATED HISTORY

*Where the ''Tennessee River breaks through the Cumberland Plateau, downstream from Chattanooga, there is a land of rugged beauty. Until the ''bad'' waters of this mountain stretch were drowned by the impounded waters of Hales Bar Dam in 1913, they seriously restricted navigation and turned Chattanooga toward a gateway to the South. Courtesy of the Tennessee Valley Authority.*

# CHATTANOOGA
## AN ILLUSTRATED HISTORY

BY JAMES W. LIVINGOOD

Sponsored by
The Chattanooga Area Historical Association
Windsor Publications, Inc.
Woodland Hills, California

ISBN 0-89781-027-9
Library of Congress Card Number: 81-51158
Windsor Publications, Woodland Hills, California

First Edition

# Contents

*"Trail of Tears," from the original painting of Robert Lindneux depicting the sad experience the Cherokee endured on the forced trek to new homes beyond the Mississippi River in 1838. Courtesy of the Woolaroc Museum, Bartlesville, Oklahoma.*

# Introduction

The complexities of writing local history—of balancing local detail with sweeping national trends—have always presented problems. Until fairly recently the task fell to genealogists or antiquarians; and this often led to an account of local affairs presented in a vacuum or colored by excessive regional pride. Gradually this has changed. The approach used in this volume stresses the concept of microcosm, but tells the story with an easy flow from era to era, including colorful episodes and personalized detail without the formality of a rigid structure.

Dr. James Livingood is the author chosen to write the script for this unfolding drama of the history of Chattanooga. As an adopted son of Chattanooga, having come from Princeton University in 1937, he is the acknowledged dean of historians in the area. He served the University of Tennessee at Chattanooga with distinction in a number of capacities as chairman of the history department, Dean of the College of Arts and Sciences, and Dean of the University. He was honored by being named Guerry Professor of History.

He has been appointed the official historian of Hamilton County.

Dr. Livingood has immersed himself in the history of the locale. He has looked carefully at the impact that the geographical location itself has had on Chattanooga history. He has carefully analyzed political trends on the national level and assessed their influence on local history. Beyond all this, he has studied carefully the personal histories of individuals, families, businesses, and institutions as they collectively made history in Chattanooga. He has brought talent and dedicated scholarship to this task.

Chattanoogans live on both sides of the Tennessee River in southeastern Tennessee and along the many ridges and valleys edging up to the border with the state of Georgia. A sense of community readily spills beyond the city limits involving places perched on the mountaintops, across the whole of Hamilton County, and even reaching into North Georgia neighborhoods.

Place has an important bearing on history, and the site of Chattanooga is no exception. Limitations of river navigation in the mountain reaches downstream from the city focused attention on a southern route where elevations proved minimal and a way around the southern shoulder of the Appalachians to the sea stood open. Ancient Indian trails used this gateway; the Cherokee in the early 19th century built the first roads for wheeled vehicular traffic this way. First settlers pointed out that Chattanooga's site marked the meeting point of the corn and cotton country and within a generation a railroad laced the corridor southward. Union military strategy emphasized the advantage of splitting the Confederacy; Chattanooga's gateway with its rail facilities offered the natural route that General Sherman took.

However, place means nothing without people and Chattanooga's story is one of a great passing parade. Stone Age natives took the longest time in passing—to be pushed aside in their closing chapter by Europeans. Spanish, French, and English peoples flew their flags proclaiming their title to the land; many never saw the region but, like some English leaders who arbitrarily drew a line on the map which today is the Georgia-Tennessee border, they had a lasting historical input.

After the American Revolution when the Tennessee country became a federal territory and then a state in 1796, vast stretches including the Chattanooga area remained Indian country. Not until long after Knoxville and Nashville were founded and not until Andrew Jackson was 71 years old did Ross's Landing become Chattanooga. Then this urban frontier assumed the role of a railroad junction that brought the soldiers of the 1860s to the region. The destiny of some 2,500 citizens at this time was definitely not in their own hands. The Reconstruction debt paid for secession followed, but local residents found a path to reunion at an early date and as the 19th turned into the 20th century, the economy gradually found its way into the American mainstream.

The inclusion of a number of appropriate pictures adds to the pleasure of reading Dr. Livingood's interesting text.

Spencer J. McCallie, Jr.
President, Chattanooga Area Historical Association

# Chronology

**1540**
(June) The Spanish expedition of Hernando De Soto passed through the area.

**1663**
The British established the colony of Carolina, which included all of the Tennessee country. About the same time French from the Mississippi Valley also claimed the land.

**1763**
England gained undisputed title to the territory at the close of the French and Indian War.

**1769** (ca.)
First permanent pioneer settlement west of the Appalachian Mountains established in upper East Tennessee.

**1777**
(Spring) Chickamauga Indians, a splinter group of Cherokee under Chief Dragging Canoe, moved to South Chickamauga Creek villages; they resisted white settlement and cooperated with the British in the American Revolution.

**1779**
(April) Frontiersmen under Col. Evan Shelby destroyed the Chickamauga villages in rear guard military action, an important phase of the Revolution.

**1785**
(Nov. 25) By the Treaty of Hopewell the U.S. government took over control of Indian affairs.

**1790**
(Apr. 2) North Carolina ceded the Tennessee country to the United States; it was established as a federal territory with William Blount as governor.

**1794**
(Sept. 13) Ignoring federal policy, militiamen destroyed the chief Chickamauga towns, ending the struggle between the Indians and the settlers, which had included several earlier engagements on Lookout Mountain.

**1796**
(June 1) Tennessee became the 16th state, but Indian lands made up about three-fourths of the area, including the Chattanooga area.

**1801-23**
Return Jonathan Meigs was appointed Cherokee Indian agent—the first government representative to reside in the area.

**1805**
(Oct. 25) The Cherokee and the U.S. agreed to open first vehicular roads in the area.

**1816** (ca.)
Ross's Landing established at the (later) site of Chattanooga.

**1817-38**
Brainerd Mission operated by the American Board of Commissioners for Foreign Missions. Its leaders encouraged Sequoyah, who presented his syllabary to the Cherokee Nation in 1821.

**1819**
(Oct. 25) Hamilton County was established on lands north of the Tennessee River; in 1820 it had 821 residents.

**1828**
(Spring) First steamboat, the *Atlas*, ascended the Tennessee River to Knoxville.

**1828**
(Oct.) John Ross was elected first Principal Chief of the Cherokee Nation. Until 1838 he successfully resisted removal of his people to the West.

**1837**
(March 22) U.S. Post Office opened at Ross's Landing with John P. Long in charge.

**1838**
(July 19) First issue of the *Hamilton Gazette*, soon called the *Chattanooga Gazette*, printed by Ferdinand A. Parham.

**1839**
(Dec. 20) The Tennessee legislature passed an act "to establish the Town of Chattanooga. . . ."

**1850**
(May 9) The Western & Atlantic Railroad ran the first through-train from Atlanta to Chattanooga.

**1854**
(Feb. 11) The Nashville & Chattanooga Railroad completed.

*This sketch, by artist Theodore R. Davis depicts a steamboat being warped through the Suck. Six men labor at the windlass. From* Harper's Weekly Magazine, *1864.*

**1857**
(Mar. 28) The last spike was driven in the Memphis & Charleston Railroad.

**1858**
The East Tennessee and Georgia Railroad completed a direct line between Chattanooga and eastern cities.

**1861**
(June 8) Tennessee voted to secede from the Union. Chattanooga favored this decision, while a Hamilton County majority voted to stay in the Union.

**1861**
(Nov. 9) Bridge burners tried to disrupt rail service in East Tennessee. Unionists destroyed two local spans; as a result, the first Confederate troops arrived in the town on Nov. 14.

**1862**
(Apr. 12) Andrews' Raid on the W&A Railroad.

**1862**
(June 7-8) Federal troops fired on Chattanooga from the north bank of the river.

**1862**
(July 27) Confederates began concentration of men in the Chattanooga area for their Kentucky Campaign.

**1863**
(Sept. 9) Confederate forces evacuated Chattanooga; advance Union units entered the city.

**1863**
(Sept. 19-20) Battle of Chickamauga.

**1863**
(Sept. 21-Nov. 25) Union army besieged in Chattanooga.

**1863**
(Nov. 24) Battle of Lookout Mountain.

**1863**
(Nov. 25) Battle of Missionary Ridge.

**1863**
(Christmas Day) General George Thomas established the National Cemetery.

**1864**
(May 5) General William Sherman with some 100,000 troops began the Georgia Campaign from his Chattanooga base.

**1865-66**
(Winter) Chattanooga troops demobilized, forts dismantled, and army surpluses disposed of.

**1867**
(March) Largest recorded flood on the Tennessee River.

**1869**
(Dec. 15) First issue of Chattanooga *Times*; ownership passed to Adolph S. Ochs on July 2, 1878.

**1870**
(Dec. 5) Hamilton County courthouse moved to Chattanooga.

**1872**
(July 18) Chattanooga started publicly supported schools; Tennessee's program began the next year.

**1878**
(Aug.-Nov.) Yellow fever epidemic.

**1880**
(July 3) Telephone exchange opened.

*James Hall represented a touch of new life when it opened in 1870 as the first theater in the city booking road attractions. (CHCBL)*

**1882**
(May 6) First electric lights.

**1885**
(Aug.) Construction of Lookout Mountain's first incline railroad begun; the present line completed Nov. 16, 1895.

**1886**
(Sept. 15) Chattanooga University enrolled first students.

**1890**
(Aug. 18) U.S. Government established Chickamauga Chattanooga National Military Park; dedicated Sept. 18-20, 1895.

**1891**
(Feb. 18) Walnut Street bridge dedicated.

**1898**
(April-Sept.) Camp George H. Thomas on Chickamauga battlefield trained Spanish-American War soldiers.

**1899**
(July 12) Ben F. Thomas and Joseph B. Whitehead signed contract for exclusive right to bottle Coca-Cola.

**1904**
(Apr. 27) U.S. agreed to building of Hales Bar Lock and Dam; completed Nov. 13, 1913.

**1904**
(Dec.) Fort Oglethorpe established as a permanent military post.

**1915**
Dixie Highway Association, led by Chattanoogans, linked the Middle West with Florida by highway.

**1917**
(Nov. 16) Market Street bridge dedicated.

**1930**
Lovell Field opened.

**1933**
(May 18) Tennessee Valley Authority created.

**1935**
(Mar. 12) Chattanooga voted for public power; Electric Power Board created a month later.

*This bustling street scene at Fountain Square provides an interesting glimpse of turn-of-the-century styles of dress and modes of transportation. Courtesy of the Chattanooga Convention and Visitors Bureau.*

**1936**
(Aug. 31) Chattanooga *Free Press* published first daily.

**1940**
(Sept. 2) President F.D. Roosevelt dedicated Chickamauga Dam.

*The unveiling of a marker identifying the community's original site; Mayor "Pat" Rose at far right.*

**1943**
(June) Fort Oglethorpe designated Third Women's Army Auxiliary Corps training center; Fort closed Dec. 31, 1946.

**1946**
(July 3) Tennessee Temple University launched.

**1954**
(Apr. 25) Chattanooga's first TV Station, Channel 12, went on the air.

**1958**
(July) Golden Gateway urban renewal began; completed Dec. 1976.

**1962**
(Aug. 29-30) Desegregation of Chattanooga and Hamilton County schools began.

**1965**
(Sept. 20) Chattanooga State Technical Community College opened.

**1969**
(July 1) University of Chattanooga became a major campus in the University of Tennessee system along with Chattanooga City College.

**1971**
(May 1) Last railroad passenger service.

**1976**
(Oct. 17) Chattanooga Hamilton County Bicentennial Library opened.

**1980**
TVA completed Raccoon Mountain Pump-Storage-Hydro Plant and the Sequoyah Nuclear Plant.

*In August 1935 the Chickamauga Dam project was assured. Courtesy of the Tennessee Valley Authority.*

On the "new" Tennessee River barges and tugs have replaced steamboats. The nine-foot channel means no more waiting for the "tide." Grain, soybeans, sand, gravel, fuel oil, asphalt, and iron-steel products make up the bulk of the tonnage. Courtesy of the Tennessee Valley Authority.

## Chapter One
# The Tennessee River, Old and New

The site of Chattanooga occupies the southern limits of the Great Valley of East Tennessee, which in turn is the southern portion of a huge geological trough extending from Pennsylvania. The valley is framed by the Unaka Mountains to the east and the Cumberland Plateau to the west. Trimming the plateau's edge under the name Walden Ridge stands an almost continuous line of cliffs broken only by occasional rocky stream-cut notches reaching back into the tableland. To the east rise the ancient Unakas—often popularly called the Great Smoky Mountains—which are a constant barrier to easy travel.

Another name for this extensive furrow is the Valley and Ridge Province; all of the land forms are generally slanted from the northeast to the southwest and within the valley proper many minor ridges and valleys of all widths, heights, and lengths variegate the pattern. To one of vivid imagination the landscape appeared "as if the Titans had plowed and forgotten to harrow it." Only

a few satisfactory passageways allowed for trails or roads "across country" (east-west); most travelers and trade moved "up and down country."

Through this valley, crowded with geologic faults and burdened with folded, twisted, and compressed rock, flowed the Tennessee River—wandering and untamed until it was put in harness after 1933 by the Tennessee Valley Authority. It gathered its waters from the hills of north Georgia, from tributaries rushing through deep wild gorges lost in the mountain fastnesses of North Carolina, and from long parallel streams with headwaters in Virginia. Although far from its mouth, the serpentine waterway was already a mature river with a wonderful timeless history. Like a true western stream, it was filled with shoals and reefs, gravel and sand bars, snags and sawyers.

Heavy seasonal rains—a yearly average of 51 inches—and the steep, rugged topography caused heavy spring freshets and recurring floods normally fol-

*On Walden Ridge, rushing streams and waterfalls match the beauty of Lookout Mountain. This picture of Falling Water Falls shows one of the more striking views. (CHCBL)*

name Tennessee was chosen to honor a Cherokee town called Tunnissee, Tanase, Tenese, or some other spelling variation.

Southwest of Chattanooga, near the entrance to a mountain gorge, the river passes a sentinel unique in its shape and grandeur. Like the many mountains nearby it has forested sides, cascading streams, a palisade crown and wears a variety of seasonal colors. But Lookout Mountain with its surroundings of mingled valleys stands out as a natural landmark which through the years has symbolized the silent strength, endurance, and beauty of nature. It is Chattanooga's logo. *(See side bar.)*

Opposite the promontory of Lookout Mountain, the Tennessee twists in every direction, outlining the shape of a giant Indian's moccasin. This gigantic fellow's footwear became the nickname for a local university's teams. Here at the bend of the river ancient Indians lived, Civil War cannon fired, and engineers moved the river to make room for a modern Interstate Highway at the mountain's base.

After the Tennessee River flows past Lookout Mountain, instead of continuing a southern course through a slight divide and on to the Gulf of Mexico, the contrary river chose to leave the East Tennessee Valley by cutting its way through the Cumberland Plateau.

The mountain which Lookout faces across the Tennessee River gorge is the southern point of Walden Ridge, where in the 20th century the town of Signal Mountain developed. Walden Ridge, named for a Tennessee long hunter of pioneer vintage, possesses many of the same rough and irregular physical features as its companion to the south.

Downstream from Lookout Mountain and Moccasin Bend the river enters a narrow canyon chiseled into the Cumberlands and curves away to the southwest, with Raccoon Mountain rising on one bank and Walden Ridge on the other. Steep wooded slopes climb from the water's edge to a ring of cliffs of gray sandstone

lowed by shirttail depths in summer and early fall. Boatmen using the old river constantly rounded bends and confronted new vistas. Early mapmakers, too, had a difficult time finding a standard name for the stream. They called the waterway or sections of it Acansea Sipi, Cusatees, Hogohegee, Callamaco, Kallamuchee or Kallamak, Cherokee or Rivière des Cheraquis. Finally, the

# LOOKOUT MOUNTAIN: TALL AND PERMANENT

*Lookout Mountain, once described as a "noble pile of stratified limestone with a huge lump of sandstone at the top," is a constant landmark in a changing world. Crowned with a ring of palisades, it affords panoramic vistas in all directions. From* Appleton's Journal, *1871.*

Only three miles of the northern end of Lookout Mountain lie in Tennessee, with the remaining 80 or more miles in Georgia and Alabama. Years ago it carried an Indian name, "Chatanuga," which was borrowed by the city in 1838. A Creek word meaning "rock that comes to a point," the word as translated from the Cherokee meant "mountains looking at each other." In the early 1800s the name Lookout Mountain came into general use.

Exactly how this change occurred is not known. A varied assortment of explanations has been offered but most seem to be mere theories. One notes that the mountain provided a natural "lookout" over the surrounding countryside; another refers to a warning to navigators of the river's rough waters in the "Narrows." A third version explains that flatboatmen never undertook to run the Suck at night but took refuge in the evening in the mouth of Chattanooga or Lookout creeks. Hidden robbers made forays on the boatmen, robbing and sometimes murdering them. Word of these desperadoes spread throughout East Tennessee and warnings were given parties planning river trips: "When you pass Ross's Landing, look out for robbers." Before long the name became fixed to the mountain itself.

When Elias Cornelius, Yale graduate and young New England minister, visited the Indian Mission at Brainerd in 1817 on church business, his inquisitive mind led him on a trip up the mountain at the time when the entire area remained Indian country. He wrote with feeling:

*The summit of Lookout Mountain overlooks the whole country. And to those who can be delighted with the view of an interminable forest, penetrated by the windings of a bold river, interspersed with hundreds of verdant prairies, and broken by many ridges and mountains, [it] furnishes in the month of May a landscape which yields to few others in extent, variety, or beauty.*

*Top*
*Elias Cornelius, never insensitive to natural beauty, visited Lookout Mountain when he stayed at Brainerd Mission. His "word picture" is the first known recorded description of the mountain. (CHCBL)*

*Above*
*Today, thousands of tourists visit the caverns on Lookout Mountain. After passing the stalactites and stalagmites along a long corridor, the visitor comes to a large room, 1,120 feet beneath the surface of the earth, where a spectacular 145-foot underground waterfall continues to amaze cavern visitors. Courtesy of Ruby Falls.*

Other mission people also made their way to the mountaintop to examine its unusual geological formations. Typical of the entire region, Lookout represents eons of geological change: tidal flats with coal-producing debris, intense disturbances and eruptions creating new mountains, the appearance of anticlinal heights followed by erosion from wind and rain that resulted in a "reversal of topography." In this process lower, weaker rock wore away until the heights became valleys and valleys became uplands. So today Lookout Mountain's exposed rock strata point upward toward the peaks which once towered over Chattanooga and Lookout valleys.

But the men from Brainerd came mainly to explore the caverns penetrating the mountain's limestone base, the cascades such as those at Lu Lu Falls, and the sculptured

sandstone formations on the top. In 1823 after visiting the region of Rock City, one missionary wrote about this "citadel of rocks":

*This is just at the top of the mountain, and is composed of rocks as high as houses, one, two, or three stories. It is so situated as to afford streets and lanes to form many convenient shelters from the heat, rain, and wind. Especially we noticed one apartment twelve by fifteen and six feet high in the highest place, arched overhead and walled on each side by solid rock, except an opening for a door, and one or two places in the corners, which would serve for chimneys. This natural fortress was formerly inhabited by the Creeks. We saw where they hung their meat and where they prepared their lodgings. Here, after viewing for a moment the wonders of the Omnipotence, being retired from all the world, we bowed with adoration before Him, whose favor is compared to the shadow of a great rock in a weary land.*

*Above*
*Montlake on Walden Ridge has for generations stimulated the imagination of visitors as to its origin and reasons for its unusual circular shape. (CHCBL)*

*Left*
*This waterfall and lake, once called Seclusion and later Lu lu, Lulah, Lula, or Lulu, attracted Civil War soldiers; today it entices hikers, picnic parties, and swimmers. Here the mountain stream pours into a wild gorge of steep cliffs and boulders. Courtesy of U.S. Signal Corps, Brady Collection, National Archives.*

*Far Left*
*This photograph, taken in 1886, depicts the rough terrain that construction workers were faced with when building the narrow gauge railway on Lookout Mountain. (CHCBL)*

1,000 feet overhead. Early rivermen called the 20 or more miles of this mountain stretch of the river the "Narrows" or sometimes the "Suck"; enthusiastic writers dubbed it the "Valley of the Whirlpool Rapids," while modern tour guides label it the "Grand Canyon of the Tennessee."

When the first steamboat from the Ohio laboriously ascended the Tennessee River in 1828, an editor noted that passage through this stretch of water downstream from Ross's Landing had been "impossible to be performed by any being or thing except the sturgeon and the catfish." *(See side bar.)*

After breaking at last through the Cumberlands, the river crosses the Sequatchie Valley and dips into northern Alabama and Mississippi before turning northward to meet the Ohio River in western Kentucky. On the way it encounters the Muscle Shoals, a second major deterrent to navigation where extensive rapids, reefs, islands, and white water produced that famous 30-mile hazard. This maelstrom along with the "Narrows" prevented the Tennessee from becoming an artery of western pioneer migration like the Ohio River, but some braved the trip.

The Tennessee resembled a stream broken into three distinct sections rather than a continuous watery highway. In the Chattanooga area these conditions helped underline the need to use an overland gateway to the south. They also inspired people who saw great

possibilities in the river itself to propose, at various times, ambitious alterations in the Tennessee's riverbed and its surrounding terrain—to result in the Chattanooga we know today as well as other developments along the length of the river.

Ross's Landing—consisting of a decrepit ferry, a crude cabin for the ferryman, and a "kind of shanty for goods" on the southern bank of the Tennessee River—marked the start of Chattanooga. About 1816 the small settlement began to serve the local trade and also became a transfer point for river traffic to roads running through a gateway to the south and on around the shoulder of the Appalachian Mountains. The Landing, surrounded by virgin forests, represented the business interests of the brothers John and Lewis Ross, youthful Cherokee Indians of mixed blood.

*Top Left*
*Moccasin Bend as viewed from Lookout Mountain. The Bend throughout the years has been a kind of Chattanooga trademark. Courtesy of the Chattanooga Convention and Visitors Bureau.*

*Above*
*The steamboat* Paint Rock, *passing through the Suck, as sketched by Fred B. Schell. The Suck remained a navigation barrier until 1913 when Hales Bar Lock and Dam drowned the turbulent waters. From* Leslie's Illustrated, *February 6, 1864.*

# THE NARROWS

Colorful local expressions early described specific sites within the Narrows section of the Tennessee south of Ross's Landing, the beginnings of Chattanooga. Turbulent waters began with the Tumbling Shoals, which in certain seasons was a wild, roaring rapid. Next came the Suck—an old English word for whirlpool. Here the channel narrowed with rocks jutting into the current throwing the water into piles and creating a gigantic whirl; at this same spot a wild mountain tributary, Suck Creek, poured its rushing waters and their burden of debris into the river. Although he never saw the place, that inquiring naturalist, Thomas Jefferson, wrote of it as a "whirlpool called Sucking-pot, which takes in trunks of trees or boats, and throws them out again half a mile below."

Farther along were other troubled waters called the Pot, the Skillet, and the Pan. Collectively the entire mountain stretch was often generically referred to as the Suck.

This spectacular area prompted the imaginative Cherokee to spin fanciful myths about the river's strange formations and frontier tellers of tall tales to exaggerate the dangers. One of these latter stories caught the attention of a scribe for *Harper's Magazine* in 1858. He told of a local river pilot engaged to guide a party through the Suck. Although night was descending, they started out without fear, for their liquor supply was good. When they passed a house where a fiddler was playing Old Zip Coon and people were dancing, the group on board drank to their health. The pilot continued:

*So we went on pretty sprightly: and, by jingo, before we got well out [of] sight and hearin' of that house we went past another, whar' they were dancin' to the same tune. "Success to 'em!" says I. "Hand us the bottle; while fun is goin', we might as well have our share." So we drank a mouthful, and before we were done talking about it we went past another place, fiddlin' and dancin' like the rest.*

By two o'clock they had passed nine houses in the "jolliest settlement ever I traveled through," according to the traveler. If they came to another, he insisted on tying up and joining the fun. Sure enough they came to another party but as they headed for the landing, the pilot realized where he was. He told it to the *Harper*'s man this way:

*Now, stranger, how do you think it was? Why, this was old Jack Cogle's house, down thar fornense the Bilin' Pot, whar some fellers and some gals were dancin' around all night; and we went bilin' around and passin' by the same place over and over agin! Now at fust it come to me like a sort of a dream; then it was all clare; and without waitin' to be cussed or laughed at, I streaked it. But it's all true, jist as I tell ye.*

Within a decade of the founding of Ross's Landing the United States government recommended a program of internal improvements including a recognition of the national significance of the Tennessee River. Colonel Stephen H. Long of the U.S. Topographical Engineers—a foremost expert in the field—surveyed the stream in 1832 and reported optimistically of its potential. Such encouragement, combined with the appearance of steamboats on the upper Tennessee, resulted in simple navigational improvements at the Suck and at other spots; Chattanoogans led the valley in cheering for this sporadic work. They also joined in the promotional talk for a "Southern Route" from the region to the Gulf of Mexico, a century and a half forerunner of the Tennessee-Tombigbee Waterway now being built.

State and national pork barrel legislation tended to minimize the work of improving the hazardous, snag-studded stream while faulty technology defeated an effort to build a canal around Muscle Shoals. A satirist relates the major problem of these early years: "I have bin to the legislator, gentlemen, and I know how this improvement bisniss works. When I ax for money to improve Tennessee river, every feller in the whole legislator wants some too to improve some branch or creek in his county; and there aint money enough. . . ."

No channel improvements were made during the 1860 war years, but immediately after peace came, the valley people petitioned the federal government for financial aid to renew work. A river convention met in Chattanooga in 1867, attended by 143 delegates: river improvements would awaken the "latent elements of prosperity" and federal help would strengthen the reunion between the North and South, their spokesmen claimed. Other meetings followed as the states' rights theme was de-emphasized.

The U.S. Army Corps of Engineers maintained an important office in Chattanooga from 1867 until 1933.

The officers assigned to this district participated in community affairs and enjoyed the support of the city in their open-channel work and in the supervision of construction of a second Muscle Shoals canal. Again, however, hopes overshadowed final accomplishments.

Before the turn of the century a new factor had a bearing on river improvement discussions: the generation of hydroelectric energy. Hales Bar Lock and Dam, 33 miles downstream from Chattanooga, became a pioneer project for multipurpose service on the entire river. Built over a period of eight years at an astronomical cost for that era, this 1,200-foot dam averaging 52 feet in height impounded waters that drowned the Suck and turned the turbulent mountain stretch of the river into a smooth waterway.

*Above Left*
*Colonel Stephen H. Long surveyed the upper Tennessee in 1832. At the mountain stretch in the "Narrows" a member of his party drowned. Courtesy of the Department of the Army, Nashville District, Corps of Engineers.*

*Above Right*
*The Corps of Engineers closed its Chattanooga District office in 1933, when major responsibilities for the Tennessee River were turned over to the TVA. This meant the loss of General Robert R. Neyland, one of the most popular officers who served here. Courtesy of the Army Corps of Engineers.*

But the Hales Bar Dam itself, authorities confessed, "became a problem, taking on a fifty-year parade of engineers and beating them every time." The dam leaked even before it was completed because of the limestone foundation. Cinders, sand, clay, baled hay, wire, and a variety of junk were dumped into the crevices as well as ladies' corsets which, it was claimed, "did not stop the leaks but may have left them in better shape." Nevertheless, the first multipurpose dam on the Tennessee River not only solved the old navigation problem but it also brought electric current to Chattanooga.

During the immediate post-World War I years the Engineers made comprehensive studies of the whole Tennessee River system and wrote up an exhaustive report. Doggedly pursued by Major Harold C. Fiske, it became the blueprint for multipurpose proposals and was available when the Tennessee Valley Authority was created on May 18, 1933. With TVA the major tasks of the Corps of Engineers on the Tennessee River were ended and the new Authority assumed responsibility. The office of the Corps in Chattanooga closed amid scenes of grief and distress; the city had not only supported their labors over the years but in 1933 the res-

*The Hales Bar Lock and Dam became the first multi-use dam on a major river in the United States. Plagued with foundation problems, construction lasted from 1905 to 1913. The dam was acquired by TVA as part of the purchase of the Tennessee Electric Power Company's facilities in 1939. The leaky dam was replaced in 1967 by Nikajack Dam and then destroyed. Courtesy of the Tennessee Valley Authority.*

ident engineer was the very popular, dynamic General Robert R. Neyland. In addition to his engineering duties, Neyland taught military science at the University of Tennessee and molded the Vols into football legend.

TVA plunged into its task of taming the Tennessee River and creating a "new geography" for the region. Main river dams cause the once unruly river to "walk" to the Ohio in giant steps and create the Great Lakes of the South. Tributary storage dams establish a steady water flow and reduce the threat of disastrous floods. Managed forests, cover crops, and modern industry line these new banks along with wooded homesites, recreational facilities, marinas, and parklands.

In the immediate Chattanooga area TVA purchased the Hales Bar Dam in 1939 with its hydro and steam-generating facilities. The dam, still leaking, was reconstructed and raised to meet minimum requirements but it continued to be a stubborn reminder of the fractious river and was finally replaced by Nickajack Dam in December 1967.

Upstream, Chickamauga Dam was the site of dedicatory exercises featuring President Franklin D. Roosevelt on Labor Day, 1940. The 5,800-foot dam with a maximum height of 129 feet and a lock-lift of 55 feet completely changed the area. It created a 58.9-mile-long lake with 810 miles of shoreline. Although the circuitous course of the river still carries commerce in a roundabout route, the Tennessee River beginning in 1933 has been engineered into a new waterway. Powerful tugs and utilitarian barges have replaced the steamboat packets; Indian tradition and place names remain, but the nostalgia of bygone days has largely disappeared.

*Chickamauga Dam with its 58.9-mile-long lake was dedicated on Labor Day of 1940. Within the city limits of modern Chattanooga, this facility mirrors the technology of 20th century America, while its name recalls past days when Indians used the river and local* *trails. Courtesy of the Tennessee Valley Authority.*

*When the Hales Bar Lock and Dam construction was undertaken, no one dreamed of the problems a limestone region would present. Locally, Josephus Guild, Sr. and Charles E. James pioneered the project, which turned the turbulent Tennessee River currents into* *hydroelectric assets. Courtesy of Anthony Cortese.*

Dallas Island, about a half mile from the mouth of Wolftever Creek, was a wilderness metropolis. This Middle Mississippian cultural center occupied the island and both shores of the river, all of which now lie beneath the waters of Chickamauga Lake. Courtesy of the University of Tennessee Press. Illustration by M. Kneberg.

## Chapter Two
# First Residents and Visitors

Neither the missionaries nor modern scholars can readily imagine the time span measured in uncounted millenia before the first humans took shelter in caves and overhangs. Scientists suggest some 15,000 to 40,000 years have now passed since anonymous hunters from out of Asia crossed the North American continent. Campsites and fluted points of stone reveal a local occupancy of these Ice Age fellows who today are called Paleo-Indians. Their culture, like that of an old Stone Age people, remained practically unchanged for centuries; their possessions, very few in number, alone tell of their presence.

A more advanced people followed them some 8,000 years ago. These aboriginal residents knew how to manage fire, dine on river mussels, and live in fairly substantial huts. The use of a spear-throwing device which increased their hunting range was the most outstanding accomplishment of these natives whose assigned name is Archaic Indians. Archaic homesites included Russell Cave in northern Alabama, areas along Nickajack Reservoir, and the lands of Moccasin Bend.

Around 1,000 B.C., a third major migratory group—the Woodland Indians—arrived in the Tennessee Valley. They possessed a much more advanced culture and technology: they domesticated plants, knew the arts of weaving and of pottery, and used the bow and arrow. Woodland people lived on Williams Island, Moccasin Bend, at Citico and South Chickamauga creeks, on Dallas and Hiwassee islands, and other river locations.

These natives are best known for their mounds, which served as ceremonial burial centers. Throughout East Tennessee they have been called by the archaeologists the Hamilton Indians because of their dominance in the local county. Their earthen mounds represent a centralized society and contain along with the remains of the deceased a rich collection of tools, jewelry, trinkets, and pottery from which today's student reads the past.

About 1,000 years ago another cultural era dawned. The new life-style of the Mississippian Indians was more sophisticated culturally and advanced technologically although fundamentally it continued to be of the Stone Age. They brought to the southeast a working knowledge of Middle American culture and emerged as the most prominent southern natives. From the Chattanooga area northward through the Tennessee Valley their presence and superiority were best expressed in majestic temple mounds.

One of these great mounds rose on Hiwassee Island, where a public square, large civic structures, and temples crowned the elevation; the entire area of some 10 acres was enclosed by a palisade. Downstream another Mississippian town stood as a rural metropolis. Located on the 84-acre Dallas Island and the two banks of the river, it once had three large temple mounds. Today this symbol of indigenous splendor lies submerged under Lake Chickamauga, with only one small portion existing as a "new" island at the site of the present Hamilton County Park.

At centers like Dallas the natives gathered in the public square to talk wilderness politics, argue over the games played at the nearby chunky-yard, and trade copper, conch shells, and other valuables brought from a distance.

*Left*
*Indian technology very slowly emerged, reinforcing early man's skill and ability to hunt. Archaic man used a contrivance for spear throwing which increased the speed and distance the weapon traveled. Courtesy of the University of Tennessee Press.*

ARCHAIC HUNTER
WITH SPEAR-THROWER

One June day in 1540 the first Caucasian wayfarers arrived in the area. Headed by the hardy Spanish conquistador Hernando De Soto, they traveled cross-country with horses, gunpowder, and tools of iron into the land of a Stone Age culture. For about two weeks they rested at Chiaha in the Chattanooga area before moving on. Another Spanish party under Juan Pardo followed, but neither left any mark on Indian legend or history. Their emperor, Charles V, did have the southeastern part of the United States incorporated into the map of his vast European holdings with the idea of examining this colonial prize more closely at a future date. But this Spanish influence was ephemeral.

Years passed. Then almost simultaneously two other European powers sent scouts into the region to trade with the natives and to challenge the Spanish claim to the land. In 1663 the English king granted the colony of Carolina to court favorites; the tract awarded extended to the Pacific Ocean, with present-day Chattanooga and Los Angeles both within its borders.

Meanwhile, the French sent their boatmen, soldiers, and priests south along the Mississippi Valley from their Canadian base; soon they established St. Louis, New Orleans, Biloxi, and Mobile. It immediately became clear that the Tennessee Valley would develop into an area of contact, rivalry, and conflict. But the difficult waters of Muscle Shoals and the Narrows kept the adversaries at arm's length during the early colonial wars. Locally the issue revolved around which country's flag represented sovereign power and which of the rivals controlled the Indians who, at least for a time, held the balance of power.

*Right*
After the arrival of European traders, the Indians sought trade goods from abroad including such items as glass beads, iron and brass bracelets and bells, as worn by this group. In payment for these and other items the Indians used pelts and deer skins. Courtesy of the University of Tennessee Press. Illustration by M. Kneberg.

*Far Right*
Dallas people did not have a long life expectancy. This young man's finery, as judged from burial accompaniments, gives a good indication of his valued personal possessions. Courtesy of the University of Tennessee Press. Illustration by M. Kneberg.

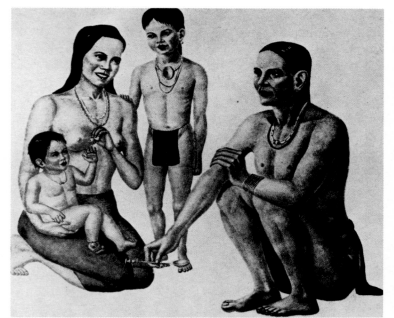

This Mississippian town stood on the island where the Hiwassee joins the Tennessee River. A scientific reconstruction shows the plaza, three community buildings, a stockade, and workers constructing a new house. Archaeologists' findings reveal that at one time the town covered about ten acres and was enclosed by a palisade. Courtesy of the University of Tennessee Press. Illustration by M. Kneberg.

Gradually the English, who offered the better and cheaper variety of trade goods, gained the loyalty of the Cherokee. The major link in this relationship was the Carolina traders, a corps of Scots associated with the Charles Town fur traders. Many of these adventurers took up residence with the Indians, married into the tribe, and sired a mixed-blood generation. According to Cherokee tradition they were welcomed as full-fledged members of the Indian nation. In addition to their business affairs, they informally represented the Crown as roving diplomats of the backwoods. Some became skilled linguists, geographers, and informed strategists in times of conflict.

The Cherokee, of Iroquois lineage, numbered some 18,000. They lived in the Unaka mountains, with only one group of villages on the western or Tennessee side: these, the Overhill Cherokee, dwelled along the Little

Tennessee, Hiwassee, and Tellico rivers. However, by 1715 they controlled all of the Tennessee country, having driven away the Creeks, Shawnee, and Yuchi tribes. From this vast hunting ground they sent furs and thousands of deerskins to the European markets through the Carolina traders.

Throughout this boundless land the redmen moved not only by the river but over the traces and trails originally engineered by the buffalo who scented the easiest way. A number of major routes ran through the local region supported by a network of minor trails, ancestral arteries of the modern interstate highways. The Great Indian Warpath drew traffic from the east, passing locally by Ooltewah over South Chickamauga Creek to Citico Creek and on around Lookout Mountain. Another, the Chickamauga Path, made it possible for braves to journey from north Georgia on to Kentucky

*From Dallas graves the archaeologist has gained an intimate picture of the prized ornaments of the day. Beads, marine conches, shell gorgets, and turtle shell rattles adorn this young woman. Courtesy of the University of Tennessee Press. Illustration by M. Kneberg.*

*The Woodland Indians, who came into the Chattanooga area around 1,000-500 B.C., are best known for their burial mounds. A large number of these relatively small mounds were left in the area, and many, which were explored by amateurs, contained fossils and artifacts which have unfortunately been widely scattered. Courtesy of Victor Hood.*

*The pursuit of "God, gold, and glory" brought the Spanish into the far interior of North America and gave them claim to the land. De Soto's (approximately) 700 followers came from the Tampa Bay area in Florida in a one year's journey. A new chapter opened for the Chattanooga area with the first visit of Europeans. (CHCBL)*

by way of the summit of the Cumberland Plateau; another from the south pointed northward from Chattanooga to the east of Walden Ridge. One more major route from Middle Tennessee to Florida passed through the local area; it has been known as the Cisco and St. Augustine trail with portions in this sector called the Nickajack Trace.

By the mid-18th century French and English thrusts for territory began to clash in the valley of the Tennessee; in the French and Indian War (1754-1763) both imperial rivals along with the Indians were caught in war's vast web. The British built Fort Loudoun on the Little Tennessee River as the Empire's westernmost defense post. They designed it to protect either the Cherokee from the French or the English from their own allies, the Cherokee. Whatever the purpose, the miserable treatment of the Indians at the hands of the British resulted in the surrender of the fort to the redmen and the massacre of many of the garrison party.

The Cherokee notified the French at New Orleans of their triumph and invited them to take possession of the abandoned fort. Boats loaded with stores and gifts started for the area but did not get beyond the mountain gorge in the Cumberlands. Here the French halted and disposed of their cargo, providing an explanation for the markings on old maps of an "Old French Store" near Chattanooga. So the French flag fluttered for the last moment. When peace came in 1763 the entire region east of the Mississippi River officially became English territory. The Union Jack now flew without challenge: the Chattanooga country and all of the Cherokee lands were a part of Britain's vast empire.

The last battle of the American Revolution, an indecisive skirmish on the slopes of Lookout Mountain involving the Chickamaugas and frontiersmen, took place in September 1792. Courtesy of the Chattanooga Convention and Visitors Bureau. Illustration by George Little.

## Chapter Three

# In the Days of the Revolution

**B**y the eve of the American Revolution, matters in the Tennessee country took on an entirely new dimension. Pioneers built their cabins to the west of the mountains; ambitious speculative interests schemed to acquire huge chunks of Indian land. Although the British in 1763 closed the western territory to white settlement and exploration, they had no possible way of enforcing this policy or of retarding the frontiersmen's tenacious quest for more land. Locally, jurisdiction over the region had passed to the colony of North Carolina when the original Carolina colony divided, and the Tarheels were now ready to utilize its unknown wealth.

Although British policy favored the Indians, all was not well within the inner circle of the Cherokee. Harsh retaliation following the fall of Fort Loudoun turned many braves to bitterness. They felt degraded, deceived, and now confused by the trouble between the English and their American colonists.

A provocation in March of 1775 brought the Amer-ican struggle for independence directly to the Chattanooga country. In violation of British policy and law a North Carolina land investor, Judge Richard Henderson, headed a group called the Transylvania Company which planned to buy some 20 million acres from the Cherokee. Amid the colorful procedures accompanying the "big talk," the older chieftains agreed to this sale of much of their ancient territorial claim. But in this crumbling world of the Cherokee Nation, one warrior stepped forward to condemn the agreement.

Dragging Canoe of Great Island of Little Tennessee River, strong and muscular, entered the speaker's circle. He voiced the ancestral passion of his people for the earth and spoke of the continuous encroachment of the whites. He denounced the transaction with Henderson as a violation of the birthright of the Nation and warned the purchaser that its price would be high. Dragging Canoe would sacrifice every pleasure and even his life to preserve the lands of his people. In disgust he turned

his back on the senior members of the tribe.

In 1777 Dragging Canoe and his adherents broke all ties with the Cherokee. From their Overhill towns they journeyed by trail and river some 100 miles southwest to the valley of South Chickamauga Creek, now within Chattanooga's city limits. Known as the Chickamaugas, they built villages, planted crops, and sallied forth to burn and kill along the extensive East Tennessee and Virginia frontier. In their new home they had the counsel of a Scottish trader, John McDonald, who held a commission to act as a British deputy agent.

This young tradesman, the first white to do business in the local area, arrived in America in 1776 and became a Carolina representative with the Cherokee. In the Overhill towns he married the mixed-blood Anna Shorey, daughter of another Scot. In 1770 the Mc-Donalds left the populated part of the Cherokee country and settled on South Chickamauga Creek along the Great Warpath. Although pelts were plentiful at the trail junction location, the trading post assumed a new significance with the coming of the Chickamaugas.

Dragging Canoe's defiance attracted malcontents from many tribes as well as Tory supporters of the British cause. Long caravans delivered guns and ammunition from Charles Town and, after the fall of that city,

*Above*
*Whatever their design, these handmade boats relied on the current of the Tennessee River to carry them downstream. Normally,*

*the canoe was the only craft that could negotiate upstream currents.*
*From TVA,* A History of Navigation in the Tennessee River System.

from Florida ports of entry. The Chickamaugas soon numbered 1,000 or more braves and the Canoe ranked as the most vigorous Indian ally of the Redcoats in the South. With firebrand, tomahawk, and rifle, he and his followers stormed the frontier, where a strong current of migration flowed in spite of the war. Black clouds hung over these outlying settlements; contempt and cruelty were mutually expressed.

The governor of the new state of Virginia understood the problem. Patrick Henry, radical political leader with a special forensic gift, planned an offensive into the Chickamaugas' lair. He sought aid from North Carolina's governor, telling that leader, "Justice and necessity demand that proper measures be taken to chastise these people, and by doing that, to anticipate the evils they meditate against us." He not only called attention to the bloody Indian forays but also to the "navigation of Tennessee River, in which your state, as well as ours, seems deeply interested, which is rendered unsafe and impracticable so long as these banditti go unpunished."

With this call the "War of the Revolution in the West" came to the Chattanooga region.

Militiamen assembled in upper East Tennessee; no draft was needed as volunteers took up the cause. Although they were not trained soldiers, all were outdoorsmen to be reckoned with under the command of Evan Shelby of Sapling Grove (Bristol, Tennessee). On April 10, 1779, they embarked in boats on the Tennessee River—there may have been 900 men in the area's first naval operation. In the valley of South Chickamauga Creek they put the torch to 11 villages, destroyed the spring crops, rounded up horses, and carried off booty from John McDonald's stand. One part of the army continued on down the Tennessee River to join George Rogers Clark in his dramatic campaign in the Old Northwest.

Shelby's scorched-earth policy had little permanent effect; the Chickamaugas' manpower losses were slight and crops were replanted. Dragging Canoe, however, correctly assessed the result. His villages lay exposed to attack. In a second trek, the Chickamaugas in large numbers moved around the base of Chatanuga Mountain (Lookout) into the river canyon and beyond. Some rebuilt the older towns; but under the protection of the mountains where the river's troubled waters helped maintain control, the warriors established new villages collectively known as the Five Lower Towns—Running Water, Nickajack, Long Island, Lookout Mountain, and Crow towns. Their rear guard offensive in the Revolution was far from over; John McDonald moved with the Canoe, and the flow of war supplies from Florida still passed through the area's southern gateway.

Despite Governor Henry's admonition about the Chickamaugas' control of the river, Shelby's punitive expedition had little effect on the use of the stream. Within the year, Chickamauga braves sighted a large flotilla of flatboats of many shapes and sizes moving downstream. The Tennessee River had never hosted such a fleet. Ignoring the wartime hazards, the settlement party sailed with a large crowd of women and children toward new homes on the exposed Cumberland River frontier. They chose the treacherous un-

known currents of the river and the wrath of marauding Indians rather than the overland route from East Tennessee, which most of the men had taken earlier with their livestock. The *Adventure,* an appropriately named craft with John Donelson as master, served as flagship; it carried among others the skipper's family, including young daughter Rachel, who later became the wife of Andrew Jackson.

On March 8th the squadron started its run through the Chattanooga area into the valley of the whirlpools, drawing fire from redmen hidden among the canebrakes. One craft with 28 people aboard sailed in the rear because of a self-imposed smallpox quarantine. The Indians intercepted this flatboat, killing or capturing the entire party.

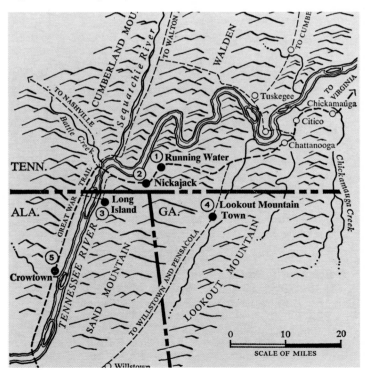

*Until 1794 the Five Lower Towns of the Chickamaugas dominated the diplomatic and military policy of the old Southwest. Numerous letters of President George Washington sought a policy of conciliation, but peace came to the local area only after the destruction of key villages by Major James Ore, whose action was in violation of federal policy. Courtesy of the University of Tennessee Press.*

The Chickamaugas tormented the voyagers from the riverbanks as they sailed by until the boats started their run through the Suck, where they fired from the bluffs overhead. One craft, while battling the relentless currents, ran aground, partly filled with water, and had to be left behind with the frightened family of Jonathan Jennings. Following a hairbreadth escape, Jennings passed on an account of his experience to the party's commander. In his journal, Donelson wrote:

*He ordered his wife, a son nearly grown, a young man who accompanied him, & his two negroes to throw all his goods into the river, to lighten their boat for the purpose of getting her off, himself returning their fire as well as he could (being a good soldier and an excellent marksman). But before they had accomplished their object, his son, the young man, & the negro man jumped out of the boat & left them. He thinks the young man & the negro were wounded before they left the boat. Mrs. Jennings, however, & the negro woman succeeded in unloading the boat, but chiefly by the exertions of Mrs. Jennings, who got out of the boat & shoved her off, but was near falling a victim to her own intrepidity on account of the boat starting so suddenly, as soon as loosened from the rock. Upon examination he appears to have made a wonderful escape, for his boat is pierced in numberless places with bullets.*

*It is to be remarked that, Mrs. Peyton who was the night before delivered of an infant, which was unfortunately killed in the hurry & confusion consequent upon such a disaster, assisted them, being frequently exposed to wet & cold then and afterwards, and that her health appears to be good at this time, & I think & hope she will do well.*

The new and badly exposed Cumberland settlements immediately became the prime target of the Chickamaugas. In the Five Lower Towns, American Revolutionary strategy continued to be made. These plans led to clever ambushes at river fords and mountain passes and by well-worn trails. The warriors of Dragging Canoe burned cabins, killed pioneer families, and re-

*Left*
*Isaac Shelby, one of the five sons of Colonel Evan Shelby, accompanied his father on the Chickamauga raid. He later became a famous citizen of the frontier and first governor of the state of Kentucky. (CHCBL)*

*Facing Page*
*The rear-guard military action of the American Revolution in 1779 brought the war to the Chattanooga area when Evan Shelby's command invaded the Chickamauga settlements. (CHCBL)*

turned to the mountain fastness of their villages with captives, slaves, and stolen horses. Their sneak assaults by 1782 were so widespread and violent that in June the governor of North Carolina wrote:

*A tribe of Cherokees called the Chicamoggies, instigated by British emissaries and tory refugees, have been very troublesome in murdering many peaceful families of this state and Virginia. I am about to form an expedition to extirpate them if possible from that country if they cannot be reclaimed. . . .*

The next month the legislature authorized the campaign against Dragging Canoe's towns: ". . . all the males therein to be killed, and the females captured for exchange; supplies to be divided among the soldiers participating." Expenses paid in "continental credit" gave the expedition official status.

A small force of transmountain men finally moved toward the Chickamauga stronghold under the frontier fighter and leader of men, Colonel John Sevier. They burned Chickamauga towns east of Lookout Mountain and were baited by the taunts of Bloody Fellow and other Indians from the opposite cliffs of Lookout. The frontiersmen answered the challenge; they crossed the river and scrambled up the boulder-strewn mountainside. A brisk fight followed before the Chickamaugas slipped away through the undergrowth. The date was

September 20, 1782, some 11 months after the war's end at Yorktown, when Sevier's militiamen fought the British-backed Indians in an engagement now designated as the last battle of the American Revolution.

The war, however, did not end for the Chickamaugas; no peace treaty was made that included Dragging Canoe, whose military aims remained unchanged. The struggle for possession of the native hills went on. Now the state of North Carolina claimed all of the Tennessee country, and its political leaders generously made land grants to soldiers and attractive proposals to speculators. More and more settlers moved into the transmontane region.

When the British could no longer furnish help to the Indians, they turned to Spain, which had gained possession of Florida in 1783. John McDonald, who had remained with Dragging Canoe, became a Spanish agent and was supported with an annual pension. McDonald's influence among the Indians steadily mounted; they found him honest and they respected him for his skillful use of their language. Tennessee's first territorial governor, William Blount, also considered him very able, stating that "he has as much or more influence with the Lower Cherokees, than any other man who resides among them."

Although the new United States government sought to create a foreign policy based on conciliation with the Chickamaugas, the Indians kept up their widespread offensive and maintained their control of navigation on the Tennessee River. Isolated traders continued to brave the journey through the region, however, and one in particular had an experience with totally unforeseen consequences.

In 1785 a trading expedition with Baltimore connections ventured down the Tennessee. The boat, which was stopped by the Indians near Lookout Mountain, caused a big stir among the natives. On board they found inviting trade goods, an unfriendly Indian chief, and a young Scot, recently from Sutherlandshire. John McDonald rescued his countryman with the fresh brogue and made the newcomer a business associate. Before long his daughter Molly married this man, whose name was Daniel Ross. He and his wife lived at various places in the Indian country and raised a family of nine. On October 3, 1790, their third child and first son was born, whom they named John; the history of his homeland would center around his career.

Other river parties also suffered attack while frontier raids from the Five Lower Towns were carried out until 1794. Although Dragging Canoe had died two years earlier of natural causes, the tribe somehow managed its affairs under new leadership. Many of his followers had interesting careers as well as intriguing names such as Bloody Fellow, the Breath, Doublehead, John Watts, Fool Warrior, the Glass, Turtle-at-Home, the Bench, Pumpkin Boy, and many others.

In September of 1794, however, a volunteer force from Middle Tennessee under Major James Ore slipped into the innermost Chickamauga stronghold, destroyed the major towns, and killed the spirit of resistance of the Chickamaugas. The loss of Spanish support as a consequence of the French Revolutionary wars and the defeat of northern tribesmen at Fallen Timbers at the hand of Anthony Wayne contributed to the demise of the Chickamaugas. There was no alternative except to make peace. The Chickamaugas under Dragging Canoe had relied on force to hold back the westward course of pioneer settlement and protect their lands. They had failed.

Sequoyah (1760?-1843), called George Gist by the whites, is possibly the only person in history to develop an entire syllabary. On presenting him the Cherokee Nation's medal for his service, Chief John Ross said: "The old and the young find no difficulty in learning to read and write in their native language. Types have been made and a printing press established in the Nation. The Scriptures have been translated and printed in Cherokee. While posterity continues to be benefitted by the discovery, your name will be held in grateful remembrance. The great good designed by the author of human existence in directing your genius to this happy discovery cannot be fully estimated — it is incalculable." From T.L. McKenney, History of the Indian Tribes of North America.

# Chapter Four
# The Cherokee– 'Principal People'

The subdued splinter tribe of Chickamaugas returned in the autumn of their defeat to membership in the Cherokee Nation amid appropriate ceremony. Although knowledge of their ancestors was dimly maintained in oral tradition, the Cherokee continued to call themselves Ani-Yunwiya, "Principal People." Under mounting pressure they had sold much of their homeland and drifted to new locations to the southwest in lower East Tennessee and north Georgia.

Ross's Landing after 1815 became a major economic hub and New Echota, in northern Georgia, the Indian capital in 1788. Under these fluid conditions the Cherokee life-style rapidly changed as the natives made a concerted effort to master the culture of the whites. Adapting nimbly to new ideas, they saw their former hunting economy give way to agriculture and trade.

The United States Indian Agent, Connecticut-reared Return Jonathan Meigs, contributed materially to this transition after his 1801 appointment. For the next 22 years he gave benevolent guidance to the Cherokee from his first residence at Southwest Point where the nearby village of Kingston grew up, and after 1807 at the Hiwassee Garrison or Agency within a convenient journey from Ross's Landing. Meigs in 1802 placed a subagent, Major William L. Lovely, at Lookout Creek in the shadow of the mountain with the same name. Here the first local representative of the federal government erected a gristmill for the use of the natives.

About 1800 the government, as stipulated in land treaties, began annual annuity payments in basic tools and in craft instruction in smithing, milling, tanning, and other skills. A native spokesman in 1826 boasted of the results. He found the Cherokee had 22,000 cattle, 7,600 horses, 46,000 swine, 2,500 sheep, 762 looms, 2,488 spinning wheels, 172 wagons, 2,942 plows, 10 sawmills, 31 grist mills, 62 blacksmith shops, 8 cotton machines, 18 schools, and the same number of ferries. "In one district," he added, "there were, last winter, upwards of 1,000 volumes of good books; and 11 different periodical papers both religious and political, which were taken and read."

Prior to the time of this inventory, the Cherokee built roads through the Nation that connected the isolated farming areas of East Tennessee and of the Cumberland settlements with the markets of the Deep South. Over them the first vehicular traffic in the region's history carried men and produce, but it was frequently delayed by herds of swine, cattle, mules, and horses or flocks of turkey making their way to an exchange mart under their own power. From the roads also came fabricated tales of ruffians, highwaymen, and carnage.

The local section of the Georgia Road into Middle Tennessee, sometimes known as the Nickajack Road, reflected the economic opportunities of wheeled traffic. John Brown's ferry tavern built in 1803 drew trade from north of the Tennessee River. On Chattanooga Creek Daniel Ross settled; he operated a stand while living as a patriarch amid his orchards, deerskin tanyard, mills, stables, and Negro cabins. A visitor in 1820 noted that "from his manners and information he might have been living the last twenty years in England or Scotland, instead of among the Cherokee."

John McDonald and his family returned to an earlier homesite at Poplar Springs in the gap of Missionary Ridge, which in time became known as Rossville. At his general store the stage changed horses and a semiweekly mail passed from Nashville to Augusta, Georgia. In 1817 a post office opened at Rossville, although it was deep in Indian country, under a favorite grandson, John Ross.

John Ross's first education was acquired at his father's home, but he later attended a frontier academy; he also got practical mercantile experience from clerking at Kingston. Although he never spoke Cherokee

*Top*
*During the Civil War the Ross House served as headquarters for Major General Gordon Granger (of the Army of the Cumberland) at the time of the Chickamauga battle. Ross's name was given to the post office and to the settlement in the gap. Courtesy of the U.S. War Department, General Staff, National Archives.*

*Above*
*John McDonald, grandfather of John Ross, built the first part of this house in the Rossville Gap (Georgia), once called Poplar Springs. Ross spent much of his youth here and inherited the property upon the death of his grandparents. (CHCBL)*

*Facing Page*
*About 1803, a Cherokee mixed-blood named John Brown established a ferry and tavern near the route of the Great War and Trading Path. Presently, the tavern is the home of Judge and Mrs. Herschel Franks, and is a classic model of preservation. (CHCBL)*

fluently and never learned their written language, Ross gained the trust of the Cherokee in his unfailing devotion to his homeland, in his enterprise, and in his integrity. In 1813 he married Elizabeth Brown Henley (called "Quatie" in Cherokee) with whom he had six children. Most likely she was of mixed blood but she was a zealous Cherokee and always used the language of the tribe. Although she was a Moravian churchmember, her husband later joined the Methodist denomination. Shortly after his marriage, Ross and his brother Lewis founded their mercantile operations on the river at Ross's Landing, which became a customary stop on the Georgia Road from Nashville to Augusta.

In addition to these prominent persons, other mixed-blood Cherokee made up the most successful element of the tribe. In 1835 an estimate indicated that 17 percent of the Indians had some white ancestry, including such residents of this locale as Joseph and James Vann, Judge James Brown, George and John Lowry, Betsy Pack, Richard and Fox Taylor, John Walker, Joseph Coody, Richard Timberlake, David Fields, William Brown, and John Hildebrand.

Most Cherokee lived in log or frame houses and dressed as the frontiersmen except for the rather common use of a turban. Many developed extensive holdings characterized by a plantation economy; 207 Cherokee had Negro slaves, with "Rich Joe" Vann of Spring Place owning as many as 110.

An interesting wedding in 1828 tells much about social developments. It was reported by Waterhunter, who served as translator. There were prayers and singing in Cherokee followed by a nuptial dinner and the marriage ceremony performed in English. Of the couple Waterhunter wrote:

*The Bride is a quarter white, possesses a fine figure, somewhat tall, beautiful complexion, with dark hair and eyes; her features bear the evidence of amiability and good nature; and altogether . . . she is an interesting woman. She is a member of the Methodist Church. The Bridegroom, a cousin of mine, is a full-blooded Indian, of Aboriginal deep copper complexion, low in stature, fine figure, but does not possess a handsome face, though depicted upon it are the marks of honesty, fidelity and good nature. He was dressed in a clean northern domestic suit, and his bride in white cambric.*

*Major George Lowrey, a popular and politically influential mixed-blood, vigorously supported the Brainerd Mission. Portrait by George Catlin, courtesy of Thomas Gilcrease Institute of American History and Art in Tulsa, Oklahoma.*

Missionaries and circuit riders, by bringing their Christian messages to the Indians, did much to help the latter along the way to civilization. Moravians, Presbyterians, Methodists, and Baptists ran schools and structured congregations. But the most influential work was conducted by the American Board of Commissioners for Foreign Missions, an interdenominational society of Congregationalists, Presbyterians, and Dutch Reformed Church members. In the midst of a wilderness on acres originally cleared by John McDonald, they built a mission station in 1817.

Ministers, teachers, and workers from New England and the Middle Atlantic states came to the school, which took the name Brainerd to honor David Brainerd, a missionary to the Indians of New England who lived a century earlier. The federal government gave them financial aid and encouragement; on May 27, 1819, President Monroe visited the remote establishment. Its chapel knew no color line as whites, Africans, and Indians worshiped together. Brainerd became the parent of 10 substations scattered throughout the Nation and deserves the fitting name Robert Sparks Walker gave it—Torchlights to the Cherokees.

In 1825 a new missionary arrived at Brainerd. Samuel Austin Worcester, a college graduate with an aptitude for language, soon had an impact on the community which reached far beyond the walls of the mission school. He became aware of the work of the perceptive mixed-blood Sequoyah in developing a Cherokee written language and encouraged its practical adoption.

Sequoyah, a native of East Tennessee, believed the white man's superior culture rested on his ability to use a written language and resolved to prepare an alphabet or syllabary in Cherokee. He labored without any knowledge of English or any formal education with the sole purpose of uplifting his people. Overcoming ridicule and frustration, he prepared 86 characters representing all the syllables of the Cherokee language. The simplicity of his system enabled uneducated Indians to learn to read and write within an extremely short time.

Worcester was instrumental in getting the Indians to have type cast in Boston; the American Board agreed

Cherokee Alphabet.

*Sounds represented by Vowels.*

*Far Left*
*A sketch of Brainerd Mission from an old wood print in "The History of American Missions to the Heathen," published in 1840. (CHCBL)*

*Left*
*Sequoyah constructed a series of 86 characters representing the sounds in the Cherokee language, which enabled the Indians to read and write in their own language within a few months. From the* 19th Annual Report of the U.S. Bureau of American Ethnology, *1900.*

to pay for all the equipment needed, including a press, to fit out a printing office for which the Cherokee Nation reimbursed the society. On February 21, 1828, the first issue of a bilingual newspaper was published; its editor, a Brainerd-trained mixed-blood who got advanced training at a New England school of the mission, was Elias Boudinot. This weekly, named the *Cherokee Phoenix*, announced in a prospectus:

*We would now commit our feeble efforts to the good will and indulgence of the public, praying that God will attend them with His blessings, and hoping for that happy period when all the Indian tribes of America shall arise Phoenix-like, from the ashes, and when the terms, "Indian depredation," "War-whoop," "scalping-knife," and the like, shall become obsolete, and forever be "buried deep under ground."*

Few persons in world history accomplished a feat unassisted comparable to that of Sequoyah. The Cherokee understood this; they awarded him an annual pension of $300 for life and presented him a medal. In a special ceremony John Ross stated: "The great good designed by the author of human existence in directing your genius to this happy discovery cannot be fully estimated—it is incalculable." The United States awarded Sequoyah $500 and later his name (spelled as Sequoia) was most properly given to the giant redwood trees and a national park in California.

Prior to the publication of the first newspaper, the Cherokee made use of Sequoyah's invention in another demonstration of their advancement. On July 26, 1827, they completed work on a written constitution establishing a democratic republic with suffrage granted to all males over 18 years of age. John Ross served as president of the convention.

Although the constitution was patterned after that of some states and the federal government, one feature was unique. Article I, Section 2, emphatically stated that the Cherokee lands "shall remain the common property of the nation"; improvements were the property of the citizens but they possessed "no right nor power to dispose of their improvements in any manner whatever to the United States, individual states, nor to individual citizens thereof. . . ."

In October 1828 John Ross was inaugurated Principal Chief under the constitution. He had served a political apprenticeship for some years and was acquainted with the leading United States statesmen. Prior to his election he left his Rossville property to Nicholas Dalton Scales, who had married Ross's niece Mary Coody. Scales, along with Pleasant H. Butler, took over Ross's Landing.

Ross moved to an area near the source of the Coosa River known as the "Head of Coosa." There as a planter he was close to the circle of influential Cherokee. He might have ended his full life in comfort and widespread recognition. Instead a bitter fate awaited him.

"Trail of Tears," from the original painting by Robert Lindneux.
Courtesy of the Woolaroc Museum, Bartlesville, Oklahoma.

## Chapter Five

# The Trail of Tears

The cultural advancement and invigorating education of the Cherokee showed exceptional gains but at a time when the mutterings of a coming storm threatened to sweep the Indians forever from their ancestral lands. Under Ross's leadership the great majority of Cherokee determined to resist all schemes and demands for their removal west of the Mississippi River. This resolve and firmness of purpose were no less than those of Dragging Canoe a generation earlier but took an entirely different course of action. Instead of using brawn, the Cherokee now chose to abide by the law and to rely on passive resistance to achieve success. For a decade they mounted a determined legal defense against removal until the national government rounded them up by the sword in one of the darkest chapters in American history.

In the first years of the 19th century the pressure of frontier settlement for Cherokee lands was an ever-present issue. It grew more intense as gold was discovered in a corner of north Georgia and as that state voiced vigorous complaints that the federal government had reneged on a pledge to invalidate Indian land claims. Then the election of Andrew Jackson to the Presidency placed a vigorous proponent of Indian removal in the executive office. And finally there was the Cherokee written constitution which focused attention on a basic question: Who actually possessed sovereign power in the area—the state, the federal government, or the Cherokee Nation? This question enraged the Georgians.

A small number of Indians had moved west voluntarily, but Georgia officials grew dissatisfied with the lack of federal initiative for removal. In December of 1828 the state legislature took action; no longer would they wait for federal dabbling. A law to take effect on June 1, 1830, along with supplementary acts, annexed that part of the Cherokee country within the state and extended jurisdiction over it. Cherokee law and custom became null and void; no Indian could be a court witness where a white was defendant. All whites in the area were obligated to take an oath of allegiance to the state—a measure aimed at the Brainerd missionaries. The land, surveyed and mapped, was to go to Georgia white citizens in a public lottery in which each resident got a ticket.

A wave of lawlessness followed as the Cherokee were crowded off their lands. Some Georgians explained that the Cherokee had more land than "intended by the Great Father of the Universe"; the Indians responded that they were unaware of the plans of the "Supreme Father in this particular." They appealed to Washington but got no aid. John Ross lost his fields, ferry, and home at the Head of Coosa; on returning home one night from a trip to Washington he found a lottery winner installed and his own family turned out. The old McDonald home at Rossville with its 160 acres passed from the Scales family to a lottery winner. The brothers McFarland, who had helped survey the area, bought it shortly after. At Spring Place the brick home and 800-acre plantation of Joe Vann changed hands as the departing Cherokee family witnessed a fight between two sets of claimants. Many of the Cherokee fled from the Georgia area into the region around Ross's Landing.

Some national humanitarians spoke out for the natives, but the people who directed Georgia policy and those who engineered matters for the Jackson administration did not listen. Georgia suppressed the *Cherokee Phoenix,* destroying the local voice of the Indians. They arrested missionary friends who refused to take an oath supporting the state, putting them in chains and forcing them to walk 22 miles to jail. Eventually the United States Supreme Court, in the case *Worcester v. the State of Georgia,* found certain Georgia laws unconstitutional; however, an obstinate president ignored the decision.

The Cherokee capital was moved to the Red Clay Council Grounds in Tennessee, but Georgia guards rode across the state line and arrested John Ross and a house guest, John Howard Payne. The federal government allowed its agency to become inactive and changed the method of paying the Cherokee annuity from a national settlement which supported schools, the newspaper, and other group projects to a per capita payment which amounted to the paltry sum of 42 cents annually.

The United States dispatched a commissioner to the Cherokee region to arrange for a removal treaty. The Reverend J. F. Schermerhorn undertook the assignment with an abundance of missionary zeal but little principle. He eventually called a meeting at New Echota in December 1835, selecting a site which Georgians had earlier ruled off limits to the Indians. Only about three percent of the men, women, and children of the Nation attended, according to the estimates of that day. But they did negotiate a document. It was endorsed by only 20 Cherokee; no representative of their government signed and only two prominent men affixed their signatures.

This so-called Treaty of New Echota or the Removal Treaty ceded all eastern Cherokee lands for territory west of the Mississippi River and a bonus of $5,000,000. The government pledged to bear the cost of removal and of subsistence for one year. The Cherokee would relocate within two years.

The Cherokee raised an almost unanimous cry of deception and fraud when they learned of the endorsement of the small minority to this document which surrendered their native lands. Ross and other national delegates carried petitions to Washington signed by nearly 16,000 Indians, protesting the deal. Cherokee resolutions denounced the methods of Schermerhorn. A representative of the national government, sent to begin enrolling the natives, agreed and angrily exposed what he had discovered in a letter to the Secretary of War:

*I now warn you and the President that if this paper of Schermerhorn's called a treaty is sent to the Senate and ratified you will bring trouble upon the government and eventually destroy this [the Cherokee] Nation. The Cherokee are a peaceable, harmless people, but you may drive them to desperation, and this treaty can not be carried into effect except by the strong arm of force.*

The U.S. Senate approved the treaty by a margin of one vote, and steps were taken to implement it. As the enrolling officer predicted, troops were sent to prevent disorders.

Ross's Landing became one of the three concentration centers from which the Cherokee would go west. (Gunter's Landing in Alabama and the Cherokee Agency were the others.) The Landing at the time consisted of possibly 30 crudely-built houses with a cluster of huts called a hotel, whose ventilation system made it possible for a guest to view the mountains through the wide cracks in the walls. The army built a stockade with cabins and stables for the soldiers and an Indian concentration center of tents and rough shelters without any provision for privacy or sanitation.

Some whites who were to become permanent residents moved to the Landing. John P. Long opened a general store and won an appointment as the first postmaster—an office which opened on March 22, 1837, some 20 months before the last Cherokee started for the West. In addition, a large crowd of transients arrived: contractors and drivers who would haul for the army, census takers, provisioners, swindlers, and others

*From the establishment of Hamilton County in 1819 until the removal of the Cherokee in 1838, the Tennessee River served as the border between the whites and the redmen. Except for the brief years when the military bridge stood at the foot of Market Street, only ferry service linked the two shores of the stream until the Walnut Street bridge was built. From* Picturesque America.

*Until the coming of the railroads in the 1850s, economic life centered on the river. To the site of Ross's Landing came homemade craft and steamboats. In addition to country products brought in for sale, many of the first settlers of the town arrived here by boat. From* Picturesque America.

who hoped to turn a fast profit. One officer described this latter group as "vultures" and concluded that it was the Indians who needed protection.

The work of enrolling the Cherokee, appraising their property, and arranging transportation and subsistence continued at a slow pace. The Indians doggedly refused to accept the treaty; Ross and associates continued to petition Washington for relief. The Principal Chief patiently ignored the threats of arrest and punishment for impeding removal. In spite of the intensity of federal pressure, only about 2,000 Cherokee voluntarily migrated prior to the expiration of the grace period before removal.

Several of these early groups left from Ross's Landing; the first departed on March 3, 1837. Steamboats with convoys of flatboats carried some into exile while at least one party began an overland journey using wagons or traveling on foot. The stubborn Cherokee's refusal to cooperate annoyed the government people so much that the head of the armed forces got orders to transfer them out by force.

President Van Buren ordered Major General Winfield Scott to take command of a force in the Cherokee country on April 10, 1838, comprised of regulars, militiamen, and volunteers, numbering 7,000 in all. Although the Indians had previously been disarmed, the troops outnumbered the adult male Cherokee.

The soldiers picked up Indians in the fields or in their kitchens or wherever they happened to find them. When a number of families were collected, the troops marched them to one of the three concentration sites.

Livestock, poultry, and pets remained behind. A few days later wagons collected household goods that looters had passed over. Cattle and horses were driven off or bought by speculators at sacrificial prices. Graves were opened for possible plunder. By early June the disgraceful business was about over; the army had rounded up all except a few spirited natives who escaped into the deep mountains.

Again, banished parties left the wharf at Ross's Landing for the West. The son of the John P. Longs later recalled the sorrowful scene between his mother and the departing Cherokee:

*Left*
*John P. Long, one of Chattanooga's first citizens, worked as storekeeper, first postmaster, town commissioner, real estate agent, city recorder, and held numerous other posts. Through his personal interest much of the early history of the settlement has been preserved. (CHCBL)*

*Below*
*The communion service of Brainerd Mission is now a treasure of the First Presbyterian Church. (CHCBL)*

*When these Indian women, many of whom were her friends, came to bid her goodbye, she said afterwards that she could not stand it and would cry as if her heart would break but these people had a comforter among them in Miss Eliza Ross, sister of Chief John Ross, who was a regal beauty. She would ride amongst them, and stooping over the neck of her black charger would comfort a mother here and a daughter there, thus giving comforting words to all.*

*These Indians stuck to their dogs to the very last. When they reached the place of embarkation and found out they could not take their dogs with them, they wandered over the town to find homes for their canine friends. They would come up to you and say: "Want dog? Good watch-dog. Take and keep dog."*

The first party to be forcibly removed by the troops left Ross's Landing on June 6, 1838, on a steamboat and six flatboats. They numbered about 800. One week later another contingent totaling 875 persons left by the water route, but death and escapes reduced the group considerably before their August 5th arrival at their new lands. A third band departed Ross's Landing on June 17; this group of 1,070 left in wagons and on foot on the first leg of their journey.

Compassion for the travelers mounted in the home community as reports of suffering filtered back from the exiles. Sickness, poor food, and sultry summer weather combined to cause such a high mortality rate that Chief Ross petitioned General Scott for a postponement of further migrations until fall. The General agreed. On June 19 he accepted the Cherokee proposal that they manage the final phase of removal themselves.

Ross's Landing quieted down after the decision to delay departure, and many of the transients drifted away. The Cherokee mentors at the Brainerd Mission on August 19, 1838, held their last communion service at the mission church. The teachers and staff then packed their possessions and prepared to go west with the Indians.

In the fall months of 1838 the epic of tragedy and shame came to a close. Chief Ross's own wife, Quatie, like hundreds of her compatriots, died before reaching a new home. The final migration did not specifically involve Ross's Landing, for the last 13,000 Cherokee departed from Rattlesnake Springs near Charleston, Tennessee.

*Built in 1860, the Brotherton house was typical of many rural homes. It stood on ground where the battle of Chickamauga raged. At that time it was home for a family with seven children, but immediately after the battle it served as a hospital. (CHCBL)*

## Chapter Six

# Bringing Forth a City

Years before the Cherokee removal saga ended, an entirely different chapter in the history of the Chattanooga area opened. Early in 1819 the United States purchased land north of the Tennessee River from the Cherokee, and on October 25 of the same year Tennessee created Hamilton County. For the next 16 years the river formed the boundary between an emerging white frontier and the Indian nation.

Actually there had been shadowy attempts to establish claims in the area much earlier on the part of the whites. Practically all of the land of north Hamilton County except mountain acres had been granted to individuals in a wave of "prodigal generosity" by North Carolina at the close of the American Revolution. These "paper owners," however, had to wait for the nullifying of Indian title before they could take up their claims. In 1819 they were ready to move in, sell their claims, or fight the legal battles over where their survey lines fell.

Another practice to gain precedence for future negotiations was Tennessee's use of "extended" county boundaries. These vague extensions reached into the far Indian country and had no immediate importance. But the area of Hamilton County was an organized appendage of Knox County from 1792 until it came under Roane in 1801 and then Rhea in 1807-1819.

When the county of Hamilton came into existence, it included a pocket of settlement in the Sale Creek Valley which had formerly been a part of Rhea County. This area naturally became the population center of the new political unit, which in 1820 reported 821 residents, including 16 free Negroes and 39 slaves. In 1840 these totals had changed to 8,175 persons, counting 93 free Negroes and 584 slaves.

What happened during these 20 years duplicated the typical American frontier process. The new settlers came chiefly from nearby counties and represented the youth from older settlements. In this case most arrived by river in craft they themselves had built; all they had to do was to load the craft and call the dogs. In their new Hamilton homes they hacked out fields from forested land and canebrakes, used the standard "wooden architecture" for their houses, and began reestablishing political and social institutions.

The act organizing the county named Charles Gamble, Robert Patterson, and William Lauderdale commissioners to decide on the location of the county seat. These three assumed the responsibility of establishing local instruments of law, order, and justice, of organizing and preserving proper records, of wrestling with taxing powers, and of arranging elections. They worked with democracy at a grass-roots level. The commissioners also chose a permanent county seat, selecting the new village of Dallas erected nearby the old prehistoric Indian community. Interestingly, during the first years the courthouse site was leased from a Cherokee Indian. (Today it lies under the waters of Lake Chickamauga.)

Many of the first settlers had pioneering experience elsewhere and had a working knowledge of organizing churches and schools. Representative early churches include the Mount Bethel Presbyterian Church of Soddy, the Sale Creek Cumberland Presbyterian Church, and the Jackson Chapel or Prairie Creek Springs Methodist Church. Religious workers apparently fared better than those who sponsored subscription schools, for the 1840 census reports that the residents supported only five "primary and common schools" with 133 students.

The early clusters of homes centered around Sale Creek, Dallas, Mountain Creek, Soddy, Poe's Crossroads (Daisy), and Hixson. The very names of the pioneer families tell much of their heritage. Most were Scotch-Irish, but some had English, German, or Irish lineage. Some typical names include: McGill, Martin, Witt, Poe, Mitchell, Gotcher, Clift, McRee, Varner, Cozby, Gann, Vandergriff, McDonald, Rawlings, Miliken, Douglass, Lusk, Connor, Yarnell, Igou, Hamil, Hixson, Beck, Miles, Williams, Hartman, Shipley, Rogers, Foust, and Brooks.

The first rumors about the Cherokee migration brought adventurous pioneers south of the Tennessee River determined to stake out squatters' claims to prime lands. Although such intrusion was illegal, no one seemed to care; before the Trail of Tears was ended, quite a number of permanent residents had gathered around Ross's Landing. The Landing itself took on new importance as many flatboats arrived loaded with produce for the army or their Indian captives, along with boats laden with salt from southwestern Virginia.

Steamboats too became an integral part of the economic and social fabric of the valley. Since the time in 1828 when the *Atlas* made the first upriver trip all the way to Knoxville, the steamboat business grew. Hampered by fluctuating depths and by the stretches of bad water, the packets made Ross's Landing a recognized division point and the community generated an ardent interest in the river and in urging river improvement.

Some of the new citizens at the Landing merely crossed the river from Hamilton County, while a majority journeyed downstream, as merchant John P. Long had done, from various parts of East Tennessee. One, a printer named Ferdinand A. Parham, brought a press along with his household goods and on July 19, 1838, from the river bank, distributed the first copy of the Hamilton *Gazette*. Actually, most business in those days seems to have been transacted on the shore, but homes stood some distance back to avoid fogs and insects.

When the United States acquired the land south of the Tennessee River, it turned the title over to Tennessee, thereby eliminating any possibility of establishing a national domain. The state created the Ocoee Land District and arranged to sell the land to individual owners at once. The policy recognized squatter or occupancy rights and graduated sales prices. Specifically, the latter pegged the price at $7.50 per acre but in numerous steps reduced it, until after 19 months all land still available would sell for one cent per acre. That became the going rate for tracts on Lookout Mountain and Missionary Ridge. At this time (1838) the land south of the river and south of Hamilton County officially became a part of Hamilton County.

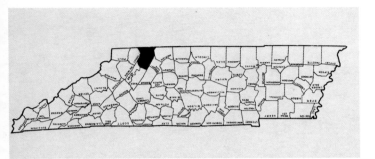

*Above*
*Hamilton, one of Tennessee's 95 counties, was named for Alexander Hamilton, first secretary of the treasury.*

*Left*
*This 1839 plat of Chattanooga does not indicate the wooded areas, duck ponds, swamplands within the town, or the twisting gully along Mulberry Street. Note that the numbered streets run perpendicular to those named for trees; Mulberry, later changed to Railroad Avenue, is now Broad Street. (CHCBL)*

*Below*
*At this 1948 gathering of old cronies in the Half Century Club, members agreed with American humorist and journalist Irvin Cobb, as well as John P. Long, that the name Chattanooga "would become familiar and pleasant." (CHCBL)*

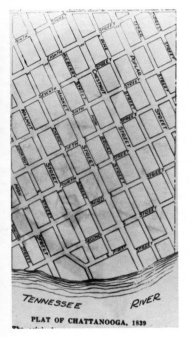

PLAT OF CHATTANOOGA, 1839

By the summer of 1837, Ross's Landing boasted 53 households; the village spread over two surveyors' sections—a quarter section and a fractional quarter section. To simplify occupancy entries of their land, the residents of these two units selected three commissioners each to transact business at the land office in Cleveland. These men—John P. Long, Aaron M. Rawlings, George W. Williams, Allen Kennedy, Albert S. Lenoir, and Reynolds A. Ramsey—became the community's founding fathers.

After the lands were properly entered, the commissioners engaged a surveyor to plat the 240-acre area and lay out streets; the boundaries extended from the winding Tennessee River to Ninth Street and from Georgia Avenue westward to the foot of Cameron Hill. Next, they issued deeds to the new owners, reserving certain designated lots for future allotment to churches. During the summer the commissioners assembled their neighbors in a log schoolhouse located at the corner of East Fifth and Lookout streets to debate and try to agree on a proper name for the place. With traditional frontier optimism they decided Ross's Landing would not do; the river bank almost anywhere could be called a landing. They sought a name in keeping with their dream for the future. John P. Long, the new postmaster and an amateur historian at heart, insisted its prosperity rested on the fact that the site was a spot where the corn and cotton country met. Believing it had "all the requirements necessary to build a future city," he had constructed a "log cabin in the woods and settled down for life."

At the town meeting, discussion centered on Lookout City, Montevideo, Albion, and Chattanooga, the old Indian name for Lookout Mountain. One speaker ridiculed the use of the latter, for it "was too uncommon, too uncouth; that strangers would miscall it. . . ." Another—most likely Long himself—responded: "The name might sound outlandish and strange to some ears, but if our city was a success, it would become familiar and pleasant, and there would not be another name like it in the world." With this the meeting voted for the local name.

*Facing Page:*
*Top Left*
*Joseph Enfield Berry, Chattanooga's first mayor in 1839, came from nearby Rhea County, known as the mother county of East Tennessee. (CHCBL)*

*Top Center*
*Dr. Milo Smith served probably seven terms as mayor of Chattanooga (1842, 1843, 1850, 1851, 1852, and again in 1862 and 1863). Dr. Smith was born at Smith's Cross Roads (Dayton) and studied medicine in Philadelphia. (CHCBL)*

*Top Right*
*Dr. Joseph S. Gillespie served as Chattanooga's mayor in 1844 and 1845. Early citizens seemed to prefer medical men as their political spokesmen. (CHCBL)*

*Bottom Left*
*William Williams, who came to Chattanooga about 1850, was in the steamboat navigation business and later became president of the city's first bank, as well as mayor in 1854. (CHCBL)*

*Bottom Center*
*David C. McMillan, mayor in 1856, arrived in Chattanooga in 1839 and opened a mercantile business. He later centered his interest on banking. (CHCBL)*

*Bottom Right*
*Charles E. Grenville, mayor in the critical year of 1860, earned his living as a miller, managing the Lookout Flour Mills. (CHCBL)*

*Right*
*The earliest representation of Chattanooga appeared in 1858 with an article by Porte Crayon (David Hunter Strothers) in* Harper's New Monthly Magazine. *Although he reported the town as a "new place, apparently just cut out of the woods," he expressed amazement at the speculative fever that appeared everywhere. The building with the cupola is the office of the Western and Atlantic Railroad. From* Harper's New Monthly Magazine.

*Below Right*
*The "Georgia Depot" of the Western and Atlantic Railroad. The first train from Atlanta on the W & A Railroad arrived on May 9, 1850, connecting the town of Chattanooga with the Atlantic seaboard at Savannah, Georgia, and Charleston, South Carolina. This technological innovation opened the gateway to the South. Courtesy of the U.S. War Department, General Staff, National Archives.*

The post office department approved the name on November 14, 1838; Parham's newspaper became the Chattanooga *Gazette*. The Tennessee legislature made it official when on December 20, 1839, it incorporated the "town" and within a month James Berry received the honor of being elected the first mayor.

Finally the commissioners sold at auction the town lots not claimed under occupancy rights. Since lands nearby in the Ocoee District had now fallen in price, many Chattanoogans invested extra funds in this real estate. Newcomers could find desirable locations, and several speculative syndicates using outside capital sought investments.

There was risk involved. Only an old swing ferry crossed the river. On the west side of Market Street, winter ponds sported wild ducks, and a ravine, maybe

15 feet deep in places, skirted along Mulberry (later Broad) Street. Crude lumber from arriving flatboats gave the town a frontier appearance; planks became sidewalks, gunwales curbing, and timbers basic housing

*With the completion of the W & A Railroad from Atlanta, packets did a lively business at Chattanooga when the "tides" were right and the channel deep enough. The people who gathered at the many small landings in East Tennessee discussed the business potential of the city. Courtesy of the U.S. Signal Corps, National Archives.*

materials. Four or five hewn log houses served as the main business places, one of which had been used by the government to store supplies during the Cherokee exodus. The area could easily have slipped into insignificance after the departure of the soldiers.

Those who put cash into real-estate ventures relied on certain reports which gradually became public knowledge: Georgia hoped to construct internal improvements to the Tennessee River. Then in December 1836 the Georgia legislature authorized construction of a railroad—the Western and Atlantic—from the center of the state (later Atlanta) northward and eventually designated Chattanooga as the northern terminal. This 137-mile line was to be the capstone of a network of roads reaching from Charleston, South Carolina, and Savannah, Georgia. Although the railroad was still a novelty and highly experimental, Georgia planned, financed, constructed, and operated the project as a state venture in an effort to capture western trade.

Engineering and financial problems delayed completion until May 9, 1850, when the first train rolled into Chattanooga. It was a day for celebration. Workers had smoothed a path through the gateway so that men and their goods could pass more cheaply, swiftly, and safely. Amid enthusiastic ceremonies the community rejoiced; "hurrah juice" added to the spirit of the hour as the chief spokesman "hic-upped" through his talk. De Bow's *Commercial Review* noted that the W & A "infused a new and progressive spirit" into the townspeople.

Through long years of anticipation, Chattanoogans had frequently despaired that the project would ever materialize; now they cheered Georgia in chorus. Local men who had stood by the scheme led this company; their numbers included James A. Whiteside, Rush Montgomery, Jesse Dugger, Thomas Crutchfield, Sr., Robert M. Hooke, Thomas McCallie, Sam Williams, John Long, Matt and Monroe Rawlings, and Ben Chandler. Most of these family surnames are familiar to Chattanoogans 130 years later.

In more distant areas, railroad buffs also had their hopes pinned to the W & A. They had been won over

to the iron horse and planned connecting links with the Georgia rails at Chattanooga. All were typically short lines joining sister cities, but fortunately all built with the same gauge, thereby permitting an exchange of equipment. During the decade of the 1850s they made Chattanooga a principal inland junction town in the southeast.

The first one completed (February 11, 1854), the 151-mile-long Nashville and Chattanooga, boasted a major engineering feat with the construction of the Tennessee River bridge at Bridgeport, Alabama. Three years later on March 28, 1857, the last spike in the Memphis and Charleston was driven, tying Chattanooga with the Mississippi River port. The next year a tunnel through Missionary Ridge opened the way for direct rail service via Knoxville with Virginia and eastern cities. Finally another, projected to Meridian, Mississippi, resulted by 1860 in the use of a nine-mile stretch to Trenton, Georgia, called the Wills Valley Railroad.

The Georgia-sponsored project of the 1840s had made Chattanooga a junction town in the 1850s and the steam locomotive had carried the town far from its Cherokee past. A common depot, generally unusual in the pioneering railroad era, served all lines and made extended journeys relatively easy.

Local reaction to such modernization was imme-

*Top Left*
*In 1838, 35-year-old James A. Whiteside arrived in Chattanooga; until his death on November 12, 1861, he ranked as the community's most outstanding citizen. As a lawyer, legislator, landowner, railroad promoter, banker, business and hotel man, cultural and religious leader, his energy touched every phase of the city's growth. (CHCBL)*

*Top Right*
*James Whiteside, owner of a large tract on the summit of Lookout*

*Mountain, readily saw the prospects of tourism with the establishment of rail connections to the lower South. In 1856 he opened the Lookout Mountain Hotel, which consisted of a large central building and satellite cottages. (CHCBL)*

*Above*
*This Cameron painting hangs in the Hunter Museum of Art. It depicts the Whiteside family against a background of Moccasin Bend and Umbrella Rock on Lookout Mountain. (CHCBL)*

diate: the "town" was chartered a "city" in 1851. Corporate limits expanded to Montgomery (Main) Street on the south to East End (Central) Avenue on the east. The city's first bank opened in 1853. Chattanooga actually felt affluent enough to think of a $50,000 pledge on behalf of the community in a bid to attract the University of the South to Lookout Mountain.

The economic impact of the railroad age reshaped the area's economy. When the W & A first ran trains, freight accumulated along Chattanooga's streets—grain, flour, cotton, bacon, whiskey, and corn; and a non-smoking ordinance was put into effect. Coal shipped in boxes went to Deep South blacksmiths. Livestock overran the town in certain seasons. One resident recalled, "I have seen every pen, lot, and even gardens in the fall of the year filled with horses, mules and hogs . . . awaiting transportation."

Rail service gave new life to river trade. In 1855 Chattanooga was made a port of delivery by the federal government, and in a practical way the place was a "sort of interior export town," although upstream traffic continued to be plagued with navigation problems. James and William Williams operated an extensive fleet of packets out of Chattanooga while managing their Tennessee River Mining, Manufacturing and Navigation Company.

To accommodate drummers and visitors, Tom Crutchfield, Sr., built a large hotel near the depot which became the center of the economic, social, and political life of the city. The railroad promoter and town booster, James A. Whiteside, also reacted to the new challenge. In 1852 he chartered a turnpike up Lookout Mountain, where he owned a considerable acreage. Four years later, to take full advantage of the "hygienic resource" found on the mountaintop, he opened the first Lookout Mountain Hotel. The city fathers issued an invitation to new industries, exempting "any mill or manufacturing company propelled by steam" from a corporate tax for five years.

It was obvious, however, that the past had not been forgotten nor had all signs of it been removed. A *Harper's* journalist in 1857 noted the "straggling and irregular streets, which are often interrupted by stumpy fields, ponds, and patches of forest timber." Blue laws, plentiful in number and meant to be enforced, prohibited business, sports, and work on Sundays and attempted to legislate morality for the rest of the week. Slave codes specifically controlled the happenings in the chattel community, and the night watch who called the hours kept an eye open for nocturnal suspicions.

According to one episode, the clergy were more successful than the law in sponsoring a moral crusade. In 1857 they successfully changed a Tuesday into Sunday, as one pastor put it, "the Lord shook the town, and sinners cried for mercy and found it." The town's three ministers sponsored a union program of evening revivals, spending one week with each church. After three weeks they started a second round, when at the end of the Monday meeting a request was made to close all business the next day and have a day-long service. All agreed.

But some folks elsewhere did not get the word. No one told Uncle Antipas Moore, who lived out Missionary Ridge way. Tuesday he brought beef to town as usual, but there were no customers; no one was on the street except another vendor. Antipas, in a fractious mood, thundered, "That town has gone crazy, there is not a house open; nobody will talk to you about business; it's just like Sunday clean down to the river. . . . Just as well take your taters back: you can't sell anything today."

The ardor of this crusade could scarcely disguise the boisterous spirit of the new junction town. The railroads had given the community an air of modernity, although most people's concerns were the daily chores of living. Little did they sense the implications of the impending national political storm.

*Left*
*Reese Bowen Brabson (1817-1863) entered the practice of law in Chattanooga. He served in the Tennessee General Assembly from 1851 to 1853, and in the U.S. Congress from 1859 to 1861. As a strong Union supporter he chose to be one of the last Southern congressmen to serve out his term, staying on until the inauguration of President Lincoln. (CHCBL)*

*Below*
*The home of Reese Bowen Brabson, called "The Mansion," stood on Brabson Hill. In addition to practicing law, the congressman raised stock and cultivated extensive orchards and vineyards.*

*Throughout East Tennessee loyal Union people secretly planned such action as the burning of railroad bridges. In this dramatic scene they are taking an oath of allegiance to the Constitution with right hands raised and left hands on the folds of the flag. From* Harper's Weekly, *1862.*

# Chapter Seven
# The Union Dissolved

Chattanooga and its East Tennessee hinterland of small farms and pioneering heritage differed markedly from the traditional cotton South. The rural population had little wealth to invest in labor, and although some landowners owned slaves, no system dependent on large numbers and absentee ownership developed. East Tennessee yeomen generally worked side by side with their help in a spirit of paternalistic concern. The city, on the other hand, did have business relations with the plantation economy of the deeper South. The strategic corridor through which the railroad into Georgia and South Carolina ran not only offered entry to good markets but also transmitted to the local commission merchants and processors a common understanding of the economic and political views that existed in the Deep South.

According to the 1860 census, 2,545 people lived in Chattanooga, while the population of Hamilton County numbered 13,258, of whom 192 were free blacks and 1,419 slaves. The Hamiltonians, about 50 percent of whom were Tennessee natives, were a young people. Altogether, 25 states and 12 foreign countries had sons or daughters in the area. Of the immigrant group, Irish railroad men and day laborers, German artisans, English mechanics and iron workers, and Welsh miners outnumbered all others. None of the residents owned many slaves and few had much wealth; only 43 persons in the county reported real estate in property and slaves valued at $15,000 or more and only 32, many the same people, had personal property worth $15,000 or more.

The county had 22 industries employing 210 men and four women. Most of these firms as well as the majority of the foreign-born lived in Chattanooga, which represented an urban frontier. Here a degree of economic specialization and social cooperation existed that was not possible in the rural hinterland. Here visitors and newcomers brought new contacts and ideas. Commission merchants did business with the Deep

South while processing plants—flour mills, distilleries, tanneries, lumber mills, and meat packing plants—sold much of their wares to the plantation country.

Ironmasters represented the most advanced technology. Webster and Mann operated the Chattanooga Foundry and Machine Works, while down by the Landing the East Tennessee Iron Manufacturing Company worked an experimental furnace fueled by coke. Robert Cravens, James A. Whiteside, Giles Edwards, and James Henderson headed this company.

The community's two leading newspapers represented opposite views on the tense political issues of the hour. James R. Hood, North Carolina-born, edited the *Gazette*, which carried the Union opinions of the 22-year-old journalist. In the *Advertiser*, H. F. Cooper, a New York native, aged 29, supported the Southern point of view. The columns of these two journals fueled the growing interest in the slave debate during the 1860 presidential campaign when Stephen Douglas, one of

the candidates, came to town to try to quiet disunion talk; the crowds enjoyed his canvass but did not vote for the Little Giant. Instead, the majority were for John Bell, Tennessee's favorite son.

South and east of Tennessee, reverberations of the campaign did not die down with Lincoln's victory; strong Southern protests led to early secession. When Georgia left the Union on January 19, 1861, the mounting pressure became very much of a local matter. Within a few miles of downtown Chattanooga ran the boundary line with an independent state, soon to become a Confederate border. Secessionists from Georgia chided their neighbors to the north for being irresolute and for harboring deep, dark dens of Lincolnism.

*The bluff furnace represented the most modern industrial plant in the region; here experiments with coke for fuel were carried on in 1861.*

*Facing Page*
*A wartime map showing the nature of the terrain and the towns of Dallas and Harrison.*

*The Reverend Thomas Hooke McCallie took up the duties as pastor of the First Presbyterian Church on the first of January 1862. (CHCBL)*

*Above*
*For a decade or so the social, economic, and political life of Chattanooga revolved around the Crutchfield House. Located across the street from the Union Station, it became strategically important to the armies during the war. (CHCBL)*

*Above Right*
*The Crutchfield brothers lived in Chattanooga through the long holocaust of war. Thomas Jr., a former mayor, moved to a secluded home at Amnicola. William worked with the Federals as guide and scout. (CHCBL)*

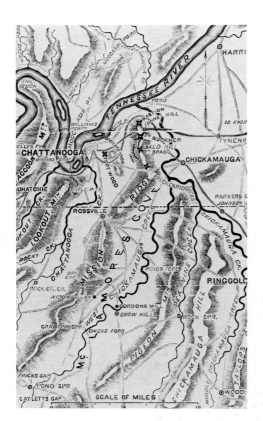

In late January, Jefferson Davis stopped for an overnight stay on his journey home, having resigned from the U.S. Senate. He spoke to a gathering at the Crutchfield House and was followed by William Crutchfield, brother of the inn's proprietor and an "uncompromising Union man." Crutchfield denounced the Mississippi statesman in a heated rebuttal. Eye witnesses reported varying details: an angry crowd shouted, women screamed, pistols were drawn. Crutchfield was ushered away by his brother; Davis sought information as to whether his assailant was an "honorable man" worthy of a duel.

No contest was fought; the Davis party entrained the next morning. But tension tenaciously gripped the town and the image of a Union community spread across the South. On February 9, 1861, the local people voted in a Tennessee referendum in relation to secession. They supported the general statewide position which decisively defeated the idea of separation from the Union. The Hamilton County vote was 1,445 for the Union to 445 for separation.

When word of the firing on Fort Sumter sped across Tennessee, this passive Unionism changed to a vocal pro-Confederate enthusiasm in Middle and West Tennessee. But in the eastern portion of the state, including the Chattanooga area and its county, aggressive Unionism remained constant. At the end of May, Hamilton County sent 24 delegates to a Union convention to attempt to find a common course of action; these men refused to bow before the storm.

The governor of Tennessee, Isham G. Harris, led the state into an active role within the Confederacy. He called for a second state-wide referendum on June 8 and expected an overwhelming majority of voters to favor separation and therefore make his efforts official.

The town of Chattanooga drifted into a military stance. Anyone looking at a map of the railroads could not miss its strategic importance, but in these early months it seemed enough to appoint a day watchman to guard the magazine, leaving night observance to the Home Guard. A vigilance committee of 12 appointed by the mayor had the responsibility to "take into consideration persons suspected of being dangerous in the community, and take such action as in their wisdom they think expedient." The slave codes were tightened respecting the movement of blacks in the nighttime hours, and a committee was dispatched to the governor to confer about arms for the city.

By June 8 the political strife, which had mounted in intensity since the presidential election, was fast escalating into a mighty upheaval. Eight weeks had passed since the attack on Fort Sumter; 10 states had already joined the Southern Confederacy, and Tennessee citizens all felt pressured to make the ultimate decision of allegiance.

In the second referendum Tennesseans voted an overwhelming endorsement for secession. Yet East Tennessee continued to favor the Union: in the eastern

counties the result was 32,923 against and 14,780 for separation. Hamilton County reported a solid Union victory: 1,260 against separation and 854 for it. The county totals, however, included Chattanooga's contrary vote of 421 to 51—in favor of secession: so the city and the county chose different roles. Locally Hamilton County and two neighboring counties, Bradley and Marion, were the southernmost political units in the United States that had a hard core of Union supporters. But everywhere neighborhoods, church congregations, and families split over the growing conflict.

Some Union men now found it to their best interests to quit the Chattanooga area. The manager of the bluff furnace, James Henderson, a native of New Jersey, departed. J. W. Wilder left after reports circulated that he was associated with a New York newspaper. James Hood of the *Gazette* found himself isolated; he stated that "as early as June 1861, a self-appointed conclave sat in judgment upon the editor . . . and nothing but the timely interference of Union friends enabled him to get away in safety."

David M. and Summerfield Key, Richard Watkins, J. W. Gillespie, Robert Berry, Frank Walker, John L. Hopkins, Robert M. Hooke, A. M. Johnson, and Samuel Williams emerged as leaders of the Confederate position. Some of their town and county neighbors who stayed loyal to the Union, although after June 8 they were an oppressed minority, were William Clift, Abel A. Pearson, Levi and D. C. Trewhitt, Ben Chandler, E. M. Cleaveland, William Crutchfield, R. C. McRee, A. M. and G. O. Cate, and S. McCaleb.

Pockets of trouble soon appeared. Tom Crutchfield, Jr., was caught in a serious dilemma at the Crutchfield House. Many volunteer troops heading for the Virginia front passed through town on the trains. In Chattanooga they expected to eat; the Confederacy, however, had no arrangements for feeding men in transit, and the recruits had no thought of paying. Crutchfield demurred. One group, the proprietor wrote, "loaded guns & fixed bayonets and marched in front of the house to mob me, calling me out and telling me that they had been told that I was a Lincolnite . . . and gave me five

minutes to explain." Crutchfield claimed he lost at least $10,000 before he sold the inn to escape the problem.

Many Union men were also on the move from north Georgia and East Tennessee to join Union units in Kentucky. Underground railways operated to help these fellows escape southern service. Colonel William Clift, a wealthy landowner from the Soddy section and formerly commander of the county militia, encouraged these volunteers with his vigorous activity which belied his better than 65 years of age. Clift used a camp meeting ground at Sale Creek in helping volunteers. Confederates in the area, attracted by this action, marched in mid-September 1861 to halt Clift's operations. Civil War among neighbors, at first with all the trappings of a comic opera, had come to the Chattanooga country.

*Facing Page*
*An 1864 photograph of a "loyal planter's" house on Lookout Mountain. Not all loyalists or Lincolnites, as they were called, lived in such comfortable quarters. Courtesy of the U.S. Signal Corps, Brady Collection, National Archives.*

*Above*
*William Clift (1794-1886), extensive landowner of the northern part of Hamilton County and head of the county militia for some years prior to the Civil War, assumed leadership of regional Union supporters in Clift's War. Some of his sons served in the Confederate army. (CHCBL)*

Friends persuaded Clift to abandon his camp; action changed to talk and a formal "Cross-Roads Treaty" resulted. The gist of this agreement signed at Smith's Cross Roads (Dayton) was that if the Union men went home and kept the peace, they would not be disturbed. Violations, however, sprouted up on both sides, and before long Clift and his followers returned to the campground. They threw up earthworks, built a cannon from a hollow log, and generally prepared for Clift's War.

All hopes that the treaty might be renewed were dashed on November 9. That night civilian Unionists attempted to disrupt rail transportation across East Tennessee by burning bridges. Five spans, including two over South Chickamauga Creek just east of Missionary Ridge, were destroyed. This "revolt of the Unionists" brought a wave of Confederate wrath into the region; fear and a revengeful spirit led to arrests with orders that drumhead court-martial trials be held and guilty parties be executed on the spot.

In Chattanooga the city resolved that all white males between the ages of 18 and 45 constitute the police force. Governor Isham Harris nervously ordered the capture of "Tory" Clift and his men "dead or alive." The Confederacy dispatched Colonel S.A.M. Wood with eight companies of his Seventh Regiment of Alabama Volunteers to the area. These first troops stationed in Chattanooga got busy at once; they sent a force to north Chickamauga Creek, "where the citizens are most disloyal and a good many in open rebellion."

Wood, working with other troops including the Rhea County Home Guard, moved against Clift's camp. But cooperation was too much to ask of these amateur soldiers who in a confused maneuver fired on their own people, inflicting the only wounds of Clift's War. Clift's men, aware of the Confederate approach, dispersed; some headed for Kentucky and Federal military service while others sought mountain seclusion.

Despite all the blunders, Colonel Wood seemed pleased. He moved his troops to Tyner "to get out of the way of whiskey, and to encamp among the Lincolnites." When he returned from the campaign against the campground, zeal flavored his report to General Braxton Bragg:

*All in confusion; a general panic; everybody running up and down, and adding to the general alarm. I issued an order taking command; put the town under martial law; shut up the groceries; forbade any exit, by railroad or otherwise without a permit from provost-marshal; had every avenue guarded; arrested about 12 persons who were talking Lincolnism before I came. . . . I have relieved all our friends in this county. All were alarmed; all are now resting easy. I have run all the Lincolnites.*

Wood's quixotic report apparently convinced his superiors that troops were not needed in Chattanooga by the year's end. Such opinions, however, soon changed, for by March 8, 1862, General John B. Floyd's command marched into Chattanooga from Fort Donelson. The onetime U.S. Secretary of War immediately found it a place "of a very considerable military importance."

*Facing Page:*
*Top*
*This artist's representation of Chattanooga from the northern bank of the Tennessee River shows the former site of Ross's Landing with the road leading to Market Street. Note "the boys" in the foreground busily engaged in a card game. From* Harper's Weekly, *September 1863.*

*Above*
*Chattanooga provided many spots for spying and wigwagging. From* Harper's Weekly.

*Facing Page:*
*Bottom*
*A magazine field artist dramatizes the awful hardships endured by men in the Civil War. From* Harper's Weekly, *November 1863.*

*An elaborate blockhouse defended the railroad yards looking toward Fort Jones. Courtesy of the Office of Chief Engineers, National Archives.*

## Chapter Eight

# The War of the 1860s

A sense of the tragic hovered over Chattanooga in 1862; possibly no other American community experienced such a variety of unforeseen and moving events.

In the wake of the February surrender of Forts Henry and Donelson, much of western and middle Tennessee was occupied by Union troops. Refugees with their pitiful belongings at once appeared at the Chattanooga depot as women and children sought solace in flight. Trainloads of sick and convalescing men from Nashville hospitals also arrived after spending frigid hours with no medical aid. Chattanooga, without Confederate personnel or funds, rallied to relieve the suffering by preparing meals and converting empty warehouses into wards.

These undreamed-of new facets of war stunned the citizenry, who discovered that they had no ready assistance. The state Confederate government by March 22 had lost its ability to govern, and law and order across the land fell into the hands of bushwhackers and guerrillas. Those with Union loyalties found new troubles by mid-April, when the first Confederate Conscription Act called all men 18 to 35 years of age into service.

On Saturday, April 12, startling news aroused the community to an unbelievable pitch of excitement. Late in the day word spread of the great locomotive chase on the W & A railroad. This exploit, "the most extraordinary and astonishing adventure of the Civil War," was designed by Union men to disrupt southern rail traffic. Disguised as civilians, they detached the engine and three boxcars from the daily train from Atlanta and sped off in it. The abortive adventure ended a few miles from the Georgia-Tennessee border when the train's engine, named the "General," had its fires go out and water ran low. Patrols and civilian posses hunted down the 22 Federal soldiers. James J. Andrews, the leader, with his "long, black, silken beard" and actor's calm, was captured, imprisoned, and sen-

tenced to death; he escaped and was recaptured in Chattanooga before his Atlanta execution. Seven others went to the gallows, eight escaped, and six were exchanged. The latter group received the Medal of Honor—the first ever presented—an honor later extended to 13 others.

On the very same Saturday that the "General" was stolen, messages arrived in town that the Yankees controlled the railroads in a different direction. Huntsville fell and then Stevenson and Bridgeport, Alabama, Jasper in neighboring Marion County, and much of the Sequatchie Valley. Local civilians who were Southern or Union men worked for their respective sides as guides, couriers, informers, and watchers over fords,

ferries, and cross-roads. Foragers for both armies raided garden patches and hen roosts.

The Confederate troops in Chattanooga had orders to make a desperate stand if needed although some had only "country weapons." On June 7 they got their first test. General James Negley's reconnaissance forces suddenly appeared on the north bank of the Tennessee River. They had crossed Walden Ridge and commenced throwing shells into the town. For a day and a half they terrorized civilians and kept the Confederate reinforcements busy. Then they left, but General Negley reported: "The Union people along the roads are wild with joy, while the rebels are panic-stricken." In town the damage proved to be mainly psychological. A de-

fender wrote to his wife:

*They threw shells and balls all through Market Street and over the town and far beyond the Crutchfield House . . . but no considerable damage was done. . . . We are still on Cameron Hill without tents or baggage. We roll up on the hillside and sleep as we can, having nothing in the world but bread and meat to eat.*

In an effort to draw the Federal troops from the South, the Confederates decided on an offensive campaign into Kentucky. Again the railroads helped determine events; General Braxton Bragg, by the last of July, began concentrating his troops for this operation

*Above Left*
*"The First Gun at Chickamauga."* This A.R. Waud wartime sketch depicts the action at Reed's bridge which opened the bloody battle of the west. From Brown, The Mountain Campaign in Georgia.

*Facing Page*
This Civil War panorama by Thomas C. Gordon depicts James Andrews' Raiders in their attempt to steal a Rebel train. From the Collections of Greenfield Village and the Henry Ford Museum.

*Above Right*
This wartime sketch by Theodore R. Davis of Harper's Weekly represents the courier line as a supplement to other signal officers' devices. Local men often served as scouts, informers, or couriers because they knew the countryside, which in many areas was without maps. From Harper's Weekly, 1863.

fell upon the ear as the train was sweeping around the base of giant Lookout."

During the ensuing lull, normal events sometimes submerged preoccupation with military matters. On Walden Ridge, for example, in February 1863 a wedding was celebrated by an all-night dance. One who attended reported that the guests were:

*. . . composed of "complicated ingredients." I do not suppose that the history of the world contains such a rare case of universal* concord *being the result of universal* discord. *The party was composed of 1st, Rebel and Union citizens; 2d, Rebel and Union soldiers; 3rd, Rebel and Union deserters; 4th, Rebel and Union spies; 5th, Rebel and Union bushwhackers.*

*Scarcely a harsh word was uttered during the whole night; all danced together as if nothing was wrong, and parted mutually the next morning, each party marching off separately.*

*Considering the great hatred between the different parties it is marvelous that bloodshed was not the immediate result.*

When Bragg's army, dislodged from its Middle Tennessee position in mid-summer of 1863, retired to Chattanooga, the *Rebel*'s headline shouted, "The Crisis Is upon Us." All that had happened now seemed long ago and of minor consequence. On their retreat the men of the Army of Tennessee heard of the Vicksburg surrender and of the events at Gettysburg. Chattanooga

at Chattanooga. Within a month some 27,000 men were camped in the vicinity. Churches and public buildings were converted to hospitals and headquarters; some citizens had to give up their homes, and residents were restricted in their movements. Water became scarce and prices rose.

On August 28, 1862, Bragg led his men across the river pontoon bridge and over Walden Ridge for an ill-starred Kentucky operation. His headquarters remained in Chattanooga as did a newspaper founded the first of the month under the name *Chattanooga Rebel*. The *Rebel* carried local news and advertisements but gave special attention to military doings. It supplied information about affairs in Kentucky and of Bragg's withdrawal, which seemed to bring war again to Chattanooga. Although Bragg's new position rested near Murfreesboro, the railroad through Chattanooga served as his main supply artery and *Rebel* reporters witnessed many interesting stories at first hand.

On December 4 General Joseph E. Johnston, newly appointed commander of the Confederate forces in the West, established Chattanooga headquarters; a few days later President Davis arrived. Together they left to review Bragg's troops; at the depot a "splendid brass band in attendance struck up 'The Bonnie Blue Flag' and broke out into 'Dixie,' the lively strains of which

*Above Left*
*General Braxton Bragg was often bitterly censured by comrades in arms who found him without the resourcefulness or personality needed for leadership. From Cirker,* Dictionary of American Portraits, *1967, Dover.*

*Above Right*
*William S. Rosecrans (1819-1898), commander of the Army of the Cumberland. From Cirker,* Dictionary of American Portraits, *1967, Dover.*

*Facing Page*
*The war of the 1860s became the first railroad war in history. Chattanooga's junction position made it a natural target. Courtesy of W.C. King.*

with its railroads tying much of the central South together assumed more and more importance.

With premeditated caution the Union army commanded by General William S. Rosecrans waited until August 16 to advance out of the Cumberland Plateau. To make the planned strategy of crossing the Tennessee River downstream from Chattanooga—at Caperton's Ferry, Bridgeport, Battle Creek, and Shellmound—the handsome, cultivated Rosecrans sent Colonel John T. Wilder with his brigade of mounted infantry directly toward the prized junction. On August 21 Wilder and his troops appeared suddenly at the river's edge where Negley had been the previous year. They surveyed the terrain, dug in their artillery on Stringer's Ridge, and shelled the town. A large congregation at the Presbyterian Church sat silently through the long prayer as the shells fell, according to some; the Federal gunners, however, claimed the people "poured out like bees from a hive."

The invading Federals also noted the Confederate positions across the river: a fort with two James rifles on Cameron Hill about 300 feet above the water, another fort with embrasures for nine guns on a neighboring lesser hill, a three-gun water battery along the river, and a nearby large distillery "pierced for muskets." At the end of Market Street stood an earthwork with

THE CAMPAIGN

two guns commanding the ferry and a pontoon bridge tied up along the levee. On the rocky bluff to the left stood another large fort and two smaller works.

Wilder's men kept up a lively demonstration, belying their numbers and purpose. They threw shells into town with special attention given to the depot, the Crutchfield House, and the office of the *Rebel*. For a time the *Rebel's* printers worked in the vault of an abandoned bank, but when conditions worsened, the management loaded the equipment on rail cars and started a new chapter in their existence as the Chattanooga *Rebel on Wheels*—with a final edition run off on April 27, 1865, in Selma, Alabama.

On September 9 Wilder's men received a semaphore message from across the river. It came from blue-clad troops of Colonel Smith D. Atkins, who commanded the 92nd Illinois mounted infantry as a unit in General Thomas L. Crittenden's 21st Corps. They had just entered Chattanooga, which had been abandoned by its Confederate defenders. The 21st immediately flew its regimental colors from the Crutchfield House as Wilder's men shouted and cheered. One of the troopers found the city had "a dirty, dreary appearance, almost deserted of citizens. . . ."

On the other hand, the young resident Presbyterian minister, Reverend Thomas McCallie, recorded events with relief and optimism in his diary:

*Chattanooga never saw a more eventful day. . . . The Confederate cavalry withdrew about 9 o'clock in the morning, and about 10 a.m. the streams of Union soldiers, the first we had seen, dressed in blue, came pouring in. Not a child was harmed, not a woman insulted, not a man killed. . . . Here was a peaceful occupation of a city without any violence or outrage of any kind.*

Wilder's brigade immediately forded the river and joined in a hastily organized chase after the Confederates. By this time all of Rosecrans' men had crossed the Tennessee River and had laboriously worked their way over the mountains of northern Alabama and Georgia only to find themselves widely scattered. In a countryside with a sparse population, few farms, and no good roads, the Federal corps were 40 miles apart. Once this dilemma became apparent, days of marching and countermarching in a "great amphitheater of hills" took place before the men in blue concentrated near Crawfish Springs (Chickamauga, Georgia).

Meanwhile the Confederates, expecting reinforcements from Mississippi and Virginia, evacuated Chattanooga for a secluded rendezvous in the hill country near Lafayette, Georgia. From this lair General Bragg sought to strike his enemy's isolated corps, but his own organization seethed with discord and lacked a cooperative spirit within the first echelon of officers. Maneuvering through the maze of forest trees, cedar thickets, and twisted undergrowth, the two antagonists anticipated a major conflict; but when small units clashed on September 18, no one realized the furor that would ensue or had a battle plan in which strategy would play the victor's ally. Instead, what followed was a "soldiers' battle," fought almost continuously over new ground and in a series of disconnected efforts by units of brigade size. No commander could see far enough to direct a larger group in the surrounding wilderness.

With the meandering, sluggish, and in places deep South Chickamauga Creek to their backs, the Confederates pushed through thickets, battle smoke, and cannon blasts. In no way was there any semblance of a stable line; units of any size were used to extend the lines if they happened to be nearby. Emphasis did fall on the Confederate right wing, as the overall scheme aimed to retake the roads back to Chattanooga and drive the Union troops into a mountain trap.

Darkness, rather than the flow of the battle, ended the Saturday fighting as men and beasts, especially on the Federal side, suffered from a lack of springs or flowing streams. That night officers planned strategy, Thomas's men cut trees for log breastworks, and General James Longstreet arrived from Virginia to take command of the Confederate left wing while wounded and fatigued men spent miserable cold hours on the field.

Action renewed on Sunday morning. About mid-day, by chance, a Longstreet charge found a gap in the Union line. General Rosecrans, two corps commanders, and the right flank of the Federal army fled the field, making their way back to Chattanooga. General George Thomas, later to be dubbed the "Rock of Chickamauga," rallied the others and in a desperate, protracted fight on Snodgrass Hill held on until evening. Then he withdrew to Rossville.

They call the conflict Chickamauga, "Bloody Battle of the West." The Confederates with troops representing all 11 southern states, Kentucky, and Missouri held the field. The price of victory matched the cost of defeat as each army listed 28 percent of its men as casualties in the two days of carnage. The Union reported 1,657 killed; the Confederates, 2,312. The Union wounded numbered 9,756; the Confederate, 14,674.

On September 20 the Chickamauga Campaign ended, but without respite for the soldiers because a new kind of struggle called the Chattanooga Campaign immediately began. Hysterical fear seemed to have gripped the Union commander that Sunday; in the agony of defeat and the weariness of exhaustion, panic tore at the Army of the Cumberland. Although Chattanooga had no defenses, within about two days a semblance of order was restored.

Rosecrans' men were all crowded within approximately one square mile; this was virtually the entire town. They razed outlying buildings and felled trees to open a line of fire; riflepits, ditches, and earthworks along with shelter tents and the baggage of an army submerged the civilian aspects of the town. The Chickamauga wounded who "could bear transportation" were sent off in ambulances while the "walking wounded" tried to get away on foot. The old residents who remained had to herd together in places unwanted by the military and exist on a daily basis under a strict master.

Meanwhile, Confederate dissidence increased as Bragg refused the pleas of subordinates to press after the disorganized Yankees. He preferred rather the concept of siege by anchoring his long line on the Tennessee River at the base of Raccoon Mountain. From there it swung across Lookout Valley, Lookout Mountain,

Chattanooga Valley, Missionary Ridge, and back to the river near the mouth of South Chickamauga Creek. Additional defenses at key sites guarded against "homemade Yankees." From this position the Confederates controlled river traffic, all railroads, and the roads on the southern side of the Tennessee River. The Federals had only one route by which to bring in food, forage, medicine, and ammunition—a 60-mile road over Walden Ridge to their railhead at Bridgeport, Alabama.

Heavy rains and cavalry raids such as General Joseph Wheeler's legendary one of early October combined to bring to a crisis the problem of survival. W. F. G. Shanks of *Harper's Magazine* graphically tells the details:

*After the third week of the siege, the men were put on quarter rations, and only two or three articles were supplied in this meager quantity. The only meat to be had was bacon, "sidebacon," or "middling," I think it was called, and a slice about the size of three larger fingers of a man's hand, sandwiched between the two halves of a "Lincoln Platform" as the four inches square cake of "hard bread" was called, and washed down by a pint of coffee, served for a meal. . . . I have often seen hundreds of soldiers following behind the wagon trains which had just arrived, picking out of the mud the crumbs of bread, coffee, rice, etc., which were wasted from the boxes and sacks by the rattling of the wagons over the stones. Nothing was wasted in those days, and though the inspectors would frequently condemn whole wagon loads of provisions as spoiled by exposure during the trip, and order the contents to be thrown away, the soldiers or citizens always found some use for it. The hundreds of citizens who were confined in the town at the same time suffered even more than the men. They were forced to huddle together in the center of town as best they could, and many of the houses occupied by them during the siege surpassed in filth, point of numbers of occupants, and general destitution the worst tenement house in New York City.*

The extreme right of the Federal position at Chickamauga was at Lee and Gordon's Mill; today it stands as a veteran landmark on the field. Courtesy of the U.S. Signal Corps, Brady Collection, National Archives.

*James Longstreet (1821-1904), a graduate of West Point in 1842, gained high personal acclaim for the charge he led at Chickamauga. From Cirker,* Dictionary of American Portraits, *1967, Dover.*

*About 12 miles south of Chattanooga, Confederate and Union soldiers clashed in the woods. For two days, September 19 and 20, the din of battle could be heard for miles around. Courtesy of W.C. King.*

During these autumn days only a rare artillery duel reminded the soldiers of war. The main participants in the noisemaking were guns on Moccasin Bend challenging pieces from Confederate positions on Lookout Mountain. Observers found little damage; only ammunition was lost. Along the picket lines, especially on Chattanooga Creek, the troopers took advantage of the quiet to exchange news, coffee, and tobacco.

Among the Confederate officers the calm concealed a serious crisis. The complaints on the part of various subordinates persisted about Bragg's failure to finalize his Chickamauga victory. The officers' view that a new commander had to be found brought President Davis to investigate. He interviewed the officers in Bragg's

presence at headquarters on Missionary Ridge. Despite their pleas, Davis retained Bragg. More Confederate subordinates were transferred to other sectors, while army morale at Chattanooga sank to a new low.

The Federal military establishment and the civilian government, meanwhile, lost no time in arranging to help the entrapped men of Rosecrans. Within 48 hours of the defeat at Chickamauga, some 23,000 men of the Army of the Potomac under General Joseph Hooker entrained in Virginia for a 1,157-mile rail trip to Bridgeport. In Mississippi General William T. Sherman got orders to bring four veteran divisions east and to repair the railroad from Memphis enroute. General Thomas replaced Rosecrans in command at Chattanooga, but

*Left*
*Ulysses S. Grant (1811-1885) graduated from West Point in 1843. During the war his leadership qualities revealed themselves in a positive way at Chattanooga. For his victory there Grant received the rank of lieutenant general. While commanding in the East in 1864, he kept in close contact with Sherman advancing from Chattanooga against Atlanta and then on to the sea. From Cirker,* Dictionary of American Portraits, *1967, Dover.*

*Facing Page*
*An 1889 Kurz & Allison version of Hooker's fight on Lookout Mountain. Courtesy of the Library of Congress.*

more significantly the entire western command district was reorganized and placed under General Ulysses S. Grant.

On October 23 Grant arrived in Chattanooga after a long wet ride from Bridgeport and took charge. He found plans for relieving the siege already prepared. Just three nights after his arrival he put into execution a three-step movement. Under the cover of night some 1,800 Union troops slipped down the Tennessee River in pontoons from Cameron Hill past Confederate pickets at Lookout Mountain to Brown's Ferry. This surprise move gained a bridgehead on the river's south shore; the men who landed were presently joined by comrades who had marched across Moccasin Bend.

The next day General Hooker traveled from Bridgeport into Lookout Valley, where his men fought a confusing night engagement called the Battle of Wauhatchie before linking up with the Brown's Ferry group. As a result of these maneuvers the Confederates lost not only their position west of Lookout Mountain but also opened the way for a new Federal supply route. From Kelly's Ferry, downstream from the rough mountain stretch of the river, roads led to Brown's Ferry where a pontoon bridge crossed to Moccasin Bend. From there a second temporary span crossed the stream into Chattanooga.

Union engineers had assembled a crude steamboat,

the *Chattanooga,* at Bridgeport and started it on its maiden voyage with loaded barges on the night of October 30. The instant it tied up at Kelly's Ferry, word swept through the camps that the "Cracker Line" was now open; full rations would follow. Supplies accumulated and the rugged days of the wagon trains were a thing of the past, during which time the Federals reported that they had "used up" 10,000 army mules.

In less than one month Grant was ready to assume the offensive. This decision came at a time when General Bragg's force suffered a reduction in numbers. Longstreet's men had marched off to campaign around Knoxville. All America turned its attention on Chattanooga. The Richmond *Dispatch* summed up the feeling: "It is an hour of fearful moment. The destinies of this generation, and of generations yet to come, may be involved in this battle."

The extended Union lines, coupled with the nature of the terrain, dictated the plan of operation—which called for three distinct yet coordinated actions. Grant initiated the assault on his besiegers in the valley. On November 23 Thomas's Army of the Cumberland marched by Fort Wood to push all Confederate pickets back to their riflepits at the western base of Missionary Ridge. In doing so they got possession of Orchard Knob before spending a rainy night without shelter in the newly won field.

The next day the plan called for General Hooker to win possession of Lookout Mountain. Amid clouds and river mist his men assaulted the Confederates' prepared position on the mountain's saddle where the Cravens family had their home. Here the Southern troops commanded an unusual prospect with some supporting artillery on the mountaintop. But their numbers were small and the odds heavily weighted against them. As the afternoon rain and fog increased, intense firing gave way to sporadic action. During the night the Southern troops withdrew from the mountain; at dawn the Yankees climbed to the summit and planted their flag. Hooker's fight was that day referred to as the battle "above the clouds," thus giving perpetual glamor to an otherwise routine action.

The culmination of the Chattanooga campaign came the next day, which dawned clear and bright after what many soldiers thought of as a symbolic eclipse. Bragg's troops, occupying long lines along Missionary Ridge under Generals J. C. Breckinridge and William J. Hardee, were outnumbered and much of their artillery was badly placed. Grant stationed Thomas in the center of his front at Orchard Knob; Hooker's orders designated a position on the right following a march from Lookout Mountain. Sherman's divisions, having just arrived in the area, successfully established a bridgehead on the southern shore of the Tennessee River near the end of Missionary Ridge. He was instructed about midnight to begin the action at "day dawn."

All morning the noise of battle reverberated across the valley from the Tunnel Hill sector where General Pat Cleburne held Sherman on even terms. Grant, at Orchard Knob, grew apprehensive. A correspondent for the New York *Tribune* saw him there:

*Enveloped in a rather huge military coat, wearing a slouching hat, which seems to have a predisposition to turn up before and down behind, with a gait slightly limping from a recent accident; giving his orders, speaking but little and in a low tone, and with an accent which partook of the slight nervousness, intensity of feeling, yet perfect self-control seen in all his movements. I thought at the time that Gen. Grant might be described best as a little, old man—yet not really old—with a keen eye, who did not intend that anything should escape his observation.*

About noon the Union commander instructed General Thomas to prepare an assault on the Confederate riflepits at the western foot of the ridge. When the Federals finally moved out with banners flying, they came into full view of the thinly held Confederate lines; the steep, boulder-strewn wooded slope lost its advantage to the psychological effect the dramatic scene ex-

*In the process of building Chattanooga into a military base, government sawmills sprang up everywhere; workers indiscriminately cut trees on private land. Courtesy of the National Archives.*

*When Ulysses S. Grant was placed in charge of all Western forces, William T. Sherman succeeded to command of the Army of the Tennessee, and took part in the Chattanooga campaign in late 1863. All photos from Cirker,* Dictionary of American Portraits, *1967, Dover.*

*Leonidas Polk, founder of the University of the South, served as major general in the Confederate army. Despite his lack of military experience, Polk served ably, seeing action mainly in the Mississippi River defenses.*

*General George Thomas succeeded Rosecrans as commander of the Army of the Cumberland prior to victory at Chattanooga, where he also played a major role. From* Harper's Weekly, October 10, 1863.

erted on the Rebel defenders. The troops in the riflepits were overwhelmed; the soldiers in blue without command pressed their advantage. No general orders directed their action. Common soldiers urged on by junior officers reached the crest, broke the Confederate lines, and forced the Confederates to retire into north Georgia. While details followed the retreating men in gray, other Union soldiers observed the next day, Thursday, November 26, as the first national Thanksgiving Day—which one described as "sad, solemn, grand."

The Chattanooga campaign offset the dearly won victory Bragg had gained at Chickamauga. A large Tennessee supply area as well as all of Chattanooga's railroads were now securely held by the Federals. General Bragg resigned his command while General Grant received the highest possible promotion. Most impor-

tantly, the gateway to the south stood ajar; Sherman was selected to exploit this route in 1864.

Immediately after Missionary Ridge, Chattanooga's role in the war changed drastically. Engineers and quartermasters continued to be the town architects but now their purpose was to build a great forward base; the community's prime business remained the war effort. The provost marshal still ran Chattanooga's affairs, having set aside the municipal government, which disappeared until October 7, 1865. Camp followers and freedmen, many at Camp Contraband just north of the river, crowded in on the remaining old residents, who struggled with poverty and want. Some relief came by spring through the Western Sanitary Commission, a forerunner of the modern Red Cross, and the East Tennessee Relief Association.

Top
Some GIs of the 1860s found leisure time to excavate this Indian mound. An account of their activity was later put into a Smithsonian Institution report. Courtesy of the Library of Congress.

Above
Chattanooga in 1864, some months after local fighting had ended. Courtesy of the office of Chief of Engineers, National Archives.

Facing Page:
Top
Sutlers' row — sometimes called "robbers' road." St. Paul's Episcopal Church can be seen on the extreme right. Courtesy of the Library of Congress.

Facing Page:
Bottom
On Christmas Day, 1863, General George H. Thomas ordered the creation of the National Cemetery, a wooded site "in commemoration of the battles of Chattanooga . . . and to provide a proper resting place for the remains of the brave men who fell." Union dead, hastily buried earlier, were re-interred in the new graveyard. Prisoners of both World Wars who died in the local camp were also interred in the cemetery. The special monument pictured here commemorates the deeds of Andrews' raiders. Courtesy of the Chattanooga Convention and Visitors Bureau.

Herculean effort was required to get ready for the Atlanta Campaign, which was supposed to begin in May when the grass was plentiful enough to support the transport teams, cavalry, and artillery mounts. The main supply rail line, the Nashville & Chattanooga, was a shambles. No track remained from Bridgeport to Chattanooga; only three of the eight spans on the Tennessee River bridge were intact; and the 800-foot trestle over the gorge at Running Water Creek was completely gone. The line was made a part of the United States Military Railroad, and Union engineers in two weeks in February had it operating; but the roadbed in general was so bad that supply trains averaged only about eight miles per hour from Nashville.

Government sawmills devoured the forests. In Chattanooga giant warehouses sprang up on vacant lots, competing for space with numerous corrals, parked transport equipment, and hospital buildings. The Federals constructed a reservoir and associated waterworks, fashioned a shipyard, built a bridge across the Tennessee River, and erected a rolling mill and foundry to reroll twisted railroad iron. Only the National Cemetery, created on Christmas Day, 1863, recalled the past.

During the first months of the new year additional soldiers arrived for Sherman's campaign until they numbered about 100,000. Sutlers—licensed merchants and service personnel who catered to both military and civilian customers—occupied vacant buildings of little pretense, newly fashioned business stands, and tents. They sold clothing, food, souvenirs, liquor, tobacco, and knickknacks; they worked as barbers, dentists, photographers, horse traders, and undertakers. When prices inflated rapidly, the government imposed a local program of price control, an early variety of OPA.

Private homes remained military headquarters. Churches were commandeered at first as hospitals and later as ordnance depots, prisons, or civilian health centers. One served as the Post Chapel, where school classes as well as religious services were held. With some free time on their hands, Yankee soldiers explored Lookout Mountain and Lula Lake as well as nearby Indian mounds. It seemed fortunate for all that editor James Hood had returned under army protection and resumed publishing the Chattanooga *Gazette* on February 29, 1864, giving the war news—of course with a Union emphasis—as well as accounts of local happenings.

Before long, most important news came from beyond the community. On September 2 Sherman entered Atlanta and later that fall broke all connections with his long thin railroad through Chattanooga when he started for the sea. At year's end the battles of Franklin and Nashville concluded major military action in Tennessee. Exciting days ensued with receipt of the word about the fall of Richmond and the surrender at Appomattox; soldiers cheered and the big guns thundered. Celebration, however, turned to emotional expressions of sorrow when it was learned that President Lincoln had been assassinated. Jenkin Lloyd Jones, a Federal soldier and an accurate observer, caught the tone in his April 16 diary entry:

*The whole town was draped in mourning, flags tied with black and white crepe exhibited in all parts of the town, while the 100-pounder Parrotts high up on Cameron Hill fired half-hour guns from 5 a.m. till 6 p.m. The gloom of yesterday still hangs over the camp.*

Facing Page:
Far Right
Point Lookout, a popular place for picture-taking, attracted soldiers with a little spare time. Letters and pictures from men stationed here made Chattanooga a household word across America. Courtesy of the office of Chief of Engineers, National Archives.

*Top*
*General U.S. Grant and his party visit Lookout Mountain prior to his transfer to the eastern theater of war. Command in the local area then went to General Sherman. (General Grant appears in the lower left of the picture with his famous cigar.) Courtesy of the National Archives.*

*Above*
*During the buildup for the Atlanta campaign as many as 100,000 men gathered in the Chattanooga area. Later a permanent force manned the base. Courtesy of the Library of Congress.*

At war's end the government gave
the city this bridge, which had been
built by Union troops. In 1867 the
greatest recorded flood on the
Tennessee River swept the bridge
away. Courtesy of the U.S. Signal
Corps, Brady Collection, National
Archives.

# Chapter Nine
# After Mars

At war's end the total concern of the military centered on demobilization. In September 1865 both the Nashville & Chattanooga and the Western & Atlantic railroads were returned to their owners. Soldiers dismantled the forts around Chattanooga and shipped artillery along with tons of munitions north. Auction sales found civilian buyers for steamboats as well as the surplus goods stored in the warehouses. The waterworks went to a private company while the fire-fighting equipment and the military bridge were presented to the city. Christopher R. Robert, a New York philanthropist, acquired government structures on Lookout Mountain and established a coeducational school for white children called the Lookout Mountain Educational Institute. Abram Hewitt, ironmaster and national political figure, with others leased the rolling mill and operated it as the Southwestern Iron Company, using battlefield scrap. Soldiers gradually disappeared from the streets, and by April 1866 most had been mustered out.

An unofficial census in 1865 reported 5,776 Chattanoogans, of whom 2,657 were blacks. Many were destitute and had wandered into the military base; old residents who had stayed on had lost slaves, businesses, and liquid assets. The columns of the newspaper were filled with announcements of sheriff sales. The town itself was described as scraggy, unkempt, worn out, and "anything but an attractive place." The streets changed with the seasons from dust to mud to dust.

The human spirit, badly crushed, had to assume the heavy load of Reconstruction. Although Tennessee was the first Confederate state to return to the Union, an interim of general lawlessness and roaming bands of desperadoes plagued the area. Chattanooga had few good dwellings and her churches remained in a dilapidated condition. The Episcopalians, for example, used a dry-goods box covered with a tablecloth for an altar; it was Easter 1867 before they could meet in their old

sanctuary. The Methodist church lacked furniture, doors, and windows; the floor was broken and weatherboarding torn from the walls. In this dark time of rebirth there appeared to be some consolation in the fact that nature's new growth covered some of the scars.

Fresh catastrophes periodically complicated the restoration of a normal existence. Fires, floods, and epidemics along with national financial panics tested the mettle of the residents. The dread of fire turned to reality in such conflagrations as those that destroyed the Thomas Webster foundry, the Crutchfield House, the Lookout Flour Mills, and the Bee Hive Store. The latter brought about the death of two firemen, to whom the Firemen's Fountain was dedicated on June 9, 1888.

On Friday night, March 8, 1867, "oceans of water" suddenly poured into the town. With no apparent warning the largest recorded flood on the Tennessee River—58.6 feet—swept away everything along the riverbank including the military bridge, leaving only ferry service for crossings until the Walnut Street bridge was finished in 1891. The waters completely isolated Chattanooga. A steamboat sailed up the main street; at the depot, water came up to the top of the freight cars. The milkman took the wheels from his wagon, making it into a boat, and paddled through the Crutchfield House. Tradition recites how men in skiffs saved St. Paul's prayer books and hymnals. Later in May the city government authorized the sale "for cash in hand to the highest bidder, after five days notice, the House now standing on Chestnut Street (left there by the receding flood of last March) between Sixth and Seventh Streets. . . ." The years 1875 and 1886 saw a repetition of the calamity in only a lesser degree.

Other gloomy times stemmed from unknown sources. In 1873 a cholera epidemic struck furiously in July: 144 deaths were reported that month, 41 in two days, from a hidden killer which prompted people to try a remarkable variety of homemade remedies. Even more serious was the 1878 invasion of yellow fever—which was not supposed to reach into the mountains. But refugees from infested areas apparently carried the disease into town in September, creating a general panic.

*Top*
*Chattanooga, always vulnerable to floods, has suffered periodic calamities, such as this one in 1886. (CHCBL)*

*Above*
*Fires like this August 1888 blaze destroyed commercial structures in town. (CHCBL)*

*Facing Page:*
*Top Left*
*Down by the river the United States army developed a "navy yard" and operated some freight packets. Courtesy of the Library of Congress.*

*Top Right*
*The numerous wooden structures put up by the government made the danger of fire so great that the military organized the city's first fire-fighting organization. Courtesy of the National Archives.*

*Bottom*
*The government constructed Chattanooga's first waterworks in the area between the east side of Cameron Hill and Reservoir Hill. Courtesy of the National Archives.*

People fled, leaving only about 1,800 persons in residence. Neighboring communities quarantined Chattanooga and, if city newspapers were delivered to rural areas, they were disinfected in labored rituals. Mayor Thomas J. Carlyle, Father Patrick Ryan, teacher Hattie Ackerman, and Henry Savage, a gambler, all fell victims to the disease while volunteering relief. Before the first frost, 366 people had died.

Skeptics found Chattanooga "an overgrown village," but one Knoxville editor read the record differently. "Chattanooga," he wrote, "has more backbone for its size and advantages than any small village we know of. She has as many lives as a cat. As to killing her, even the floods have failed. . . . Her pluck has saved her and is likely to make her one of the most flourishing and prosperous cities of the South."

Although his conclusions certainly were overly optimistic, there was an unconquerable spirit among the residents. Prewar citizens, who formerly held opposing views, returned. In their company were William Crutchfield, John P. Long, John L. Divine, Robert Cravens, A. Malone Johnson, James Hood, Dr. J. S. Gillespie, Mrs. James A. Whiteside, D. M. Key, Dr. Milo Smith, Robert M. Hooke, the Reverend Thomas McCallie, and others. Representing newcomers from the South, many of whom were Confederate veterans, were Josiah Bryan, Jonathan W. Bachman, L. T. Dickinson, Garnett Andrews, Tomlinson Fort, Adolph S. Ochs, Amos Judd, and Jack Gahagan.

A surprisingly large number of Union soldiers and other young men from northern states decided to make the region their home. Some took a liking to the area during campaign days; others like Xenophon Wheeler reasoned that if the strategic location of the town produced military campaigns, surely in peacetime it would produce economic opportunity. A few brought money, others special skills, and entrepreneurial talent, giving major emphasis to the manufacturing development of the new era. A representative few include John T. Wilder, Hiram Chamberlain, T. H. Payne, Z. C. Pat-

Xenophon Wheeler arrived in the city shortly after graduating from Yale in 1865. His profession was law; his avocation, civic affairs of a rich variety. (CHCBL)

These three pioneers of the 1870s represented the youthful spirit of the "new" city. Shown here standing: John B. Nicklin, mayor and druggist; left, Charles Whitney, construction contractor on the Alabama Great Southern Railroad; right Z.C. Patten, merchant, manufacturer, and civic leader. (CHCBL)

ten, John B. Nicklin, J. E. MacGowan, Theodore Montague, Theodore Richmond, Dr. E. M. Wight, Newell Sanders, H. Clay Evans, Alonzo G. Sharp, Jason Wiltse, H. D. Wyatt, W. P. Rathburn, S. Bartow Strang, and Wheeler.

From this unusual population mix emerged many persons of genuinely independent spirit. *Gazette* editor James Hood, elected to the Reconstruction state legislature in 1865, proved to be less a Radical than most and was expelled because he "has on several occasions insulted this Body by taking up his hat and cane and leaving the House in order to reduce its numbers below a quorum and when sent after and brought back by order of this House refused to answer to his name in

utter disrespect of this Body. . . ."

D. M. Key, an ex-Confederate colonel and Independent Democrat, moved back to resume his Chattanooga law practice on the advice of his former Union friend William Crutchfield. Paradoxically, his services were retained by the city in a lawsuit with the state's Radical government. Key then became chancellor and in 1870 represented his home region at the state constitutional convention that ended postwar restrictions on Tennessee suffrage. Key, who entertained no personal animosity about the past, refused to make any political concessions to sectional or rebel emotionalism and strove to eliminate the color line in politics.

A third person who cherished independence was General John T. Wilder; he made his career in the area where he had fought. He never showed any sectional prejudice although he was always a very willing leader of Union veterans' affairs. In 1884 he freely praised his adopted city:

*Chattanooga is not a Southern city nor a Northern city. . . . One's politics, religion or section is not called into question here. This is the freest town on the map. All join together here for the general good and strive, to a man, for the upbuilding of the city.*

*Above Left*
*Fassnacht's Coach and Wagon Works, 1875. (CHCBL)*

*Above Right*
*Chattanooga's oldest continuing business, first called T.H. Payne and Z.C. Patten. An early ad stresses that the company had a "Full Line of Stationer's Sundries and Fancy Goods." (CHCBL)*

*Left*
*General John T. Wilder was one of the foremost developers of the iron industry in East Tennessee and Chattanooga. In 1871 he was chosen mayor of the city. (CHCBL)*

The real issue for most Chattanoogans was how to structure the region's economy. General agreement focused on the value of manufacturing as a supplement to agriculture, and in particular this centered on the development of the iron and coal business. The old government rolling mill became the nucleus for this effort; the initiative came from the two ex-Union soldiers, General John T. Wilder and Captain Hiram Chamberlain. They found financial support for a furnace at Rockwood and added the Chattanooga mill to their firm in 1870 under the name Roane Iron Company.

For the next 20 years Chattanooga served as the hub of the East Tennessee iron industry. Promoters, investors, and mining scouts swarmed over the area; two furnaces were built in Chattanooga while Dayton, Tracy City, and South Pittsburg grew around major installations. In Chattanooga, a variety of satellite industries appeared, such as the Vulcan Iron and Nail Works, Wesson Car Foundry Company, Chattanooga Boiler Factory, Wheland Machine Works, Chattanooga Plow Company, Cahill Iron Company, Ross-Meehan Malleable Iron, Casey & Hedges Manufacturing Company.

During these decades a vexing problem confronted

*Top Left*
*Originally built by the government to "reroll twisted railroad iron," this mill, after the war, became the property of Roane Iron Company. The economy of the community depended for a quarter century or more on this company and its leaders. Courtesy of the National Archives.*

*Top Right*
*Hiram S. Chamberlain, soldier and industrialist, generously used his abilities and talents in building his adopted city culturally and economically. He served as president of the Board of Trustees of Chattanooga University for 25 years; he and his son gave their name to the school's athletic field. (CHCBL)*

the business: local ores with their impurities did not produce quality steel. The open-hearth process proved deficient, the Bessemer method was found wanting, and finally a "basic steel" process failed in 1891 after a fancy tin plate dinner prematurely launched this latest technology as a great triumph. About this same time competition from the rich Birmingham, Alabama, region spelled final defeat for the local effort.

Meanwhile, more railroads came to Chattanooga and river trade reached its zenith. The Alabama and Chattanooga, a jerry-built line financed by Alabama Reconstruction money, was later reorganized as the Alabama Great Southern. A Cincinnati line finished in 1880 by the Ohio River city was known as the Cincinnati Southern. The Chattanooga, Rome & Columbus road completed in 1890 and the Chattanooga Southern to Gadsden, Alabama, later reorganized as the TAG, were added to the iron network.

The economic and romantic lure of the river was enhanced during these postwar days. Rivermen traded, rebuilt, bought and sold steamboats like horsetraders. Some "elegant" packets boasted low fares and excellent meals. They frequented the Chattanooga landing along with homemade flatboats, some 60 to 75 feet by 20 feet in size, with their cargoes of flour, whiskey, corn, and other country products, and giant timber rafts.

Chattanoogans again took the lead in working for federal funds to improve the channel and optimistically invested in packet companies. They cheered the 1875 plans for a second Muscle Shoals canal, but the failure of this project in the 1890s left the bubble of river fervor badly deflated throughout the valley.

Such failure was foreign to one young newcomer who personified the era in which he gained professional training and experience. In 1878 the 20-year-old Adolph S. Ochs bought the Chattanooga *Times*. Full of energy and confidence, Ochs did not consider the four-page, six-column, nine-year-old newspaper as anything but a journal with a future and viewed the shabby building which was its home base with rosy prospects. His deal for controlling half interest for $250 with an option to complete the purchase later tells much about Chattanooga's business history at the time. Ochs as publisher believed in economic diversification, conservative Democratic politics, and the prosperity and general welfare of the community and its surroundings. The columns of his paper celebrated every business advance; competitors claimed they shouted the joyous word with each new peanut stand. Ochs's enthusiasm did not stop with words; he took a lead in every community project from a new opera house to a madcap real-estate boom.

Chattanoogans organized a board of trade in 1870, which became the Iron, Coal and Manufacturers Association before emerging as the Chamber of Commerce in 1887 under the presidency of D. B. Loveman.

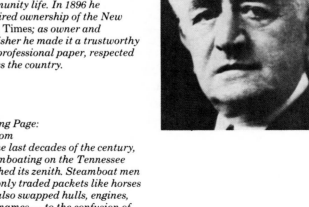

*Right*
*In 1878 Adolph Simon Ochs, at the age of 20, gained control of the decrepit Chattanooga* Times. *While developing his journal into a leading Southern newspaper, Ochs participated in all phases of community life. In 1896 he acquired ownership of the New York* Times; *as owner and publisher he made it a trustworthy and professional paper, respected across the country.*

*Facing Page:*
*Bottom*
*In the last decades of the century, steamboating on the Tennessee reached its zenith. Steamboat men not only traded packets like horses but also swapped hulls, engines, and names — to the confusion of the chronicler. Pictured at the Chattanooga wharf are the N.B. Forrest (in front), with the figure of a horseman between the smokestacks, and the* Avalon, *with the star between the "chimneys."*
*(CHCBL)*

The year 1870 also witnessed a transfer of the county seat to Chattanooga from Harrison, where it was located for 30 years after having been moved from Dallas. Existing buildings in town housed the offices until 1879, when a suitable courthouse was erected on the splendid site still in use today. The first building was destroyed in a 1910 fire and replaced three years later by a $350,000 structure of classical design. (In 1976 the Criminal Justice Building was added to the complex.)

The referendum seeking removal of the courthouse to Chattanooga infuriated many folk in the eastern part of the county. In protest they supported legislation for a new county to be formed from parts of Bradley and Hamilton counties and named James (or, affectionately,

*Top*
*A county courthouse, costing slightly over $100,000, was built on the present courthouse grounds in 1879. A fire started by a violent electrical storm destroyed the building on the night of May 7, 1910. Courtesy of the Chattanooga Convention and Visitors Bureau.*

*Facing Page:*
*Left*
*For several years after the war, Christopher Robert placed philanthropic moneys in a school for Southern whites, using buildings on Lookout Mountain purchased from the government. Personal health problems, coupled with a desire to use all funds for Robert College in Constantinople, led to the closing of the Lookout Mountain Institute. (CHCBL)*

*Right*
*Henry D. Wyatt arrived in Chattanooga with a master's degree from Dartmouth College and a discharge from the Federal army. Wyatt was associated with the public school system for approximately 45 years.*

*Above*
*H. Clay Evans settled in Chattanooga in 1870 at the age of 27. He pursued an active political career, and in 1911 served as the first commissioner of education. (CHCBL)*

"Jim") to confer honor on the Reverend Jesse J. James, father of the legislator who presented the act. Created on January 30, 1871, the new county chose the village of Ooltewah for the site of its courthouse. The sparse, rural population experienced constant fiscal problems, which in 1919 influenced another referendum vote, this one to return James to Hamilton County. This merger represents one of the very few examples of an American county voting itself out of existence.

The most important Reconstruction development in the Chattanooga area was the establishment of a tax-supported system of public schools. Immediately after the war the federal government continued the Post School for a short time, and Robert's Lookout Mountain Educational Institute held classes for a while. A few small subscription schools also existed, and in 1871 the Howard School for freedmen was started in Chattanooga. Finally, under the leadership of H. Clay Evans, the city adopted a tax-supported plan for primary grades; this system, limited to whites, got started on

January 1, 1873. Classes met for five months; the value of the school property was listed at $5,000.

School superintendent Henry D. Wyatt, a New England veteran of the Union army who had won the respect of the community as a schoolman, musician, and lover of the classics, organized Chattanooga High School in 1874. In 1883 Howard High School's curriculum was inaugurated. In the case of both primary and secondary programs, the city's efforts predated state systems of tax-supported education. In 1890 Chattanooga employed 54 white and 29 black teachers.

Recognizing the advantages of higher education, local civic leaders cooperated with the Methodist Episcopal Church to charter a central university in 1886. The lack of an educational tradition and disturbing racial problems caused delays; not until 1904 was an undergraduate program firmly established. Within a few years of that date the church deeded its property to a self-perpetuating board of trustees and adopted the name University of Chattanooga.

*This monument, commemorating the 1st Ohio Infantry, stands in the Chickamauga Chattanooga National Military Park — the nation's oldest and largest military park, consisting of some 8,000 acres. On display are 256 mounted guns, about 550 historical markers, and 667 monuments contributed by various states. Courtesy of the National Park Service.*

1st. OHIO INFANTRY,
BALDWIN'S BRIGADE,
JOHNSON'S DIVISION

20th
ARM
CORP

## Chapter Ten

# Reunion and the National Military Park

Thce nation's Centennial Fourth of July is remembered as a banner day in Chattanooga's annals. In 1876 some 10,000 persons came by packet, train, and carriage to witness the grand parade, fireworks, races, and the high jinks of the Horribles, Mulligan Guards, Indians, and other "clans." At the rally in the courthouse grove the master of ceremonies first presented veterans of the War of 1812 and the Mexican War. Accompanied by deafening cheers, he went on: "Permit me to introduce to you hundreds of soldiers of both armies in the late war, who are now in the audience surrounding me, and are here united in the celebration of the Centennial 4th of July, and have shaken hands across the bloody chasm. . . ."

Many of these veterans had worked side by side in preparing for the big day which included a tableau of a Union soldier presenting an olive branch to an ex-Confederate. Actually only a few strident voices had been heard locally since the end of the war. A small-

town spirit of understanding and neighborliness had been encouraged by the Reverend Thomas McCallie, who enjoyed the excellent support after 1873 of the former Confederate soldier and Presbyterian minister Jonathan W. Bachman, affectionately called the Pastor of Chattanooga. Furthermore, the local press consistently denounced political adventurism.

Some social differences did surface, and in the days when wealth made possible the building of fine homes on the terraces surrounding the city, some Northern ladies who lived there were labeled social climbers. Much more evident, however, was the early association of all residents along the way to reunion which was publicly acclaimed at the Centennial outing.

A year later, on Decoration Day, Union veterans took part in exercises at the Confederate Cemetery when the cornerstone was placed. The very next day former Confederate soldiers inquired if they could return the courtesy on Memorial Day "to testify [to] our

*Left*
*Outings on Lookout Mountain usually led to picture-taking. This 1884 holiday party at Sunset Rock included families of George W. Wheland, H.F. Temple, H. Clay Evans, and John B. Nicklin. Courtesy of the Chattanooga Hamilton County Bicentennial Library.*

*Bottom Left*
*The Reverend Jonathan W. Bachman, a veteran who had worn the gray, through his compassion and humanity did much to promote a spirit of reunion. For more than 50 years he enjoyed the affection of his congregation at the First Presbyterian Church and of the citizens generally as the "Pastor of Chattanooga." His son Nathan won a seat in the U.S. Senate. (CHCBL)*

*Bottom Center*
*David McKendree Key, pioneer citizen, Confederate colonel, chancellor, U.S. judge, Postmaster General of the United States, and U.S. senator, earned the high respect of his contemporaries. Upon his death General Henry V. Boynton, a Union veteran, wrote to Mrs. Key: "When the inside story of the policy looking to a more thorough reuniting of the sections becomes known . . . Judge Key will stand as one of the historic characters of an epoch in the life of the Republic." (CHCBL)*

*Bottom Right*
*Henry V. Boynton sparked the idea of creating a military park where he had fought 25 years before. Boynton served as park historian and then as a commissioner. (CHCBL)*

appreciation of the liberal sentiment manifested by the Federal soldiers on the 10th inst. in the decoration of the graves of the Confederate dead, and our willingness to show to them and the people of the United States that we cherish none of the bad feelings engendered by the late war. . . ."

The request, warmly received, led to a second gracious local act of brotherliness that May, prompting an editorial in the Chattanooga *Times* entitled, "The Harmony," which states in part: "The hearts of the people of this community had no room for hypocrisy on these two glorious days. There was no time, no need for it—sincerity was the guiding star of our actions."

The image of a city seeking to forget past hurts gained national attention in the career of D.M. Key. In 1875 this moderate Democrat received a recess appointment to the U.S. Senate seat of the late Andrew Johnson. The next year, in the compromise settlement of the Hayes-Tilden presidential dispute, the Republican Rutherford Hayes promised to bring Reconstruction to an end. Among other things, he pledged to place a Southerner in his cabinet. Hayes singled out Key to be postmaster general: the first Southerner, first Democrat, and first Confederate officer to receive such a high appointment after the war.

OFFICIAL PROGRAM.

20th
ANNUAL REUNION
— OF THE —
SOCIETY
— OF THE —

Army Cumberland,
September 18, 19 & 20,
— AT —
Chattanooga, Tennessee.
1889.

Published by
THE BRADT PRINTING COMPANY
Compiled by C. W. Norwood.
CHATTANOOGA,
1889.

Entered according to Act of Congress by Geo. M. Bradt in the Office
of the Librarian of Congress, Washington, D. C.

*Above*
*A band of eminent Chattanoogans sat for a group picture in the early 1880s. Front row, left to right: George H. Patten, H.S. Chamberlain, Xenophon Wheeler, John T. Wilder, unknown, W.J. Colburn. Standing, left to right: unknown, Francis Tyler, unknown, unknown, and A.J. Gahagan. (CHCBL)*

*Left*
*The program for the 1889 reunion presented a special feature: a meeting of a committee "on the Chickamauga Memorial Association, and the permanent organization of the Chickamauga National Park Association." At a barbecue the next day, the program called for addresses by leading ex-Federals and ex-Confederates and a "general participation in smoking the 'pipe of peace'— the pipes made of wood from the Chickamauga battlefield will be presented as souvenirs."*

In 1881 this image was refreshed during the meeting of the Society of the Army of the Cumberland in Chattanooga, when the first reunion of a Union army was held in the South. Local veterans from both armies worked on the planning committees, but when the convention opened the reunion suddenly was changed into a memorial service. News came that President James A. Garfield, a member of the society and General Rosecrans's chief-of-staff at Chickamauga, had died from an assassin's bullet. A large flagpole on Cameron Hill drew everyone's attention as four Federal and four Confederate veterans hoisted the flag to half-mast. Captain Summerfield Key then spoke on behalf of his Southern comrades and the governor of Ohio for the Union men.

As the barriers of sectional prejudice fell in a convincing fashion in Chattanooga, the mutual confidence and respect of the people received inspiration from outside sources. In 1888 the idea of marking the Chickamauga battlefield gained popularity as a topic of discussion. It originated with Henry V. Boynton, a Union regimental commander in the battle and now a journalist and strong leader in veterans' affairs. His idea took hold and was expanded into a plan to mark both Union and Confederate lines and from a private venture into one sponsored by the federal government. On August 19, 1890, legislation creating the Chickamauga Chattanooga Military Park became law.

This first national military park included a major

*A scene at the exercises of dedication in 1895 when General Boynton was recognized. The Vice President of the United States, Adlai Stevenson, participated as master of ceremonies. Courtesy of the National Park Service.*

*Right*
*General Alexander Peter Stewart, a Confederate general who taught at Cumberland University prior to the war, served for a time as chancellor of the University of Mississippi in postwar days and was one of the first commissioners of the Chickamauga Chattanooga National Military Park (1890-1908). (CHCBL)*

*Facing Page*
*In addition to the major tract at Chickamauga, Orchard Knob was a part of the original park. The central monument, erected by the state of Illinois, honors the fallen sons of that state. Courtesy of the Chattanooga Convention and Visitors Bureau.*

portion of the Chickamauga field, Orchard Knob, and three reservations on Missionary Ridge along with certain access roads. It assured that the names Chickamauga and Chattanooga, which were national household words in 1863, would always maintain their historic significance. The park, not designed to be a pleasure ground, was to be preserved as a laboratory with fields, woods, and battlegrounds left as nearly as possible the way they were in 1863.

In September 1895 the area, with a number of monuments in place, was ready for the dedication ceremony. As a crowd estimated between 40,000 and 60,000 swarmed over the town, Chattanoogans began to appreciate the incalculable value of the project. It was a festive occasion marked by gray-haired veterans reminiscing about service days and speakers sounding the "gospel of concord." Every orator, and there were many, praised the valor and sacrifice of former days but put his emphasis on the "broader fraternity" of the conflict. The local people pledged themselves to be the guardians of the traditions and heritage of the park, and on Boynton's death showed their gratitude by constructing a Cameron Hill park in his honor.

Over the years additions have been made to the military park, which is the largest of its kind in the country. In the 1890s two tracts, Cravens Terrace and Point Park, were added to commemorate the action on Lookout Mountain; later the addition of 2,700 acres on the mountain slopes in 1935 was made possible by a gift from area residents. Adolph S. Ochs, having played a dominant role in acquiring these important additions, was posthumously honored when the Ochs Museum at Point Park was dedicated to him in 1940. Since that time Sunset Rock and Signal Point (Signal Mountain) have been donated to the park.

Unexpectedly, the park assumed a new role in 1898 when war with Spain developed. The strategic Chattanooga rail junction, the proximity of the region to Florida debarkation ports, and the available land at Chickamauga led to the creation in April of Camp George H. Thomas. Before the short war ended in mid-September, about 72,000 trainees received some instruction at the hastily built facility. Miserable sanitary arrangements were blamed, however, for 425 deaths from typhoid fever—more than died in combat in the entire war. Critics carped about the location as the cause of the epidemic while others with different views worked to get a permanent base on the site. In 1902 the latter group gained success when the federal government authorized the construction of a camp on the edge of the Chickamauga Chattanooga National Military Park in north Georgia. Two years later they named it Fort Oglethorpe.

*Above*
*In 1896 the government acquired the home of Robert Cravens, called the "White House," and the surrounding 85 acres to be added to the original military park. It was here that the Battle Above the Clouds was fought. (CHCBL)*

*Facing Page:*
*Top*
*Everything at Camp Thomas showed that it was hastily built and very primitive including this "2nd Nebraska Post Exchange." Courtesy of the National Park Service.*

*Bottom*
*The Tennessee National Guard Camp under the command of Colonel J. Percy Fyffe in training camp in Chattanooga, 1898.*

*Chattanooga citizens representative of the black community during the turn of the century. Clockwise from top left: Styles L. Hutchins, Hiram Tyree, Dr. O.L. Davis, Thomas William Haigler, (center) Randolph Miller. From White,* Biography and Achievements of the Colored Citizens of Chattanooga.

## Chapter Eleven
# Before and After Jim Crow

Living patterns after the Civil War required a major racial readjustment as well as economic and political reconstruction. The old social order had completely collapsed; slave codes and regulations relating to "free persons of color" suddenly held no significance. Except for school segregation, law did not govern the new relationship: general custom, prejudice, and local mores largely dictated race relations, which differed greatly across the land. In Chattanooga the people at a very early time recognized the new political role of the freedmen, which predated the time the blacks were enfranchised or could hold state office in Tennessee.

In 1866 all male adults could vote in Chattanooga city elections and in 1868 C. P. Letcher became the first black to win a seat on the Board of Aldermen. Later Clem Shaw, George Shaw, D. Medow, and J. W. Sewell gained places on the board. Most blacks naturally voted Republican and although they had no political experience, little money, and no strong fraternal or church organizations to support them, they had sufficient numbers—the percentage of blacks, 36.5 in 1870 and 43 in 1890—to be decisive in elections in which the local Republicans and Democrats were almost equally balanced. Moreover, the business leaders of the community, desirous of maintaining a peaceful economic climate, favored a paternalistic attitude rather than one of resistance.

The political strength of the black community gained for these freedmen numerous offices and patronage jobs. In 1881 seven of the 12-man police force were black; other Negroes served with the fire companies, as justices of the peace, poor commissioners, deputy sheriffs, and members of the Board of Education.

Although an abortive effort in the 1880s to reduce black influence actually went as far as to call for the repeal of the city charter, an accommodation was found to continue black and Republican cooperation. In 1886

*Left*
*This scene in 1903 marks a high point in the social season. The "Midway," which was located on 11th Street near Market in the immediate vicinity of the old customs house and post office, played a major role in the Spring Festival for a number of years. (CHCBL)*

*Below*
*Roller skating at the Stoops Rink became a popular sport in the 1880s, leading to the organization of polo clubs on skates. Front row, left to right: Clint Hulse, Will S. Griscom; back row, left to right: Harry F. Van Dusen, Charley Etzil(?), Oliver Hubbard, B. Rawlings, and Frank Esterbrook. (CHCBL)*

J. J. Irvine won the circuit court clerkship, the first black elected to a county office. Also in the 1880s William C. Hodge and Styles L. Hutchins represented the district in the state General Assembly. They were two of only 12 blacks to serve in the Tennessee legislature in these years; after 1887 none were elected until 1965.

The emergence of Jim Crow laws and a nationwide municipal reform movement diluted black political clout by the turn of the century, although Chattanooga freedmen continued to be active. Eugene Reid, Charles Grigsby, and Hiram Tyree, the leading black politician for a decade or more, held city offices, and Dr. T. Edinburg served in 1904 as school commissioner. All such opportunities, however, ceased on April 25, 1911, when a new city government, a mayor/commission form, providing for city-wide elections came into being.

A highly selective survey of representative blacks of this 46-year period outside the field of politics includes: E. O. Tade, educator, banker, and first Hamilton County superintendent of schools; Dr. T. W. Haigler, physician and minister; Dr. O. L. Davis, a 1902

graduate of the Meharry Medical College, who is believed to be the first colored woman dentist to practice in the South; Randolph Miller, flamboyant newsman; the Reverend H. J. Johnson; and Hodge, Hutchins, and J. W. White, lawyers.

*Several times a year the entire community seemed to turn out for a celebration. This gathering shows a part of the 1906 May Festival parade and spectators. (CHCBL)*

When Jim Crow laws designed to limit racial contacts spread across the South, Chattanooga encountered change in its relations with the black community. As elsewhere, signs marked white and black limits at waiting and rest rooms, on public carriers, at water fountains, and on all other public facilities. While relations did not harden as in some regions, they did grow less flexible, and episodes of violence and tragedy followed. There were black lynchings in 1893 and 1906 in the city and one in 1897 in the county.

One such episode became a cause célèbre. In 1906 a jury found Ed Johnson guilty of assaulting a white woman and sentenced him to be executed. Two black attorneys managed to have the United States Supreme Court review the case and thus delay the execution. Local officials, immediately informed, were handed the responsibility of guarding the prisoner for the court. That very night, however, a mob lynched Johnson. The Justice Department sent agents to investigate and, after long delays, in 1909 four men were found guilty of participating in the lynching. The sheriff and his jailor were sentenced for contempt of court because of neglect of duty, and the two county officials were imprisoned in Washington. This case is said to be the first in American history in which men were jailed for contempt of the Supreme Court of the United States, as well as the first instance in which the government placed men in custody as an outcome of a Negro lynching.

A Jim Crow law governing riders on streetcars led to an interesting episode. Chattanooga blacks on July 5, 1905, set in motion a boycott. Although this move was not popular throughout the black community, some promoters started a hack line to accommodate former riders and planned to buy buses. Their scheme failed; rumor had it that the promoters were more interested in a new business venture than in the boycott, which soon drifted into the forgotten past.

*The First Baptist Church, located at 506 East 8th Street, was started around 1885 and completed a decade later. Courtesy of the Chattanooga/Hamilton County Regional Planning Commission.*

Following World War I Chattanooga joined a national movement in establishing a biracial committee under the leadership of Mayor T. C. Thompson. This effort set up constructive dialogues and encouraged such developments as the creation of Lincoln Park for blacks and later the construction of a modern high school. However, it scarcely touched the fundamental questions raised by the Jim Crow laws or such glaring trouble areas as human rights, housing, and health care. Biracial attempts at understanding the need for compassion and compromise did give continuity to the heritage of earlier decades.

The blacks at this stage found genuine pride in the accomplishments of individuals often made at great sacrifice and against tremendous odds. Among those saluted by the entire community were: James A. Henry, first Negro school principal; William Jasper Hale, educator who became president of the Tennessee Agricultural and Industrial State University; the Reverend Joseph E. Smith, minister and civic leader; Dr. Emma R. Wheeler, Meharry Medical School graduate and founder about 1918 of the Walden Hospital for blacks; Almira S. Steele, founder of the Steele Orphan Home for black children; Walter C. Robinson, a dominant figure in Republican politics; Bessie Smith, who in the 1920s was hailed as the "greatest blues singer of all time"; and Roland Hayes—son of slaves, Fisk Jubilee Singer, and internationally acclaimed lyric tenor—who contributed greatly to the integration of both the European and American stage in the field of serious music.

*Above*
*Chattanooga-born Bessie Smith has been called the "greatest blues singer of all time." Her career ended abruptly in 1937 in a tragic highway accident. Courtesy of Roy Noel.*

*Above*
*The son of former slaves, Roland Hayes used his remarkable talent to integrate the professional music stage and to gain world recognition for black artists. In 1968 the University of Chattanooga awarded him an honorary degree. In this picture, those in the front row are: Dr. William H. Masterson, university president; Dr. Loren Eiseley, visiting speaker; Dr. Hayes; and Dr. LeRoy Martin, university chancellor.*

*This Fourth of July parade of 1890 passed down Market Street near 9th Street. The many tall poles tell of change in the life-style of the citizens, but horses continued to monopolize transportation; their sound and smell were pervasive. (CHCBL)*

# Chapter Twelve
# Into the 20th Century

On September 4, 1875, a horsecar operating over a 15-block route from the river to Montgomery Avenue (Main Street) made its maiden run to the cheers of practically the entire population of the town. The Chattanooga Street Railroad Company started business with an "experienced" four-windowed car and a mule with a tinkling bell. Although one could walk almost as fast as the car moved, it gave a kind of metropolitan tone to the street. It marked not only the beginning of a rapid transit system but also, in a primitive way, it gave birth to a local technological revolution destined to transform life in the 20th century.

The car line mushroomed in every direction, and in the next decade promoters talked of using electric cars, as in other progressive cities. Because of a fear of "electrical leakage" from overhead wires, an injunction delayed the inaugural day of the genie's newest marvel until June 22, 1887, when car #1 tackled the 7th Street grade to Georgia Avenue and ran on through the open countryside to Missionary Ridge. New lines, mergers, and receiverships describe the building of a rambling system; the trolley held its own for years, even climbing Signal Mountain, before the motor coach won a final victory in 1947.

Other pioneers interested in the advancement of applied science attracted enough capital to mount fascinating projects. On July 3, 1878, a message from the Stanton House to a livery stable ordering a carriage introduced the telephone, which two years later boasted an exchange with 52 subscribers. And on the evening of May 6, 1882, an inquisitive crowd watched in amazement as 26 electric lights flashed on from power produced by a 125-horsepower generator. Three globes, used primarily for advertising, illuminated the Read House and Loveman's store while the *Times,* having placed its light on a pole, bragged of the "highest light on Market Street." For some years, however, the gaslight continued in general use.

In this same expansive era C. E. "Charlie" James, a local man of finance and blueprints, projected a belt line railroad around the city, lacing the various railroads into a chain. This company hauled freight and passengers and soon changed outlying cornfields and woodlands into suburban building lots. In town a fanciful scheme would transform Cameron Hill into a complex complete with incline, hotel, pagoda, park, and beer garden, while throughout the community a madcap 1888 real-estate boom promised riches but left many broken dreams.

Technology and investment capital combined to attack Lookout Mountain at this time because it was held that more than horse-drawn vehicles were needed to reach the summit. On March 21, 1887, Incline #1 ran cars from St. Elmo to the foot of the bluffs below Point Park. An elaborate resort hotel opened there the next year from which a narrow gauge railroad twisted precariously along the brink westward to Sunset Rock. A broad gauge line carrying regular railroad cars to the mountaintop joined the competition soon after this, as

well as a second swank hotel with the whimsical name, Lookout Inn, which operated with fleeting success until destroyed by fire in 1908. Incline #2, the railway which runs today, entered the contest for passengers when chartered in 1895; it was then, as it is now, a most amazing mile, daily carrying residents, workers, and tourists up its steep, wooded slopes.

And there were other less glamorous transportation developments. Major trunk rail lines—the N.C. & St. L. and the Southern—united the numerous shorter roads in the 1890s into regional systems. On the riverfront, packet lines organized and reorganized to keep financially afloat, with John A. Patten the main promoter of river usage and improvements.

In town, the Walnut Street bridge, designed simply to get people across the river, robbed the old ferries of their monopoly in 1891. But it was the automobile that revolutionized travel. The auto, slowly at first, expanded business opportunities; widened the scope of churches, schools, and health care; made the sheriff's job more difficult; called for engineered roads; and spelled real disappointment for livery-stable men and horselovers.

The 1903 city directory first listed auto sales and service establishments; the announcement of the Wallace Buggy Company as agent for the Cartercar, the Maxwell, and the Stoddard-Dayton tells what was happening. In 1909 about 250 cars could be counted in town. On April 22 of that year the Lookout Mountain Automobile Club sponsored a spring spectacular that attracted national press coverage when it scheduled a race up Lookout Mountain over a 4.9-mile unpaved course containing 63 turns and curves. The national Buick racing team sent its drivers, several millionaire sportsmen entered special cars, and local "hot-rodders" including Clarence James, Ernest Holmes, Charles Duffy, Fred Joyce, and Eddy Kenyon competed.

*Facing Page*
*The livery stable business of L.J. Sharp & Company at the corner of Georgia Avenue and East 9th Street occupied the site of the Volunteer State Life Insurance Company building erected in 1917. (CHCBL)*

*Top*
*This popular resort inn opened in 1890 opposite the present mountain incline station. Its 365 rooms and reputation for gracious service brought many guests, including Presidents Cleveland, McKinley, and T.R. Roosevelt. The hotel burned down on November 17, 1908. (CHCBL)*

*Above*
*The Nyberg, an early model car, was manufactured about 1909 in Chattanooga. At the wheel is William Orton. (CHCBL)*

A huge crowd of onlookers lined the roadway in the general area of the Scenic Highway. The state militia handled the spectators; surgeons and ambulances were on hand; and one fellow tried to sell accident insurance policies to the watchers. Louis Chevrolet, the popular French driver, successfully negotiated such places as "Undertaker's Delight" and "Spine Stretcher" in the best time: 6 minutes, 30²/₅ seconds, but this was ruled unofficial because he had to make three starts.

The race brought the motorcar into the Chattanooga spotlight. Enthusiasts started sponsoring campaigns for better roads and gave impetus to a demand for another Tennessee River bridge, which eventually was dedicated on November 16, 1917, as the Market Street span. And it led to easing the way into the city via ridge tunnels: Stringer's in 1910, Missionary in 1913, and later the Bachman Tubes in 1927, and the Wilcox route in 1930. More car dealers set up in business; at least one took a bicycle as down payment, riding it back to the agency after delivering the car. By 1920 horse-drawn vehicles were legislated off Market Street, trucks delivered the mail, and the last police horse was retired to permanent pasture.

Some promoters of the automobile revolution reached out beyond the city and took a hand in organizing the Dixie Highway Association, which met in Chattanooga in 1915 with seven concerned governors in attendance. They chose Judge Michael M. Allison as president and vigorously promoted a major north-south highway from Detroit to Miami which was to run directly through the Chattanooga gateway.

Chattanooga's population in 1900 totaled only 30,154. A few pioneers had their homes wired for electricity, but the small generators of the Chattanooga Electric Light Company, a consolidation of the first two small firms in 1886, could hardly be expected to provide the service demanded by the potential growth of the business. Discussion of hydroelectric generation of energy was a popular national topic of interest when Congressman John A. Moon advocated multipurpose development of the Tennessee River. In 1904 he sponsored legislation providing for a dam in Marion County,

some 33 miles downstream from Chattanooga, where the strong flow of water in the "Narrows" seemed a most desirable site: it would generate power and eliminate the hazardous waters which plagued the steamboat men.

A private company, the Chattanooga and Tennessee River Power Company, undertook construction of the Hales Bar Lock and Dam. The local leaders included Charles James and Jo Conn Guild, Jr., who replaced his father on the latter's death. On November 13, 1913, with every whistle on the river and in Chattanooga's factories sounding a blast, the structure was dedicated. The ageless Suck disappeared under the impounded waters.

Before this date, however, Chattanooga received electricity from the dams and flume system on the Ocoee River to the east; five-foot-tall letters on one of Chattanooga's tallest buildings had spelled out the word "Ocoee" to announce to the assembled citizens that the first switch had been thrown. The two rival companies soon consolidated as the Tennessee Electric Power Company while their chief market city, Chattanooga, took pride in a new nickname, "The Dynamo of Dixie."

The onset of the 20th century saw not only the growth of the utilities but also the emergence of the modern city. New preparatory schools opened: Notre

*In the late 1880s young ladies gathered on the L.J. Sharp lawn for tennis. In this group, from left to right: Miss Margaret Key, Mrs. Cornelia Carlisle Read, Mrs. Stella Hutcheson Dabney, Miss Florence Eckert, Mrs. Elise Hutcheson Chapin, Mrs. Sarah Key Patten, and Mrs. Elsie Finlay Payne. (CHCBL)*

*The Market Street bridge, later named the Chief John Ross bridge, formally opened at 3:18 p.m., November 16, 1917. At the time, engineers claimed it was the longest movable bridge in the world (bascule lift). A newsman wrote of this marvel, ''Like a huge monster of primeval days, the big steel girders and beams . . . at a given signal and without apparent assistance of human craft, began . . . to slowly leave their resting place.'' (CHCBL)*

*Facing Page*
*Prince Henry of Prussia (front left with military cap) visited Lookout Mountain in March 1902. Wearing hats prescribed by the fashion of the day, his local escorts included Dr. Henry Berlin (next to the guest) and (on extreme right) Captain H.S. Chamberlain with the Honorable Newell Saunders and J.T. Lupton. General Boynton (in the center) is bareheaded. (CHCBL)*

Dame (1886), Baylor School (1893), McCallie School (1905), and Girls' Preparatory School (1906). The University of Chattanooga in 1904 again returned to an undergraduate program which has been continuous since that time. Joseph Cadek, master musician, took up residence in 1892 before opening a conservatory. The cornerstone of the Carnegie Library went into its proper niche in 1904, marking the maturing of a fitful library movement. Only a few years earlier (1899) the Baroness Erlanger Hospital became the health care foundationstone for the city and its environs.

The opera house at the corner of Sixth and Market streets had sponsored an annual season in a blaze of glory since 1886. This playhouse, later called the Lyric, continued to be used until 1917 when, with a touch of nostalgia, a reporter noted, "There is probably no building in all of Chattanooga which is dearer to old residents. . . ." By that date two other theaters, the Shubert and the Bijou, presented seasonal schedules.

An interesting episode marked the Shubert's start in 1906. The cornerstone ceremonies were planned for a time when the great Sarah Bernhardt came to town for a performance. Since she was slated to participate, a large crowd waited patiently amid the mud and water of Eleventh Street in a frigid March wind. Time passed; Bernhardt failed to appear. Eventually the mayor, the master of ceremonies, dismissed the disappointed people. A note had explained the artist's absence, but since the city's chief executive could not read French, he simply pocketed the letter; getting it translated would have exposed his linguistic limitations.

A changing skyline clearly revealed the burgeoning city's growth. Old Civil War landmarks including the Stone Fort, Fort Wood, and College Hill structures

*Top*
*A summer home built in 1883 by D.M. Key in Summertown.*

*Center*
*The Gaskill House, built around 1883, represents "Italianate" style. It is located at 427 East 5th Street.*

*Bottom*
*This Victorian mansion built by Frank Hutcheson in 1894 stands at 360 South Crest Road.*

*All photos courtesy of the Chattanooga/Hamilton County Regional Planning Commission.*

*Above*
In town, the leveling of the area of the old Stone Fort revolutionized that part of the city. The old post office and the Park Plaza building can be seen in the background. (CHCBL)

*Top Left*
Three ''old cronies'' and prominent citizens on one of their regular fishing trips. From left to right: T.H. Payne, J.L. McCollum, and Dr. J.W. Bachman. (CHCBL)

*Top Right*
The automobile could not be of practical use until improved highways came into existence. Chattanoogans spearheaded the development of the Dixie Highway and in 1915, at a celebration, the local auto club float dramatized the changes taking place. (CHCBL)

disappeared. New residential housing at the river bluff, Fort Wood, Riverside, and Missionary Ridge gave special character to the community.

Contractors of buildings for public usage turned to Reuben Harrison Hunt, architect, who came to the city at the age of 20 in 1882. His long and distinguished professional career, which ended in death in 1937, earned him the title, "master builder of Chattanooga." His work, reflecting the popular styles of the day, represented a variety of design areas and attracted commissions for church, office, government, school, bank, and college buildings across the South. His early career until World War I is recalled locally in the Second Presbyterian Church (1890), Tucker Baptist Church (1899), Carnegie Library (1904), Pound Building (1906), James Building (1906), Chattanooga Car Barns (1907), City Hall (1908), Asbury United Methodist Church (1900), and County Courthouse (1912).

In addition to Hunt's work, other new edifices mark this period of building expansion including Central High School in Ridgedale (1908), First Presbyterian Church (1910), Christ Episcopal Church (1908), Patten Hotel (1909), and Southern Railway Terminal Station (1909)—now the Choo-Choo.

The business world was also stimulated by this same wave of brisk activity. Labor organizations, gradually losing their designation as "secret societies," chartered in 1897 the Central Labor Union, which was affiliated with A. F. of L. A surprising number of trade unions were formed, giving Chattanooga an early image of an "organized" community. A plethora of serious problems arose as a result. One occurred during World War I, when trolley car workers desperately strove to unionize and carried their demonstrations to the downtown streets, where violence went on display in a "public showcase."

In 1909 George Fort Milton, Sr., acquired from Jerome Pound the *Evening News*, first published in 1888, giving the town's readers a strong liberal voice. The textile industry got its first real start and three major insurance companies established home offices, the foundations of rapidly expanding enterprises. And

three new banks became the progenitors of present-day institutions.

A tiny advertisement in the newspaper of November 12, 1899, gave notice of a different kind of venture: the bottling of Coca-Cola. Three young men, Ben F. Thomas, Joseph B. Whitehead, and John Thomas Lupton, secured a contract to bottle this beverage from the Atlanta owner of the fountain-syrup recipe. After they divided the country into territories and adopted a franchise arrangement for bottling and marketing their product, sales grew steadily in response to a vigorous, well-planned advertising policy. Diligence and patience brought success. Allied industry—glass and case making, and cooler manufacturing—benefited by a profitable association with the Coca-Cola people. As the years passed, Chattanooga enjoyed and appreciated the generous philanthropies of foundations created by the original pioneers of this worldwide business.

*The old Market House off Georgia Avenue near 9th Street served as the city hall for a time. By 1908 it was functioning again as a market center. (CHCBL)*

*A new fleet of government-owned motor vehicles. The Romanesque structure seen in the background housed the Chattanooga post office from 1893 to 1933. Today, Tennessee Valley Authority offices occupy the building. (CHCBL)*

*"Preparedness Parades" of 1916 gave way to "Liberty Loan Parades" after the United States entered World War I. Volunteers riding on this Red Cross float pass along Market Street between 7th and 8th. (CHCBL)*

## Chapter Thirteen
# World War I and Beyond

The church bells and factory whistles sounded a continuous chorus on an April day in 1917, not in celebration of any major joyous occasion or new undertaking, but as an announcement of Chattanooga's participation in democracy's crusade in Europe. Since few residents had any close ties with the Germans or their supporters, their sympathies naturally were placed with the Allies. A majority of the people had voted for President Woodrow Wilson's reelection the previous November; already a few young men had volunteered for foreign service, and some factories by this time were in the throes of retooling for the nation's preparedness effort.

As in almost every corner of the country, Chattanoogans joined in an unrestrained outpouring of patriotism. Almost 10,000 men from the county entered service under the Selective Service Act, of whom some 200 gave their lives. Vacant lots became victory gardens, and everyone felt the pinch of shortages: gasless Sundays, heatless Mondays, and meatless days. Campaigns for the sale of bonds and stamps led to unrestrained pressure to meet quotas, and zeal was mistaken for staunch loyalty. People with foreign speech patterns became suspect; even the teaching of the German language was thought of in some strange way as contributing to the enemy's strength and was eliminated from school and college programs.

Home-front experience in Chattanooga differed from most communities because of proximity to Fort Oglethorpe and the vacant parklands in neighboring north Georgia. An incredibly large construction program in preparation for the training of thousands of troops ushered in boom days. In addition to Fort Oglethorpe the army created Camps Nathan Bedford Forrest, Warden McLean, and Greenleaf, along with the War Prisoner Barracks and quarters for civilian enemy aliens.

Virtually the entire local population mobilized for

volunteer work under the leadership of Genevieve Allan (Mrs. D. P.) Montague. Individuals, churches, and fraternal groups all pitched in. Some rolled bandages or gathered clothing; some worked in hospitals, travelers' aid stations or recreation centers. Others taught classes, gave lectures, and strove to reduce homesickness among the troops. Entertainment for Sunday dinner made many lasting friendships. At war's end the volunteers came under very heavy demands because of the influenza epidemic which swept through the camps and the town.

Chattanooga long celebrated the final victory as troops arrived for demobilization at Fort Oglethorpe. They paraded through the city streets in battle gear, with flags flying as great throngs of well-wishers lined the route. On July 4 a big peace pageant at Warner Park attracted an appreciative crowd. Later, the city, in a gesture of enduring thanks, built the Soldiers and Sailors Memorial Auditorium in memory of all who had served from the area.

The war rapidly acquainted the country with certain technical advances which could be developed for civilian usage. Radio underwent a sudden change from hobby to commercial application. On August 13, 1925, Earl Winger and Norman Thomas brought the new

medium to Chattanooga when station WDOD went on the air from its Patten Hotel studio. Even more dramatic is the story of what happened in aviation.

Chattanoogans George B. David, Johnny Green, Carl Morefield and other amateurs spearheaded experimentation in flying as far back as 1904. David, with the help of a carpenter, built a monoplane of bamboo and canvas that year. It had no motor but was a kind of glider which he attempted to launch at Olympia Park (now Warner Park) with a tow car. It had cost $73. Instead of flying, it immediately wrecked. The pilot broke both arms and the remains of the craft were gathered up and burned on the spot.

Barnstormers used fields off Rossville Boulevard and in Brainerd until an official airport called Marr Field was constructed in 1919 in East Chattanooga. It came about through the efforts of John Lovell and Walter S. Marr, a flying enthusiast who had been a designer for the Buick Motor Company. Lovell, who moved to Chattanooga in 1910 as a hotel man, served as chairman of the aeronautical committee of the Chamber of Commerce and frequently traveled with local pilots in their fragile craft. Interstate Airlines ferrying passengers and mail between Chicago and Atlanta used Marr Field. Major Fiske of the U.S. Army Corps of

Engineers chartered aircraft as early as 1921 in order to map the valley of East Tennessee for the Engineers' survey.

Marr Field unfortunately became the scene of several bad air crashes and was abandoned. John Lovell at once busied himself promoting a bond issue which eventually made possible the purchase of 130 acres for a municipal airport. The new facility, unpaved and boasting only a small administrative building, opened in 1930 as Lovell Field. For a time, aviation suffered a setback locally with the accident which took the life of Tarbell Patten, Sr., a leader in the Southern Flyers, Inc., and the first local air business group. By 1936 the needed improvements at Lovell Field were finally completed.

The contributions women made in war work led to the resurgence of a vigorous suffrage movement after peace came. Chattanooga's first concerns with the movement, the dedicated efforts of Catherine J. Wester and Margaret Ervin in 1911, had resulted in comparatively slow growth. In 1917, however, a municipal enfranchisement act allowed the town of Lookout Mountain to permit women to vote. The next year on April 2, Mrs. Corinne Dodds Sanders—wife of Newell Sanders, an industrialist and short-term U.S. Senator (first Republican senator from Tennessee in 40 years)—became the first woman to cast a ballot in the state.

In 1919 Chattanooga women voters went to the polls for the first time, but this right tended to be overshadowed by the intense effort to get the 19th Amendment to the Constitution ratified. The spotlight turned on Tennessee, where a vote of the legislature was needed to make the amendment a part of the nation's basic law. Locally, Abby Crawford Milton ably led the forces for ratification. Her efforts were rewarded by the affirmative vote of the Assembly. Shortly after this, on February 1, 1922, Sadie Watson assumed her duties as county register, the first woman to hold an elective county office. In 1926 Sarah Frazier won a seat in the General Assembly, the first woman from the district and the third in the state to win election to Tennessee's legislature.

*Top*
*Daisy Adelaide Barrett started work in the Department of Education in June 1893 and stayed on the job for 26 years. It is reported that she was the first woman to enter city hall service in any department. (CHCBL)*

*Above*
*"Bombs" fired from the Hotel Patten and the Times Building launched a celebration at war's end. The feverish activity of the previous months gave way to spirited festivities on Broad Street between 8th and 9th streets. (CHCBL)*

*Above*
*Sarah Ruth Frazier, a graduate of the Cumberland University Law School, won election in 1926 to the 65th Tennessee General Assembly. During her term this active Democratic member sponsored the Tennessee Confederate veterans' pension bill. (CHCBL)*

*Facing Page*
*Johnny Green, one of the city's first aviators, used an improvised airfield off Rossville Boulevard; he often carried John E. Lovell as a passenger. On December 5, 1919, an airstrip called Marr Field was dedicated in East Chattanooga. A new airport, Lovell Field, opened in 1930. (CHCBL)*

In the aftermath of World War I, a second wave of construction of major buildings revived the activity of the teen years. Again the community turned to that prolific and superior craftsman Reuben H. Hunt; actually between 1895 and 1935 every major governmental building in Chattanooga carried his design. Prime examples include the Tivoli Theater (1921), claimed at the time to be the "finest theater in the entire South." This was followed by the Memorial Auditorium (1922), Richard Hardy Junior High School (1925), First Baptist Church Educational Building (1927), and Frances Willard Building (1928). That same year Hunt, in a gradual transition from neo-classicism to an Art Deco style, designed the Medical Arts and Chattanooga Bank buildings.

In 1930 the Hunt firm drew plans for the Brainerd Junior High School and in 1932 the U.S. Federal Building, the best example of Art Deco in the city, and selected in 1938 by the American Institute of Architects as one of the finest 150 buildings in the country constructed within the previous 20 years. All downtown Chattanooga was enriched by the talent of this artistic professional of whom the Chattanooga *Free Press* wrote in 1937, "No man's life has been more thoroughly woven into the progress of Chattanooga during the past half-century than that of R. H. Hunt."

The '20s also found structures modifying the skyline other than those with a Hunt stamp. A few include: T. C. Thompson Children's Hospital (1929), John A. Patten Memorial Chapel at the University of Chattanooga (1919), Centenary Methodist Church (1922), Ochs Memorial Temple (1928), American National Bank Building (1928), Fort Wood Apartments (1928), and Engel Stadium (1929), the baseball park built by Joseph William "Joe" Engel.

A legendary figure during his lifetime, popular Joe Engel had been a professional player, vaudeville performer, and fighter against juvenile delinquency through his sponsorship of the Knot Hole Gang. He put Chattanooga on the national sports map with successful teams and with his love for ballyhoo. On various occasions he placed a rose garden in center field, gave a

house away at a game, staged elephant hunts, and put a girl into a lineup of an exhibition game to strike out Babe Ruth and Lou Gehrig. On his death in 1969 a link to Chattanooga's past was broken; fittingly his many keepsakes went to the baseball Hall of Fame at Cooperstown, New York.

In at least one case the city's physical appearance was changed by tearing down buildings. Many years had passed since the state of Georgia had built its railroad to Chattanooga and had acquired property south of the city limits at Ninth Street with rail connections to the river. In 1879 the city regained the use of Railroad Avenue, renamed Broad Street. The street, however, ended abruptly at Ninth because Georgia owned a row

of small buildings lining the south side of that thoroughfare. Over the years negotiations to open Broad Street and provide a direct route to Lookout Mountain had failed.

Chattanooga eventually decided to take action. On the night of May 6, 1926, when no injunction legally blocked their plan, city workers demolished enough of the buildings to drive a car through, thereby establishing a right-of-way. The noise attracted a crowd; among them were some bandsmen who struck up the tune "Marching through Georgia." The city won its point, but Georgia officials did not soon forget that music. They fussed and fumed for many years; only recently did Georgia sell all of its property located in the heart of the city.

The economic boom of the '20s spread to the neighboring mountains as the automobile made access not only possible but also comfortable. On Lookout, the Scenic Highway was paved and the other mountain road greatly improved and renamed Ochs. A post office had opened as long ago as 1867 and the village on the Tennessee side of the state boundary incorporated in 1890. A generation later Garnet Carter and his wife Frieda, and Paul Carter, joined by several associates, developed the modern mountaintop. A residential area called Fairyland clustered around the Fairyland Inn. During this time Garnet Carter invented and promoted commercially the game of Tom Thumb golf.

*Facing Page*
*Buildings owned by the state of Georgia along 9th Street blocked a direct route to Lookout Mountain from Broad Street. This bottleneck was finally removed in May of 1926 when city demolition crews opened a right-of-way through the property. (CHCBL)*

*Above*
*On June 14, 1927, ground was broken for a new generation of Lookout Mountain hotels by developer Paul Carter and associates. Depression days limited the success of the "Castle Above the Clouds"; after changing hands several times, it became the property of Covenant College in 1964. R.H. Hunt designed the structure. (CHCBL)*

*The popular "Joe" Engel, one-time president of the Chattanooga Lookouts, the Southern Baseball League, the Chattanooga Fair Association, and head of WDEF radio, also organized the Joe Engel Knothole Gang of boys. He settled in Chattanooga in 1929 and built the stadium named in his honor. (CHCBL)*

A palatial hotel was built in 1928, reminiscent of earlier days when guests came by train, but, like those prior ventures, the Lookout Mountain Hotel fell on lean days during the Depression. (The building ultimately became the nucleus of Covenant College in 1964.) More lasting in public appeal was the development of Rock City Gardens in May 1932. Like the Brainerd missionaries of old, visitors still find the spot exciting and alluring as they stroll through the natural gardens which grow on the edge of space.

Another nationally advertised attraction nearby on the mountain is the boldly engineered and carefully groomed property of Ruby Falls, with its striking underground waterfall. Leo Lambert, an amateur spelunker, discovered a way to this secret resource, which he named for his wife and opened to the public in June of 1930.

Change also came to Signal Mountain, a few miles from downtown Chattanooga but close enough to be thought of as community. For some years city dwellers had spent summers in this forested retreat. The association of urban residents with the mountain folk especially stimulated the thinking of a perceptive young lady of the mountain, Emma Bell Miles, whose native but largely untrained talent in art and literature had earned the respect of all. In 1905, she published a book entitled, *The Spirit of the Mountains,* a collection of stories and vignettes in which she evaluated the merits of frontier life and advocated a retention of the best of the more simple values of the mountain people without forsaking everything in imitating the ways of urban people.

*Emma Bell Miles, a "product and interpreter of the old mountain," caught the true spirit of Walden Ridge in her paintings, poems, and writings. Born in Rabbit Hash, Kentucky, in 1879, she accompanied her parents to this area as a child. Until her death in 1919 she lived close to nature, interpreted its whims and its beauties, and implored the mountain people to develop their native talents. Courtesy of Kay Gaston.*

*Another promoter of suburban Chattanooga was the Confederate veteran Captain S.J.A. Frazier, a lawyer who pioneered the development of Hill City (North Chattanooga). (CHCBL)*

*The interests of Sarah Key Patten (Mrs. Z.C. Patten) were not centered on real-estate development, but on the maturing of a sense of cultural and historic values in all with whom she associated. As a naturalist and conservationist she gave of her talents and funds to a rich variety of projects and associations. (CHCBL*

*In the development of the town of Signal Mountain and the Signal Mountain Inn, Charlie James had to construct a 13-mile trolley line up the mountain. This scenic route, where the highway scales the mountain today, was as unique as the engineering work was bold. (CHCBL)*

A practical Chattanooga developer saw the mountain from a different point of view. Long interested in its charming and breath-taking setting, he succeeded in 1913 in completing a 13-mile-long streetcar line from Chattanooga to a splendid inn on the edge of the canyon of the Tennessee River. Charlie James also built homes, and within a few years added a golf course, stables, and a casino. In 1919 the town of Signal Mountain was incorporated, with special attention given to legislating cattle off the golf course and away from the village lawns. In recent years the Inn has become the Alexian Brothers Rest Home and the town a rapidly growing suburban area pledged to retain the natural beauty of the forested mountain.

Despite the unrelenting economic whirl of the '20s, Chattanooga leaders expressed concern about the very slow growth of the population and advocated the annexation of neighboring suburban areas. They pointed out that the city's boundaries had not changed for about 50 years before Highland Park and Orchard Knob joined the community in 1905. Some other territory was annexed eight years later, but the census of 1920 showed no more than 57,895 persons living within the city.

Five years passed before the annexation of East Chattanooga, Avondale, and the Negro hamlets of Bushtown and Churchville. The long campaign by the Chamber of Commerce to add territory and population to the city, however, did not come to an end until September 30, 1929, when a celebration party welcomed Alton Park, Brainerd, Missionary Ridge, North Chattanooga, Riverview, and St. Elmo. Of this group Missionary Ridge was unique; strictly a residential area, it measured four and one-half miles long, 600 feet in width to the west of Crest Road and 500 feet in width to the east of this national government-maintained highway. As a result of these major annexations, Chattanooga census-takers reported in 1930 a total of 119,798 citizens.

*Nebraska Senator George Norris, advocate of political reform and of public ownership of hydroelectric power plants, introduced legislation for the establishment of TVA; he is called the "father" of this vast project. (CHCBL)*

## Chapter Fourteen

# The Tennessee Valley Authority

**D**uring the middle decades of the century the word Chattanooga again became a household name across the land as people whistled or sang of a shoe-shine boy or a choo-choo. The gay mood and the optimistic spirit of the '20s, however, ended abruptly in the '30s as the dreary weight of a national depression settled throughout the valley. Chattanooga found itself within a region labeled as the number one economic problem of the country.

For some time signs of trouble had been showing up in marginal activities like coal mining, textiles, and agriculture. In Chattanooga's hinterland the burden of post-Civil War poverty lingered; people wrestled with subsistence living, soil erosion, and drudgery. In the city, as the bubble of more prosperous days burst, numerous families experienced a brush with financial ruin.

Massive unemployment overpowered the community as industry slipped into the doldrums. Men who had jobs often walked miles to work to save a nickel in carfare. "Old clothes days" were common; barter returned as a way of business. Vacant houses were attacked for firewood. Along the railroad yards and under viaducts hobo jungles sprouted up where wanderers clustered together for company. Some localities like Onion Bottom and Blue Goose Hollow were the home places for people in abject poverty. The Lookout Mountain Hotel, Ruby Falls, the Signal Mountain Inn, and other attractions changed hands. One bank failed to reopen after the bank holiday. The city, although curtailing services in many areas, did support municipal food stations.

New hope surfaced on May 18, 1933. A "bedlam of noise" greeted the arrival of word that President Franklin D. Roosevelt had signed legislation creating the Tennessee Valley Authority. Although the comprehensive nature and scope of this gigantic project were unknown, it meant that national recognition had come to the area, that a goodly supply of money for

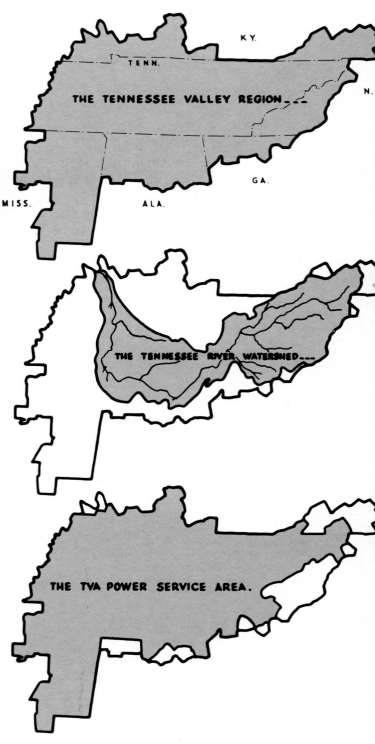

THE TENNESSEE VALLEY REGION

THE TENNESSEE RIVER WATERSHED

THE TVA POWER SERVICE AREA.

*Above*
Robert Sparks Walker, a lifetime Chattanoogan, naturalist and author, taught appreciation of the region's grandeur and of local history. (CHCBL)

*Right*
The TVA regional boundaries extend far beyond Chattanooga, but the "thorax" of the butterfly-shaped watershed falls within the city's immediate area. Courtesy of the Tennessee Valley Authority.

jobs and wages would be forthcoming, and that better days lay ahead. Chattanooga, in the center of the TVA country and with an historical record of being in the vanguard of river improvement, had reason to rejoice.

The symbol TVA represented a web of multipurpose projects related to navigation, flood control, and the generation of electric energy. It called for new ideas for land usage, wildlife management, reforestation, marginal land utilization, and scientific farming. In addition, the TVA proposed policies to promote the "economic and social well-being of the people" of the river basin. All this was to be managed by a board of three directors who believed in the "feasibility and wisdom" of the program and who would be responsible to the President, with stewardship to Congress only relating to matters of appropriations.

Echoes of the cheering had scarcely died down before some residents expressed caution about the plan, which soon turned to outspoken criticism stemming from a dislike for the "socialistic element" of the law and the "idealistic engineers" in charge. Some in opposition owned securities in the local power company; others feared a new competitor for labor. People with such views got encouragement from Jo Conn Guild, Jr., president of the Tennessee Electric Power Company (TEPCO) and from Wendell Willkie, president of Commonwealth and Southern, the holding company involved, along with the electric utilities of the whole country.

Early TVA supporters included George Fort Milton, publisher of the *News,* Senator William Brock, the majority of the Kiwanis Club, and members of the County Council. Of the situation at the time it was said: "Chattanooga is the center of the Tennessee Valley, is the center of the TVA storm, and like the center of the storm it is dead center."

Many Chattanoogans concluded that the deeply serious community split would forfeit all potential gains TVA had to offer. They hoped for the placing of some new offices in town; they wanted a dam just upstream from the city and a municipally owned electric power distribution system to peddle cheap power.

TVA placed their Maps and Surveys Division, the General Engineering and Geological Department, and the Electrical Division in Chattanooga. Chattanoogans battled over the distribution system in a referendum held on March 12, 1935. The question related to whether the city should sell $8,000,000 in bonds to finance the acquisition of a municipal system which would handle TVA power.

Lines were drawn. The Public Power League, short of money but long on enthusiasm, debated the Citizen & Tax Payers Association, closely linked to and financially aided by the power company: "Good old Americanism" vs. socialistic planning; bankruptcy of the city and high taxes vs. the experience of the old utility. Charges of fraud and columns of nasty gossip marred the campaign which found two newspapers, the *Times* and the *Free Press,* opposed to and the *News* in favor of public power. One desperate tactic took advantage of the city law which allowed property owners within the city to vote although they were not residents. Some 162 persons living outside the city jointly bought a $50 lot and qualified to vote at the cost of 33 cents each.

*Public-spirited John A. Patten headed the Chattanooga Medicine Company in formative years. The president of three packet lines operating on the Tennessee River, he championed the efforts of the Tennessee River Improvement Association and won praise as the "dominating river spirit of the whole Tennessee Valley." (CHCBL)*

*John A. Moon (1855-1921) moved to the city in 1874 and later served the district as congressman for 24 years. One of his major legislative interests centered on the systematic improvement of the entire length of the Tennessee River. In 1906 a local journalist wrote, "No real progress had been made in Tennessee River improvement until he came to Congress." (CHCBL)*

The public power people won 19,056 to 8,096 and the Electric Power Board of Chattanooga was established, with Colonel Harold C. Fiske placed in charge. However, several years passed before the Board serviced any customers. Their logical goal was to acquire TEPCO's lines and equipment, but the private company refused to sell. Finally the Board began constructing a costly duplicate system and served a few homes by January of 1939. It was now increasingly evident, however, that the Board would erode the value of TEPCO and that a sale was inevitable. On August 15, 1939, the transfer of property was made; the Power Board acquired the so-called Chattanooga District for $10,850,000. That midnight the Board became the sole distributor of electricity in a district about 500 square miles in size; it comprises practically all of Hamilton County and small areas beyond. (TVA acquired the Hales Bar Dam from TEPCO in the same sale.)

The growth of the business under the Board in its 41 years of operation has been as amazing as the inventions on which the industry is built. The number of customers grew from 42,234 to 120,221 in 1979-80 while the sale in kilowatt-hours rose from about 432 million to 4,957 million. The Board's 41st annual report gives the average cost of electricity to all its users as 72 percent of the national average and reflects on the fact that its residential customers use 17,554 kilowatt-hours compared with about 8,700 for the entire country. The Board has not only been remarkably free of political pressure but is also the largest payer in lieu of taxes to the city and the county: its payments to all districts have risen from $279,000 to $4,873,000.

In addition to municipally owned distribution and the locating of some TVA offices in Chattanooga, early advocates of the Authority wanted a dam upstream from the city. This latter objective was not easily achieved. As a matter of fact, TVA's early construction priorities called for tributary storage dams instead of main river structures. Local politicians led by County Judge Will Cummings turned their guns on the Directors and on the national government; they felt abandoned and embittered because construction funds had not helped fight the Depression locally. Finally a dam was assured and on January 13, 1936, work started on the $39,000,000 project to be known as Chickamauga Dam. Unemployment figures tumbled. President Roosevelt stopped in Chattanooga at the time and addressed the workers in characteristic fashion:

*You are not merely putting an obstruction across a river just to make a few kilowatts of electricity. We are doing a much bigger job than that. We are not only improving navigation and stopping floods, we are not only helping to reforest cut-over lands and conserving soil, but, taking it by and large, we are doing something constructive that will affect the lives of our grandchildren in the United States. . . . TVA is a demonstration of what a democracy at work can do, of a people uniting in a war against waste and insecurity.*

On Labor Day 1940 the President returned to dedicate Chickamauga Dam and all of the TVA reservoirs as the Great Lakes of the South. The occasion, preceded by parades, balls, and pageants, brought an estimated 80,000 persons out into the broiling sun for one of Chattanooga's red-letter days. Three major radio networks carried the chief executive's remarks, in which he referred to earlier visits when:

*The TVA installations attract thousands of tourists, journalists, and political leaders, many from foreign lands. President Miguel Aleman of Mexico and his party visited Chickamauga Dam on May 6, 1947. (CHCBL)*

*Far Left*
*President Roosevelt, who kept in close touch with the progress of TVA, dedicated Chickamauga Dam on Labor Day, 1940. Governor Prentice Cooper of Tennessee sits between Mrs. Roosevelt and the President; the fourth passenger is Senator Kenneth McKellar. Courtesy of the Tennessee Valley Authority.*

*Left*
*Charles H. Coolidge, Medal of Honor recipient. This photograph was taken at the time the medal was awarded. Courtesy of Charles H. Coolidge.*

*. . . There flowed here a vagrant stream, sometimes useless, sometimes turbulent and in flood, always dark with soil it had washed from the eroding hills. . . . But, worst of all, I have seen the splendid people living in parts of seven states fighting against nature instead of fighting with nature.*

The personal assessment of the President was underscored years later by the historian Henry Steele Commager, who said that TVA was "probably the greatest peacetime achievement of twentieth century America."

In the fall of 1940 there were signs that the United States could not much longer remain out of the expanding European war. Chattanooga soon had to gear up for the struggle. From Hamilton County 25,258 persons went off to war; 695 died in service. World War II resembled a crusade of sacrifice and duty rather than a public display of patriotism as in 1917. On the homefront price control, rationing, and volunteer work dominated the conversation of the day. The 446 manufacturing plants within a 25-mile radius turned out textiles, blankets, shells, tanks, artillery parts, boilers, and alloys of steel products. "K" rations were packaged, and at a new plant occupying some 7,500 acres at Tyner, the Volunteer Ordnance Works, operated by the Hercules Powder Company, produced about 8,233 million pounds of TNT before it ceased operations in August 1945.

Chattanoogans were also caught up in the frantic pace set by TVA. At the Maps and Surveys Department more than one-half million square miles of enemy country—Italy, France, and Pacific Islands—were mapped. A construction schedule designed to build the dams and power facilities planned for years ahead was rushed to completion. The engineers of the power division headquartered in Chattanooga found themselves managing one of the largest utilities in the world while planning to meet the gigantic requirements of the war-produced newcomer on the line—Oak Ridge, homeplace of America's nuclear program.

Proximity to Fort Oglethorpe and a new camp at Tullahoma again gave the city a martial air. In January 1943 a dramatic change occurred when the north Georgia post was converted to the Third Woman's Army Auxiliary Corps Training Center. Uniformed women crowded the city's entertainment and public facilities as shopkeepers hastily stocked a different inventory.

At war's end a memorial was erected in Patten Parkway to the local persons who had served their country. With gratitude and pride the community still honors Technical Sergeant Charles H. Coolidge of Signal Mountain, winner of the Medal of Honor for heroic conduct on October 24-28, 1944. His citation reads:

*With a handful of new reinforcements he directed a 4-day battle against a superior German force during which time he dueled two tanks with his carbine, advanced alone to stop a German attack with two cases of grenades and frustrated an attempt to turn the flank of his battalion.*

Finally, on December 31, 1946, another military chapter closed in Chattanooga's history: on that day taps sounded for the last time at the Fort Oglethorpe installation.

Throughout the Tennessee Valley the demand for electric power continued to grow after the war; huge steam plants in a short time were producing more current than the original hydro facilities. Protests again rolled in from private enterprise supporters and utility organizations claiming that TVA was exceeding the role which government should properly play in business. A renewal of the early legal battles loomed; many advocated the idea of selling the Authority, but friends rallied around TVA.

The local U.S. Senator, Estes Kefauver, was a warm supporter of TVA. The tall, folksy Kefauver had entered Congress from Chattanooga in 1939 and then nine years later moved to the Senate. Closely associated with his coonskin cap symbol—the coon had rings in its tail and not in its nose—he got the reputation of being a maverick politician among his constituents. But Kefauver had a solid national following, which brought him

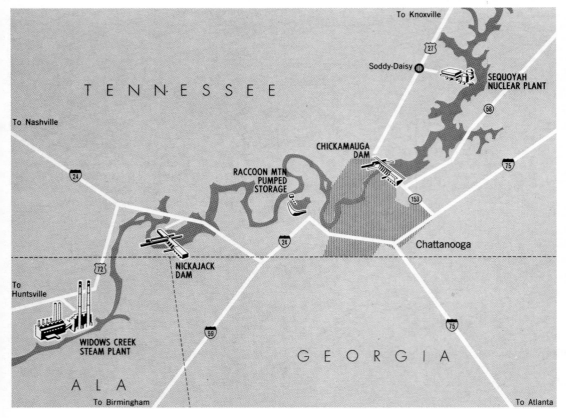

*Above*
*Chickamauga Lake, with its wooded, irregular shoreline and its adjacent hills, has offered an opportunity for a new life-style for the people since 1940. TVA's recreational by-products have been a boon to the area's tourist industry and provide a greater choice of outdoor activities for residents. Courtesy of the Tennessee Valley Authority.*

*Left*
*Chattanooga is headquarters for TVA's power division and a geographic center for the unique assemblage of energy development facilities: hydro, steam, nuclear, and pumped-storage. Engineers in hard hats have replaced pioneers in their coonskin caps both in the urban and the rural areas. Courtesy of the Tennessee Valley Authority.*

*Facing Page*
*The "old river" sported only a very few pleasure craft, such as the Tomlinson Fort. The many marinas on the "new river" have few if any vacant slips. (CHCBL)*

the nomination for vice-president in 1956. Until his sudden death in 1963 the senator was a firm backer of TVA. The most significant accomplishment was the approval of self-financing legislation in 1959, which authorizes TVA to sell revenue bonds for construction projects. This put the Authority in a stronger position than ever because it permitted systematic future planning without the problems of annual appropriations.

Over the years, TVA has brought many advantages to Chattanooga. Hundreds of new citizens associated with it moved to the community. A flood control project on South Chickamauga Creek, within the city limits,

*Within 20 miles of the city to the northeast, the cooling towers of the Sequoyah Nuclear plant symbolize an awesome power for a nation short of energy. The name is a most appropriate reminder of the Cherokee Indian who found power in the written word. Courtesy of the Tennessee Valley Authority.*

lessens fears of another 1973 flood. Beyond the urban borders cover crops replace bare, row-crop fields, and numerous small managed forests stand in place of unkempt woodlands. The lakes and their parklands prove a boon to navigation, recreation, and tourism.

As TVA nears its 50th birthday, however, power continues to be the most controversial phase of its operation. The specter of shortages appeared about 1970 and, for a time four years later, Chattanooga experienced a limited Christmastime brownout. To prepare for the future, the Authority began planning an extensive nuclear program, including the Sequoyah plant some 18 miles to the northeast of the city. After a decade, construction of this 2.5-million-kilowatt facility has been completed and the necessary licenses acquired to put it on line.

In 1970, the same year ground was broken at Sequoyah, TVA started work on the Raccoon Mountain Pumped-Storage Hydro Plant six miles west of Chattanooga to supply "peaking power." It includes a 528-acre lake on top of Raccoon Mountain filled with water pumped from Nickajack Lake a thousand feet below; this water will generate electricity when needed at expensive periods of high demand. The pump-turbine units are housed in a chamber 470 feet long and 72 feet wide carved into the mountain fastness. At full operation this gigantic engineering facility, located in a rugged natural setting, has a capacity equal to 14 Chickamauga Dams.

These developments, undreamed of in 1933, form a partial response to the nation's energy crisis. TVA has been called upon to serve as a model of regional economic and energy development and act as a sort of laboratory for experimental projects. But contention and controversy still surround the program. The Authority in its early days demonstrated great pride in its mission and won valley allegiance by encouraging the large-scale use of its cheap power. Low rates became a tradition as well as a working economic philosophy. As inflation, big environmental costs, and high interest rates challenge the old pricing policy, rates to consumers are increasing amidst a chorus of protest.

*High fences enclose a construction area in the south-central business section where an enormous office complex and computer center will house TVA's power center. This architects' drawing barely suggests the scale and technology of this project of the future. Courtesy of the Tennessee Valley Authority.*

*This R.H. Hunt Courthouse of neo-classical design boasts a lavish use of Tennessee marble and a three-story, colored-glass dome. Completed in 1913 for $350,000, its graceful lines stand as a masterful example of the architect's talent. In 1975-1976 a six-story Criminal Justice Building was added to the Hamilton County Building complex. (CHCBL)*

## Chapter Fifteen

# Yesterday's Last Hours

The hour of midnight had passed that Tuesday, September 12, 1967. In the night's darkness, an attack on the railroad yards at Wauhatchie, exhilarating and successful, bordered on sheer fiction. It could have been a ghost raid by the braves of Dragging Canoe, pilfering in their native haunts; it could have been bushwhackers several generations later; or it could have been shades of James Andrews, captor of the famed Civil War locomotive. Rather, it was the mayor of Chattanooga, Ralph H. Kelley, with a cadre of raiders made up of city commissioners, police officials, the county sheriff, and a squad of his aides. Their purpose: to hijack a major freight train carrying the little Civil War locomotive, the "General," southward to a permanent new home at Kennesaw Mountain, Georgia.

For more than 75 years the "General" had stood in the city's Union Depot as a relic of history and an attraction for the tourists. For years it had been emblazoned on the city's seal as a local heirloom. The railroad people removed it from its accustomed corner to display during the Civil War Centennial. Then, contrary to earlier suggestions, word came that the engine would not be returned but, being the property of the state-owned railroad, would be placed in a Georgia shrine. To prevent this, Kelley's raiders went into action. Although their escapade proved successful, the mayor's supporters lost a spirited legal battle later, and with it the "General." The city did get extensive publicity over the prank, with one admirer wiring the mayor, "Even if you lose, you got class."

The second capture of the "General" proved to be an omen. The iron horse had brought a certain identification to the city for more than a century. Following the Wauhatchie episode on August 4, 1970, the Southern's *Birmingham Special* made its last scheduled call to Chattanooga and on May 1, 1971, the L & N's *Georgian* ceased to run; all rail passenger service ended. The old Union Depot and the Georgia railroad lands in the

heart of the city were sold and the station razed, despite the protests of buffs who treasured historic landmarks.

Freight trains continue to carry their burdens over the rails through the old gateway, but most of the nostalgia of past times must now be sought at the Tennessee Valley Railroad Museum, opened in 1970, and at the Choo-Choo, the refurbished Terminal Station where gaslight, sleeping cars, and special "railway menus" keep a corner of the past alive.

The past, present, and future have always been but one thread on which history is laced. The only constant found in it is change—sometimes very slow, often abrupt, or what historians refer to as "deep change." Since mid-century, Chattanooga, like all America, has been in the midst of accelerated social, economic, political, and cultural transformation that is so extensive as to make the historian's task most difficult and his findings very inconclusive.

*Above Left*
*For 75 years this famed Civil War locomotive, captured by Andrews' Raiders in their attempt to sabotage the Confederate railroad, had been on display at Union Depot. In 1967 a new raid was perpetrated by Chattanoogans; led by their mayor, they vainly tried to prevent the return of the "General" to Georgia. Courtesy of the Chattanooga Convention and Visitors Bureau.*

*Above Right*
*This Italian Renaissance office building was constructed in 1891 to house the offices of the* Chattanooga Times. *Originally called the Ochs or Times Building, with new occupants and restoration it has become known as the Dome Building. Courtesy of the Greater Chattanooga Chamber of Commerce.*

*Facing Page*
*The Great Lakes of the South generated a vast increase in recreational opportunities. Unlike the rudimentary use of the river by pioneer forebears, modern Chattanoogans find boating, fishing, and camping enjoyable outdoor pastimes during a long period of the year. The waters of Lake Chickamauga have brought vacation lands within a short distance of home. Courtesy of the Tennessee Valley Authority.*

In economic affairs Chattanooga moved closer to the mainstream of American business during these decades. They were, on the whole, years of growth although confidence was periodically shaken by distant, unpredictable events or by local signals of distress when a bank closed or a veteran company like Coca-Cola Bottling Company (Thomas) moved away.

Manufacturing remained the chief occupation, but mergers and purchases by outside interests of established local enterprises revealed a constant trend: in 1977, among the 47 larger firms, 31 had headquarters elsewhere. Changing technology brought new activities. Broadcast television, for example, accompanied by a cluster of service and retail businesses, was pioneered by WDEF's Channel 12 in 1954. Combustion Engineering's production of nuclear components, the Du Pont organization's development of modern fabrics, and the enormous growth of the carpet industry centered in Dalton, Georgia, represent the "deep change" in many industries.

In newspaper circles business consolidation reduced competitive costs while preserving a continuity of two strong independent editorial voices representing two local family interests. In 1969 the Chattanooga *Times* celebrated the centennial of that journal. At that time the news market was also served by a conservative evening publication which had started as a Depression throwaway to advertise the food stores of Roy McDonald.

McDonald's efforts culminated in the Chattanooga *Free Press* on August 31, 1936. Within three years of the launching of this first edition, the new venture was expanded with the purchase of the financially troubled Chattanooga *News*, and the combined name *News-Free Press* was adopted. During the years 1942-66 the evening paper merged with the morning *Times* in a joint agreement of all business-related activities. This association, dissolved in 1966, was renewed in 1980 after receipt of a grant of immunity from antitrust suits by the federal government.

Left
Lookout Mountain, once described as a ''noble pile of stratified limestone with a huge lump of sandstone at the top,'' never ceases to attract visitors. From the valley to the west, Sunset Rock resembles the profile of an Indian. Courtesy of the Greater Chattanooga Chamber of Commerce.

Below
The Tennessee Valley Railroad Museum was incorporated in 1961 to keep the spirit of the railroad era alive. Today, its steam locomotives and passenger cars operate over a six-mile track which includes the historic tunnel through Missionary Ridge. Courtesy of the Chattanooga Convention and Visitors Bureau.

Facing Page:
Top Left
On December 11, 1950, Margaret Truman sang as guest artist with the Chattanooga Symphony. (CHCBL)

Top Right
Admirers of Grace Moore gather after a concert on March 9, 1935, at the city's Memorial Auditorium to congratulate the area's most celebrated artist and to offer her a key to her hometown. A screen star, Broadway actress, and grand opera prima donna, she died in a tragic plane crash near Copenhagen, Denmark, in January 1947. In this photo Tommy Thompson stands to Miss Moore's left and Mrs. John L. Hutcheson, Jr., to her right. (CHCBL)

Bottom
This art complex, which houses both permanent and visiting collections, was completed in 1975 on a site overlooking the Tennessee River from the bluff. It originally consisted only of the Faxton-Thomas Mansion, a Georgian Revival home, built 1906-1908 by Ross Steele Faxton, and designed by Abram Garfield, son of the President. Courtesy of Michael C. Crawford.

The interstate highways, following closely the old Indian traces, were also newcomers, offering panoramic scenery to the vast numbers of persons hurrying by. More than one-half of the nation's population reside within a day's journey of the city and, guided by numerous "Rock City" signs, many stop to view the scenery, historic spots, and natural attractions. Even the current craze of the followers of Icarus brings guests, who as hang-gliding fans find their "home mountain" here or come to witness international competition in this burgeoning sport.

The economic activity of the area could scarcely match the constant growth in the performing arts, health care, and higher education. Excellent and some-

times heroic triumphs mark the range and richness of amateur and professional presentations in music, drama, and the dance. All have been encouraged by local patrons and foundations, by the renovation of the Memorial Auditorium, and the city's purchase of the Tivoli Theater, long known as a "little gem." Summer pop concerts in the national park and midday programs at downtown Miller Park draw spontaneous audience approval.

Chattanoogans also found pride in the success and fame of an adopted daughter with a golden voice and gracious manner. Associated with the area from 1932, when her parents made the city their home, until her tragic death 15 years later, Grace Moore—screen star,

Broadway actress, and grand opera prima donna—won the love and admiration of the city and, in turn, encouraged other talented singers to seek instruction.

Consecutive successful seasons of the Symphony Orchestra, Opera Association, Festival Players, and Little Theater not only complemented local collegiate offerings but also surpassed all earlier experiences in the variety and professionalism of their offerings. The Hunter Museum of Art from its river bluff location adds to this legacy of cultural leadership and community cooperation. Other organizations—the Chattanooga Museum of Regional History, Chattanooga Nature Center, Houston Antique Museum, and the Tennessee Valley Railroad Museum—illustrate the variety of interests in the past along with the Society for the Preservation of Tennessee Antiquities, Landmarks, the Area Historical Association, and many patriotic societies. All combine in drawing more closely to Chattanooga such regional communities as South Pittsburg, Dayton, Cleveland, Athens, Collegedale, and Dalton.

Growth also marks the story of higher education. The University of Chattanooga and City College for blacks merged in 1969 with the state university, to become a major campus under the name University of Tennessee at Chattanooga. As a public institution, programs, campus, and student body expanded annually at an unprecedented pace.

New state institutions are represented by the Chattanooga Area Vocational Technical School, founded in 1970, and the Chattanooga State Technical Community College, begun in 1965. The privately supported Bible school and junior college, founded in 1946 by the Highland Park Baptist Church, has grown into Tennessee Temple University, with some 4,000 students. (Within commuting distance are Covenant College, Southern Missionary College, Bryan College, Tennessee Wesleyan, Cleveland State Community College, Dalton Junior College, Lee College, Tomlinson College, and the University of the South.)

Three special organizations have brought distinction to themselves and acclaim to the city. The Rehabilitation Center of the Siskin Memorial Foundation, started in 1950, has earned national and international recognition for its speech, hearing, dental, and physical therapy programs. So too has the Orange Grove Center for the Retarded with its school, day care, and workshop programs as it expanded from painfully small beginnings in 1952 to a modern plant with about 700 students. Some 35 local and national health and social agencies get financial support from the United Fund, which has established a national record by surpassing its annual giving objective for 59 consecutive years.

The idea of expansion became a goal for the city fathers, Chamber of Commerce leaders, and community boosters when they realized that Chattanooga's size and population had stagnated. Practically no annexation occurred since 1929, but vigorous suburban areas had sprouted up on all sides beyond the reach of city planners and tax gatherers and wanted to stay that way. City spokesmen, on the other hand, fussed about "daylight citizens," "bedroom satellites," and the municipal expenses that commuters avoided.

Tennessee came to the aid of its cities in 1955 by making it easy for urban centers to annex; all the city had to do was to pass an ordinance to this effect. No consent of parties concerned was needed; the only alternative for private citizens was to prove at their own expense that annexation was unreasonable. A wail of protest arose as Chattanooga made a move to add land and people. Legal battles flared up. Some sections of the county—Red Bank, White Oak, Soddy, Daisy, Collegedale, Lakesite, and Walden—incorporated in order to avoid annexation. Others such as East Ridge and Ridgeside reaffirmed their earlier corporate independence.

The "annexation wars" continued year after year. From the city's point of view expansion became more pressing because federal assistance funds were based on size. Mayor Robert Kirk Walker, despite political obstacles, gave special attention to the annexation movement.

When the air cleared by June 1977, Chattanooga

claimed 170,046 citizens, a gain of more than 50,000 since 1970, and a sprawling territory of 126.9 square miles. In addition, the city acquired an abundant crop of new problems. In the name of Chattanooga, promises of service to the annexed people had been made: the city and county seriously feuded over school property that had to be transferred along with countless other problems; and city engineers and maintenance personnel discovered that kudzu vines and blackberry bushes grow inside corporate limits as well as in the hinterland.

These annexation troubles, however, were compounded by the complex urban agonies which struck locally as they did across America. An awakened conscience after World War II exposed the harsh side of society: deterioration of the inner city; pollution of air and water; the need for interceptor sewers; deplorable housing; and interurban transportation problems headed the list. Such matters got but slight attention before the 1950s; conservative views and fiscal policy dismissed them from society's concern.

*The "county bridge" was a topic of fiery debate in the 1880s; Chattanooga and Hill City people north of the river wanted it but many county folks objected. Finally, in July 1889, contracts were let and on February 18, 1891, a festive celebration marked its completion. In 1929 Chattanooga inherited the span, with the annexation of Hill City. Presently, the Walnut Street Bridge is considered to be unsafe and has been closed. Its future provokes the same vigorous civic debates it did nearly 100 years ago. Courtesy of the Chattanooga Convention and Visitors Bureau.*

In the face of vigorous opposition, the new mayor in 1951 "picked up and shook" the city. Under P. R. Olgiati, Chattanooga, known as one of America's dirtiest cities, after frustrating attempts, got control of its air and water. Residents whose memories reach back to the Depression years appreciate the tremendous strides made, although newer citizens continue to point to pockets of suspended particulate from in-town heavy industry and to the natural atmospheric temperature inversions which no amount of legislation can prevent.

Meanwhile Olgiati, who insisted that urban social and physical problems were everyone's problems, sparked

*Above*
This view of downtown Chattanooga, although several years old, shows clearly the renewal area of the Golden Gateway (beyond the interstate), and the modifications made by the decapitation of Cameron Hill. Despite all these changes and modern improvements, the Tennessee River continues to twist its way through this man-made world. (CHCBL)

*Facing Page:*
*Left*
Time has modified the type of craft that sails the river through the Canyon of the Tennessee, but the surrounding hills present the same picturesque, ever-green landscape. Courtesy of the Chattanooga Convention and Visitors Bureau.

*Facing Page:*
*Top Right*
The Federal Building, built in 1932, represents the last major design of architect R.H. Hunt. It is acclaimed the "most outstanding example of Art Deco architecture" in the city, featuring geometric, plant, and animal motifs. Courtesy of the Chattanooga/Hamilton County Regional Planning Commission.

*Facing Page:*
*Bottom Right*
The Cravens House, home of the pioneer ironmaster Robert Cravens (1805-1888), is the oldest surviving structure on Lookout Mountain. The Battle Above the Clouds centered on this spot, at which time the name "White House" was generally used. Acquired as part of the National Military Park in 1896, the deteriorating house was later restored as a shrine. Courtesy of the Chattanooga Convention and Visitors Bureau.

the momentum in housing. As for the building of interstate highways involving Chattanooga, he campaigned for speedy completion and insisted that a river bridge, called by some "Olgiati's footlog," was to be included. "Chattanooga Roundabout," a program to move downtown rail yards, eliminate street crossings, relocate Chattanooga Creek, and build street bridges, turned into a major public-private cooperative face-lifting operation.

The high point in renewal of the core city, however, was the Golden Gateway urban renewal project comprising 403 acres of the dying west side. Families numbering about 1,400 had to move; 1,170 buildings had to be razed. As the cleared land slowly returned to private ownership, professional planning with emphasis on open spaces and modern construction provided the stimulus for renewal in other areas. With steel and concrete, it was said, the mayor "altered the face and heart of Chattanooga."

The new spirit spread; in recent years more than 20 major downtown structures have changed the city skyline. Vintage buildings of distinctive lines—the Tivoli Theater, Terminal Station, Carnegie Library, Dome Building, Patten Hotel, Park Plaza, and the Volunteer Building—have been refurbished with an eye for preserving their original character. Some private homes, churches, commercial structures and residential districts on the National Register have joined with such historic sites as the Cravens House, Brown's Tavern, and the John Ross House as guarded treasures of the past.

Prominent in the inner city's rebirth is the attention given to the architectural use of space. Market Center features planters, plazas, no street parking, and a curving thoroughfare. It complements the John Ross Landing Park by the river, the mini-Boynton Park on Cameron Hill, and the relaxed atmosphere of Miller Park. First floor false fronts, unfinished walls exposed by razing neighboring buildings, and cluttered off-street parking with its glaze of blacktop, however, serve as reminders that the task is not yet finished.

Since the days of Ross's Landing the physical appearance of the area has changed many times. Human institutions, however, cannot be so readily torn down and replaced because emotions, self-interest, and pride surface very readily. Both the barest fears and the noblest idealism often race to extreme positions and on to violence. When the social revolution of the mid-century erupted across America, Chattanooga was not immune from its consequences; the population included a large black minority and a considerable number of persons living below the poverty level. Civil rights, social adjustments, and political tensions challenged the traditional spirit of community and moderation.

Dissatisfaction with government arose but was not a vital issue. Chattanooga's political structure remained the same as in 1911; Hamilton County, on the other hand, experienced two complete changes. In 1941 a council/manager plan was put into effect and lasted until 1978, when it was replaced by a commission/executive form with the nine commissioners selected in district elections.

A more fundamental political development came in 1972 when the U.S. Supreme Court ruled on reapportionment: the one man, one vote concept. Tennessee's urban centers consequently gained legislative seats denied them for years by the rural majority; in addition, political and racial minorities gained through a requirement for district voting. After the changeover, Chattanooga and the county both seated black officials, and Clarence B. Robinson, a black, gained a seat in the General Assembly in 1974, the first black to represent the area since 1887.

Another relevant "first," although not necessarily associated with the reapportionment question: the Congressional District in 1976 sent its first woman, Marilyn Lloyd Bouchard, to Congress and has reelected her twice since that date.

A local reform movement favoring Metro government gained supporters by 1962. Although Chattanooga and Hamilton County had cooperated in health care, library service, and police work, advocates of the new concept claimed a more efficient and less expensive single government could best serve the region as it became more urbanized. Within the next eight years two referendums in which concurrent city and county majorities were required for success were held. Metro lost in both elections although in the 1970 voting Chattanooga supported the change.

*Left*
*Lookout Mountain Incline No. 2 has climbed the 72.7 percent grade regularly since November 16, 1895. The thrilling ride and panoramic scenery attract the touring public to "America's Most Amazing Mile." Designed by Josephus Conn Guild, it operated as a private attraction until 1973, when it became a facility of the Chattanooga Area Regional Transportation Authority (CARTA). (CHCBL)*

*Above*
*Thousands of visitors tour the Chickamauga Chattanooga Military Park administration and museum building each year. Located on the battlefield in north Georgia, it serves as headquarters of the many park sites in the Chattanooga area and houses the splendid Fuller collection of shoulder arms. Courtesy of the Chattanooga Convention and Visitors Bureau.*

Much more serious were the events associated with civil rights and desegregation. Agitation, fear, and violence poured from the nation's urban centers. Sit-ins in 1960 at Chattanooga downtown lunch counters followed by stand-ins at theaters generated mob scenes. The city's agony increased in intensity. Only the calm leadership of Mayor Kelley and the gracious understanding of William E. Brock, Jr., who led a diligent biracial group, prevented a violent clash. Within a relatively short time segregated bus seating was ruled out, city services were made available, and public facilities officially opened to all citizens.

Tension mounted anew, however, when delayed plans for school desegregation were finally implemented. In the fall of 1962, 44 blacks attended six formerly white city schools in the lower three grades;

Hamilton County voluntarily followed a similar program at the same time. Within four years the "separate" school system ceased to exist, but the "mix" did not provide true integration; the court answered with busing demands. By this time fresh signs of social torment broke out; racial scuffles grew into community hostility. Fire bombings, sniper attacks, and incoherent rumor required curfews and national guard presence before tension eased. The impact of social change has left an image of civic apprehension; it has also left a record of racial interaction recalling earlier days along the "road to reunion" when people cultivated the will to live with compromise and community.

According to the 1980 final census reports, Chattanooga's population numbers 169,565; the county, 287,740. Blueprints of economic growth indicate a continuing renewal and expansion. Potential energy supplies seem assured; planners talk of a riverport and a renewal program for East Ninth Street. Several major private buildings have been announced and preliminary work has begun on a TVA office complex and computer center designed to be a "showcase of alternative energy use."

Recently Mayor Charles (Pat) Rose stated: "Chattanooga ... offers the basic ingredients of a larger city but is small enough to offer an attractive life-style that is lost in larger metropolitan areas." Actually the city and its environs present a unique blend of the urban and the rural, of lakes, mountains, and woodlands. The wonders of nature are near at hand: Audubon Acres, Reflection Riding, state parks, and wildlife management areas.

A proud history is on daily display in Chattanooga in place names and the commemorative acres of the national military park. Many families have lived in the region for several generations and thus have put down roots which are firmly embedded here. And newcomers over the years have found it a good place to live; like early settler John P. Long they have built their "cabins in the woods" with the intention of staying.

# Color
# Plates

The city of Chattanooga, as seen from the superior vantage point of Lookout Mountain. Photograph by Robert Fuschetto.

*Above*
*Situated in Georgia a short distance south of the Tennessee border, Rock City Gardens with trails, swinging bridges, and giant sandstones carved by nature was opened to the public on May 8, 1932. Wildflowers indigenous to the region grow along the trails, while wide vistas on a clear day extend to the Great Smoky Mountains. Courtesy of the Chattanooga Convention and Visitors Bureau.*

*Right*
*The spring flowers and fall colors of the mountains are at times matched by a different kind of natural beauty. The ice, freezing temperatures, and shimmering sunshine transform the summit of Lookout Mountain into a winter wonderland as in March 1960. Courtesy of the Chattanooga Convention and Visitors Bureau.*

*Above*
*At the Choo Choo, flower gardens, fountains, gaslights, and the Hilton Hotel now stand where trains once backed into the station. Sleeping and dining cars stand by for the nostalgic traveler to slip back into another age. A great variety of specialty shops have transformed the utility areas of former days. Courtesy of the Chattanooga Convention and Visitors Bureau.*

*Left*
*Leo Lambert had an obsession for mysteries. Following the closing of an old Lookout Mountain cave, he headed a search for a new entrance to the scenic underworld by drilling from above. The unexpected result was the discovery of Ruby Falls. On December 31, 1928, the cavern was opened for the public to inspect the 145-foot underground waterfall. Courtesy of the Chattanooga Convention and Visitors Bureau.*

*Top Left*
*Major Ridge, a wealthy and influential Cherokee, served with the whites under Andrew Jackson at the Battle of Horseshoe Bend and afterward used the title "Major" as his first name. He became one of the leading figures in opposing Ross's resistance to removal to the West, believing sincerely that the Indians' only salvation lay in moving beyond white contact. He was killed in 1839 for signing the Removal Treaty. From T.L. McKenney,* History of the Indian Tribes of North America.

*Top Right*
*John Ross (1790-1866) lived in the Chattanooga area for 48 years. He served his people as a leader in the Cherokee cultural revolution, and in 1828 the Nation elected him Principal Chief under the terms of*

*its new written constitution. Using a policy of passive resistance, he led the opposition to the westward removal of his people. Ross's physical features reveal the small Cherokee strain in this son of a Scottish trader. From T.L. McKenney,* History of the Indian Tribes of North America.

*Above and Right*
*Artifacts of the Mississippian Period, from the Audubon Society Site in Hamilton County. The great temple mounds of the Mississippians have disappeared, but archaeologists find evidence of their highly developed shell industry and implement trade which possibly centered in the strategically located town on Dallas Island. Courtesy of Victor P. Hood.*

*Top Left*
In the ''Narrows'' the Suck was the most difficult stretch of water. Cherokee myths undertook to explain the unusual problems created by this giant whirlpool; later boatmen cursed its existence.

*Top Right*
The beauty of Lake Seclusion has been enjoyed by generations of visitors.

*Bottom Left*
Tucker & Perkins' photographic scenery of the South series, made about 1860, featured this gathering at Leonora Spring on Lookout Mountain. Discovered and named for Harriet Leonora Whiteside, it was a site of festive occasions as well as a source of water for some early mountain residents of the Summertown area.

*Bottom Right*
One of Lookout Mountain's unusual natural creations is Umbrella Rock at Point Park. At one time called Noah's Umbrella, it attracted mountain visitors in pre-Civil War days. Today it is off limits to tourists because of its delicate balance.

*Top*
*Hang-gliding sportsmen from many distant states, finding the launching sites on Lookout and Raccoon mountains ideal, have adopted the area as their "home hill." International competition for the annual American Cup races attracts teams from Great Britain, Canada, and Japan, as well as the United States. Courtesy of the Chattanooga Convention and Visitors Bureau.*

*Bottom*
*Moccasin Bend of the Tennessee River and Chattanooga, as seen from Point Park. Courtesy of Terry C. Henson.*

*Facing Page:*
*Top*
*A spectacular night scene in downtown Chattanooga. Photograph by Robert Fuschetto.*

*Facing Page:*
*Bottom*
*Dressed in spring flowers or fall colors, or basking in the pastoral quiet of a summer afternoon, Reflection Riding brings the visitor in close touch with nature's grandeur. The park land, founded by John A. Chambliss, is the home of the Chattanooga Nature Center. Courtesy of the Chattanooga Convention and Visitors Bureau.*

*An early 1900s Lookout Mountain work crew. (CHCBL)*

## Chapter Sixteen

# Partners in Progress

Nestled in a valley beneath the ever-looming presence of famed Lookout Mountain and bounded by Missionary Ridge on the east and Elder and Signal mountains on the west, Chattanooga possesses abundant natural resources, geographical advantages, mild climate, and human talent. The combination of the Tennessee River and the natural passes out of the valley to the northeast, west, and south made the city a natural junction point on the Southeast's growing transportation network.

As railroads snaked their way through the mountains and into the valley they met on the banks of the Tennessee River. Near their stations enterprising people established the business required to serve the voracious needs of the "iron horse" and the goods and passengers it brought to the once-quiet area. The city's natural development was rudely interrupted, however, by the Civil War, during which both the blue- and gray-clad armies, following the new railroads, fought for possession of the strategic terrain.

The war spread widespread destruction and suffering through the valley even as it brought new opportunities in its wake. Military authorities introduced the first heavy industry to the city to support the continuing war effort and numerous Yankees recognized undeveloped opportunities in the city. They took home their memories and some of the more ambitious and enterprising returned after the war, started businesses and industries, and settled down to stay.

Hundreds of new concerns were started in Chattanooga during what Mark Twain labeled the "Gilded Age." Many failed, but some grew and prospered. Chattanooga industries remained largely immune to the great consolidation movement at the turn of the 20th century; they remained largely family-owned businesses, although by the "Great War" some of them were operating, thanks to the convenient transportation facilities, in national markets. During the following two decades the city's financial leaders continued to invest in the basic manufacturing industries that had proved the backbone of the local economy, although there was rapid growth in the fields of banking and insurance.

While the Great Depression brought economic tribulations everywhere, it brought renewal and hope to the Tennessee Valley in the guise of the Tennessee Valley Authority. Cheap energy, combined with the city's other resources, helped propel the area into the mainstream of 20th-century America. New businesses and industries were attracted to the city as older enterprises modernized, merged, and consolidated. A new middle class emerged to promote improved and expanded educational opportunities, the arts, health care, political reforms, and a demand for consumer goods. A new city developed, built upon the tradition and heritage of the old—a vibrant, awakening urban entity, with its roots sunk deeply in the past. This is what the following pages are all about.

# AMERICAN NATIONAL BANK AND TRUST COMPANY

American National Bank's origins reach back to a banker in Lawrenceburg, Indiana. Three years after Harry S. Probasco moved to Chattanooga in 1885, he formed a partnership and opened the Bank of Chattanooga. The little bank prospered under Probasco's presidency and in 1905, with new partners, he chartered another bank, American National, which absorbed all but the trust business of his earlier venture. His new institution operated under the American name until 1911 when it was absorbed by First National, a local bank that had been organized right after the cessation of civil hostilities.

Shortly, Probasco had a yen to re-enter the banking business and in 1912 with his son, Scott L. Probasco, and E.Y. Chapin chartered American Trust and Banking Company. In its first year of business, at 8th and Broad streets with eight employees and a capitalization of $200,000, the bank attracted $381,000 in deposits. Only three years later the value of its first year's deposits had doubled; the firm grew apace and moved to more spacious quarters at 734 Market Street. At the same time the partners increased their bank's capitalization by 50 percent to bring its total resources very close to one million dollars.

A conservative banker, Probasco paid no dividends on the bank's earnings for over five years, making profits as well as capital available to his patrons. When he finally declared a dividend in mid-1917, accumulated earnings were almost $200,000, 66 percent of the bank's capital. At that date its deposits exceeded one million dollars.

Probasco died in 1919 and Chapin succeeded him as president. A year later he increased the bank's capital to $5 million, positioning the firm well to share in the prosperity of the postwar decade. Success, however, brought problems, chief among them a continuing need for more space in a convenient downtown Chattanooga location. The bank first bought a 4-story building on the northeast corner of 8th and Market streets and then proceeded to purchase additional land along Market and East 8th streets upon which in 1928 it erected its own 4-story headquarters.

American Trust and Banking Company weathered the stock market's disastrous plunge in 1929 and the ensuing Depression quite well. In 1933 it became a member of the Federal Reserve System. Five years later Chapin became chairman of the board and D.H. Griswold was elected president. On the eve of America's entry into World War II, the bank merged with Commercial National, a concern founded in 1933 by Z.C. Patten and others. Patten, whose father had been a Probasco partner back in 1905, joined American as chairman of its executive committee and Harry Probasco's son, Scott L. Probasco, Sr., was named chairman of the board. The merger brought almost $5 million in resources into the American bank.

The years immediately after the war witnessed momentous changes at the bank. In June 1946 it opened its first

*After World War I, American Trust and Banking Company moved to more spacious quarters at 8th and Broad streets.*

*Harry S. Probasco chartered the American Trust and Banking Company, forerunner of today's American National Bank and Trust Company, in 1912.*

*Current headquarters of American National Bank and Trust Company is located at 8th and Market streets.*

American National's deposits increased from $73 million to $123 million, while its capital, surplus, and undistributed profits grew from $4.7 million to $10.1 million. In 1957 Chapin Jr. became chairman of the executive committee and Sam I. Yarnell assumed the bank's presidency. Five years later, after Scott L. Probasco's death, Yarnell became chairman of the board; Scott L. Probasco, Jr., vice-chairman; and John P. Wright, president.

By that date the bank's officers realized that the organization had again outgrown its quarters. After extensive discussion they decided to build a new facility on the same site. Early in 1966 the bank moved its millions to temporary quarters in a dime store while its building was demolished and a 20-story, 300,000-square-foot tower with parking spaces for 300 automobiles was constructed. In September 1968 American National Bank moved into its new headquarters, a downtown Chattanooga landmark.

The very nature of the banking business changed in the 1970s and American National Bank was in the forefront of the movement. In May 1972 its officers chartered a new corporation, Ancorp Bancshares, Inc., a registered bank holding company, creating the seventh largest bank in Tennessee. The new firm's principal assets are its Chattanooga bank and the Hamilton Bank of Johnson City, the largest bank in that metropolitan area. Ancorp also operates the Ancorp Insurance Company, which provides credit life, accident, and health insurance. Although the holding company's assets reach $8 billion, it is still very much a Chattanooga firm; its president is the Hoosier banker's grandson, Scott L. Probasco, Jr.

branch office, followed soon thereafter by seven more. The bank's rapidly growing business made it necessary to extend its quarters through to Cherry Street that fall and afterwards into the Cherry Street side of the building adjoining the bank on its north side. Two years later, on September 30, 1948, American Trust and Banking Company was chartered as American National Bank and Trust Company of Chattanooga, a name that more accurately reflected its status.

Within a month, the bank absorbed St. Elmo Bank and Trust Company, a firm founded by Patten back in 1913. To cap off a year of change, Griswold retired and E.Y. Chapin, Jr. became president of American National.

The decade of the 1950s was one of steady growth for the Chattanooga bank.

# THE ANTIQUE ARMORY

To some people a gun is merely a weapon to bring down a buck or to carry for personal safety—for Theodore Hutcheson, owner of The Antique Armory, it is a piece of fine art. Following a boyhood bent for collecting old guns, Hutcheson left his family's business to strike out on his own and within a decade became one of the top five gun dealers in the country who handle famous high-quality and expensive firearms.

Hutcheson opened his first gun shop in Rossville, Georgia, in 1968; two years later he purchased a store in Atlanta that dealt in both antique and modern firearms. At the same time he opened yet a third store at 105 West 8th Street in Chattanooga. In 1972 he consolidated the Rossville and Chattanooga stores in a new structure he built at 1936 Dayton Boulevard, which he soon expanded to 15,000 square feet.

In 1973 Hutcheson made his first big gun purchase; for several million dollars he acquired 1,400 guns of what was probably the finest gun collection in private hands. He coauthored a book, *The William M. Locke Collection*, while selling the collection and broke even a mere 36 days after making the deal. The scope of the transaction and the quality of the guns earned Hutcheson instant national recognition. Two years later he made another major acquisition, 1,000 to 1,200 pieces of the R.Q. Sutherland collection, one of the major accumulations of Colt arms in private hands in the United States, for about one million dollars. He sold it off and recouped his investment in about 90 days. Shortly thereafter he bought the Sportsmen's Den, a gun-oriented, fishing, and general sporting goods business, which he closed two years later to concentrate on dealing in antique guns.

In a complicated transaction in 1979, Hutcheson purchased 44 guns for almost $1.5 million from John Solley and then traded six of them to the Connecticut State Library for a portion of Sam Colt's original collection valued at about a million dollars. Included in that deal was

a Gatling gun—Sam Colt purchased Gatling's patents and manufactured the guns—which is still operable.

The Antique Armory is one of the 10 or 12 dealers in the country that is serious enough and has access to capital to invest a million or more dollars in a collection. Over the past 10 years it has purchased more large collections than any other dealer in the country. The most expensive gun The Antique Armory has handled was a small, profusely engraved, pre-Patterson Colt revolver; it lacks even a serial number. The Armory also deals in modern firearms, in less expensive guns—those used in the Civil War for example—and will locate a desired piece for any interested party. For the discerning collector anywhere, however, it is a prime source of truly rare firearms.

*Colt Experimental Zig-Zag Revolver, part of the original Colt Factory Collection.*

*Colt 1862 Police, Bookcased, Presentation gun, inscribed on backstrap, "To Mrs. Howell Cobb from Col. Colt."*

# ARCADE, INC.

Printing companies commonly conjure up images of sleepy shops in which workers wearing long, ink-stained aprons set up presses to print stationery headings. A look into the deceptively plain brick building filling the 1800 block of East Main Street that houses Arcade,

*This illustration shows an early printing press, and in the background is the shop on Market Street which Arcade, Inc. first occupied in 1902.*

Inc. soon dispels that image—a 100-foot-long machine prints 4-color sheets at a rate of 25,000 per hour. It is a highly mechanized, up-to-date printing business successfully competing in national markets.

It was not quite that way back in 1902 when Charles Douglas, a skilled printer, opened his own shop in what was called the Arcade, a small row of shops running from the 700 block of Market Street through to Broad Street. For over 40 years Douglas operated a job-printing

shop, printing letterheads, envelopes, price lists, and posters for local business and professional people.

Gaines P. Campbell, who operated a stationery supply business in Chattanooga, bought Douglas out in 1946. When Gaines Jr. took over as president of the firm with six employees in 1951 he purchased machinery to enable the company to print in four colors, moved its operations into its 60,000-square-foot home on East Main, and expanded the firm's capabilities to print advertising materials.

In 1974 Gaines Campbell, Jr. sold his firm's job-printing business to concentrate wholly on printed advertising. Since then Arcade has primarily produced direct mail-related advertising for national firms and in numbers that stagger the imagination. One of its biggest products is the 4-color remittance envelope; in an average year Arcade will ship in excess of 100 million of them. These various printed items begin as a roll of paper, are printed, folded, glued, and delivered finished in one continuous operation. Its latest product, introduced in 1980, is "Scent-Strip," incorporated in brochures which, when opened, release the scent of the advertised product.

Arcade is still a family business. Gaines Campbell, Jr. moved up to become chairman of the board in 1975 and John Gass, who came to the printing business via the insurance industry, became president. James Campbell, brother of the chairman, is also in the firm, as is Gaines III who joined it in 1980 as its computer programmer. The company's 80 employees are still ink-stained, but in rainbow hues, and are more at home dealing with hundreds of thousands of pieces than with a ream or two of stationery.

# ASSOCIATED GENERAL AGENCY, INC.

The insurance business is one in which personal contact and service is of the utmost importance. A small office can easily provide such attention to its clients; the trick is to maintain the personal touch after the firm has vastly expanded. Associated General Agency has been able to do this through its unique, carefully planned expansion.

Back in 1926 "Polly" Boyd, who had been an assistant general agent of Provident's Life Agency, joined with Henry Trotter to form an independent agency to sell accident and health insurance. Only a year later Trotter set what was thought to be a world's record for commercial accident applications written in a month—219 of them, or approximately one every hour. In 1930 Will Keese, Jr. joined the two to form the Trotter, Boyd & Keese Agency.

The agency's business grew in the late 1920s and continued to expand at a slower rate in the following depression-ridden decade. With World War II and gas rationing, the firm maintained its personal touch by depending on the tele-

*The headquarters of Associated General Agency, Inc. is located at 620 Lindsay Street in Chattanooga.*

phone to a greater degree and streamlined its office procedures to squeeze every ounce of efficiency from its limited personnel. By its 25th anniversary in 1951 the company was one of the leaders among the city's agencies.

Two years later Llewellyn Boyd, Polly's son, joined the firm and little over a decade later became president of the company. With an eye to expansion, Boyd, with associates Don Jordan, Ted King, and Buck Rudisill, formed AGA, which is wholly owned by the original firm, in 1970. AGA acquired its first agency in Spring City barely two years later, followed soon thereafter by businesses in Rockwood, Harriman, Cleveland, Dayton, Pikeville, Athens, and Knoxville. The idea behind the expansion was to acquire East Tennessee and later Georgia businesses staffed by local agents who were known, responsible members of their communities and to stick to the smaller towns, thereby retaining the personal elements of service while centralizing other functions such as marketing in Chattanooga to achieve greater efficiency.

AGA represents dozens of national insurance companies and tailors coverages to fit the specific needs of its clients from personal insurance to the largest commercial businesses, including property, casualty, life, health, group, estate planning, risk management, and safety engineering. The firm's ability to arrange proper protection at competitive rates, its wide range of insurance products—especially property and casualty coverage, the largest part of its business—and most of all its tradition of service, have made it the area's largest locally owned independent insurance agency. With 24 producing agents and 21,000 customers, its service has paid off.

# BLUE CROSS AND BLUE SHIELD OF TENNESSEE

On a blustery December day in 1946, Murfreesboro Police Chief N.W. Powers was shot twice by a crazed gunman. One of the bullets wounded the chief; the other struck him squarely in the chest but bounced off after hitting the new Blue Cross hospitalization policy he was carrying in his breast pocket.

Only a year earlier, Blue Cross and Blue Shield of Tennessee had been chartered by a special legislative act under the state's public welfare laws to provide health care protection for the citizens of the Volunteer State. While the legislators did not envision such literal protection as the policy afforded Chief Powers, they did stipulate that the new corporation be not for profit, not investor owned, non-dividend paying, and placed under the supervision of the Tennessee State Insurance Department.

The impetus for bringing the Blue Cross and Blue Shield concept to Tennessee came from Roy McDonald, chairman of the board of Baroness Erlanger Hospital in Chattanooga, who recognized the need for a prepayment health plan. On November 19, 1945, the Chattanooga firm became the nation's 55th Blue Cross Plan. From only 16,000 members at the end of 1945, the Plan has expanded almost exponentially until today it covers more than two million citizens, 60 percent of all the people in the 90-county area the company serves. Blue Cross and Blue Shield of Tennessee now serves groups as diverse as some of the state's largest employers to dependents of military personnel and med-

*The headquarters of Blue Cross and Blue Shield of Tennessee is located in Chattanooga.*

icare recipients. In addition to traditional hospital prepayment coverage and coverge for physicians' services, the company provides dental protection, broad major medical programs, and other innovative health care financing programs.

In the mid-1960s, long before the national outcry over rising health care costs, Blue Cross and Blue Shield of Tennessee took steps to hold down costs by covering pre-admission testing, skilled nursing facility expenses, and home health agency services. The company has also developed other cost containment programs to encourage efficient

use of the health care system and the maintenance of healthy personal lifestyles. Perhaps the strongest indication of the company's serious commitment to cost containment is the fact that since 1949 it has held its own operating costs to below 10 percent of its premium income.

The company's efficient operation has been guided from the first by its board of directors, local citizens who voluntarily donate their time to serve their fellow Tennesseans. They oversee the largest health care protection company in the state. In each year since 1978 the Plan has paid out over $5 billion in benefits—$3 million each working day—quite an impressive record of service.

# GARNET CARTER COMPANY

The Garnet Carter Company was an extension of its founder, a man who was a bit of an iconoclast brimming with ideas, one willing to take financial plunges, a fellow characterized by all who knew him as the quintessential salesman. His personal style served him and his company well.

A school dropout at 16, Carter held various jobs in Chattanooga before becoming a candy salesman. After he married Frieda Utermoehlen, an accomplished musician, he quit his job and moved to Cincinnati where he took to the road for his family's wholesale novelty business. When Carter and his family returned to Chattanooga about 1907 he brought with him the germ of an idea.

He had heard of the decades-old European practice of merchants giving their customers profit-sharing coupons. Carter imported the idea and inevitably gave it his own personal twist. He established Garnet Carter Company about 1910, used his considerable powers of persuasion to recruit participating merchants, and instituted a line of redemption products including the newly

*Garnet Carter, second from right, putts at Tom Thumb Golf Course on Lookout Mountain with friends.*

introduced aluminum cookware. The cookware proved so popular that its manufacturer had to install a post office in its building just to handle Carter's orders.

Always abreast or a little ahead of his times, Carter noted the growing concern of American industrialists for keeping workers happy to encourage high production. He sold his coupon idea to factory owners as a means to keep down absenteeism, and punctual and reliable workers received coupons with their paychecks. His success, however, proved his company's undoing. By the early 1920s the rate of redemption was soaring—in one year alone he sold $3 million of his cookware—a flourishing counterfeit coupon industry had sprung up, and merchants' interest in the incentives began to lag. Later his idea would reappear as trading stamps.

Carter closed out his company in 1923 and by accident soon created another business that became a worldwide mania. Behind his office on Lookout Mountain he had a putting green for relaxation. To make it more challenging he added hole after hole, and to make his wagers more interesting he added obstructions between the greens, thereby creating miniature golf. He called it "Tom Thumb Golf" and built a few courses for friends. The idea snowballed and in 1928 he organized a company to manufacture the courses and obstructions, copyrighted the trademark, and worked out an agreement with those who held the patents on the cotton seed greens. Fearing that miniature golf was only a fad, he sold all his rights in 1929 to executives of a Pittsburgh pickle company for $200,000, after having made $300,000 from manufacturing the courses. The sale freed him to embark on his most popular and lasting promotion—Rock City Gardens.

*J.I. Carter (sitting at desk in foreground), father of Garnet Carter, and Garnet Carter (sitting at desk, far right), pose with employees of the Garnet Carter Company in this early photograph.*

# ROCK CITY GARDENS

Garnet Carter had an uncanny knack for creating fantasy, promoting pleasure, and making a living doing both. And he was able to do it either in the midst of prosperity or in the depths of a depression.

Rock City Gardens properly started with the Fairyland Company. In 1923 Carter and his friend Oliver Andrews bought an option on 300 acres straddling the Tennessee-Georgia line atop Lookout Mountain. With high hopes for profits but short of working capital, they hit upon a unique sales strategy; they divided the area into lots, offered them for sale at $2,750 each, and after 100 had been sold held a public drawing to determine who had bought what lots. They used the income to build a road to the property, bring in water, and to build the promised Fairyland Inn and golf course. The Fairyland development became a prestigious address and financial success.

The Great Depression stopped the land boom all over the nation, and Carter, who had made a considerable fortune with his "Tom Thumb Golf" only to lose it all in the great crash, looked around for an interesting and profitable enterprise. Like miniature golf, he found it right in his back yard. Literally. His wife Frieda had begun a project to make a garden in a 10-acre area. She laid out a path to what became the famous Lovers' Leap and had a swinging bridge built across the chasm, separating the projection from the rest of the rock formations. A conservationist long before it was popular, she collected indigenous wildflowers and plants on the mountain and planted them for preservation along the trails she kept lengthening in her garden.

In 1930 Carter realized how much other people might enjoy a stroll through Frieda's handiwork. He, his wife, and a small crew expanded trails all through Rock City, placed fairyland characters, especially elves, at appropriate places throughout, built a small stone house at the entrance, and on May 21, 1932, in the worst year of the Depression, opened their creation for the first time to the public. Business grew slowly through the 1930s as Carter improved and expanded their creation.

The attraction gave Carter a chance to display his promotional talents on a national scale with everything from free soap to motel welcome mats. In a brilliant move, he hired Clark Byers to paint advertisements on barn roofs, initially free since farmers needed their roofs painted anyway, and later for a very nominal fee. Byers painted 12,000 miles of advertising making "See Rock City" and "See Seven States" national bywords. When the job became too big for Carter after the war he brought his nephew, E.Y. Chapin III, into the venture. Chapin modernized the attraction's business end and created Rock City Gardens Incorporated in 1948, later merging the Fairyland Company into the new entity. What began as a backyard hobby has afforded pleasure to millions of people. Carter, who died in 1954, left a monument to his creativity.

*This is the Undercliff Terrace at Rock City Gardens.*

*High Falls and Lovers' Leap are part of the inspiring rock formations at Rock City.*

# CHATTANOOGA AREA HISTORICAL ASSOCIATION

The Chattanooga Area Historical Association, one of this volume's sponsors, has itself a long and varied history. Originally chartered in 1889 as the Chattanooga Historical Association, it soon disappeared into the historical mists. The second organization, chartered in 1905 as the Chattanooga Historical Society, fared little better, although its members did have the foresight to donate its records to the Chattanooga Public Library when the Society disbanded.

The number three has long been thought to have magical properties and in the instance of the Chattanooga Area Historical Association that certainly

proved to be the case. Under the impetus of Z. Cartter Patten, five Chattanoogans met in 1948 and organized the area's historical association. They set for themselves the ambitious goals of "acquiring, marking, and preserving historical points or sites; establishing and maintaining historical museums; collecting and preserving . . . materials; . . . and printing, publishing, and distribution of pamphlets, books, and papers of historical nature."

Much of the organization's life and zest has emanated from the long line of enthusiastic, knowledgeable, and creative presidents, many of whom were community leaders and professional historians. Among the noteworthy were Patten, his son, Z. Cartter III, Joshua Warner, Mrs. Alice Warner Milton, and from The University of Tennessee at Chattanooga (formerly the University of Chattanooga) Drs. Culver Smith, James Livingood, Gilbert Govan, William

Masterson, and Albert Bowman.

Over the years the organization that now numbers about 200 members has admirably succeeded not only in meeting its lofty goals but has also initiated other worthy historical projects. The Association's members have been indefatigable in locating, identifying, interpreting, and gaining recognition for all types of local historical sites. It has amassed an invaluable collection of local lore and records and just as importantly, has made this material availble to the public in the Chattanooga Bicentennial Public Library. These holdings range from local corporate records and publications, personal letters, diaries, memoirs, and photographs, to oral histories taken by Association members. The Association helped sponsor the Chattanooga Museum of Regional History located at 176 South Crest Road. Through members' efforts in attaining grants, the Association has at its disposal a modest amount of money to subsidize the publication of worthy manuscripts on area historical topics. In the past it awarded annual prizes to outstanding history students at the University of Chattanooga and the University of the South at Sewanee; resumption of these awards is under discussion. The Association also aids individuals seeking grants for personal projects, has published a historical tour guide to Chattanooga, and provides evidence on behalf of private preservation efforts. Its most important achievement, however, is intangible; the Chattanooga Area Historical Association has given untold numbers of people a much deeper appreciation of their own heritage.

*Lookout Mountain, with an elevation of 2,100 feet, overlooks a land of rugged beauty. It is said that one can see seven states from the brow.*

# CHATTANOOGA COCA-COLA BOTTLING COMPANY

Benjamin F. Thomas and Joseph B. Whitehead, Chattanooga attorneys, struck one of the most profitable deals in American history when they signed a contract with Asa Candler, president of the fledgling Coca-Cola Company, on July 21, 1899. For the munificent sum of one dollar, which Candler never bothered to collect, the two Chattanoogans bought the exclusive bottling rights for Coca-Cola for all of the United States except New England, Mississippi, and Texas.

In the fall of that year the two men started their first bottling company on Patten Parkway in Chattanooga. Its sales of about 10 cases a day of the bottled drink that was to revolutionize the business were distributed throughout the city in two mule-drawn wagons. Little did the partners know that sales of Coke in bottles would soon surpass the drink's fountain sales. Thomas and Whitehead soon realized, however, that it would be more profitable to become "parent bottlers" to supply local bottlers with the syrup and went on to accumulate vast personal fortunes in that business. In 1901 they sold their Chattanooga bottling plant to a fellow stockholder in the operation, James F. Johnston. Over the next 20 years Johnston slowly developed the Chattanooga plant's business. By 1909 he had four teams out in the streets; a short time later he purchased his first gasoline-powered truck; in the midst of World War I he intro-

duced the now-familiar bottle, designed in Indiana, to the area; and in 1924 he sold his Chattanooga franchise to a Birmingham bottler, Crawford T. Johnson.

Johnson, who it is claimed started his first bottling business "wearing trousers with a patch on the seat," formed a family stock company that still owns the Chattanooga bottling company. On the eve of the Great Depression he moved the plant to its third home, the site of the old Chattanooga Brewery Company at 201 Broad Street. Sales of Coca-Cola held up well during the depression-wracked 1930s and continued to expand over the next two decades in the Chattanooga bottling company's territory, which includes Hamilton County and portions of Dade and Walker counties in Georgia. By the 1970s the Chattanooga franchise ranked in the top 100 of the nation's 800 Coca-Cola bottlers, quenching the thirst of the 325,000 peo-

ple in the 3-county area.

The modern bottling plant, which moved to its present multimillion-dollar home at 4000 Amnicola Highway in 1971, bears a resemblance to the original works only in that it still bottles Coca-Cola made from the original formula. The Chattanooga company now owns the Dr Pepper franchise in addition to bottling the "allied products," Sprite, Tab, and Fresca. The firm also owns a subsidiary, Chatco Vending, which has launched it into the snacks and food business. Employing about 325 persons in the area, Chattanooga Bottling Company's fleet has grown from two mules to 150 trucks, symbolic of how the carefully nurtured and tended family business has prospered over the years.

*Shown here are three of the Mack trucks used in 1928 by the Chattanooga Coca-Cola Bottling Company to meet the needs of thirsty consumers in the Chattanooga area.*

# CHATTANOOGA COKE & CHEMICALS CO., INC.

Coke, the carbonization of coal, has long been vitally important to America's industrial system. Used primarily in the manufacture of iron and steel, this basic industrial raw material is produced on Central Avenue in Chattanooga for customers all over North and Central America.

The manufacture of coke in the city started in 1913 when the Chattanooga Gas & Coal Products Company built Roberts-type coke ovens primarily to extract gases; coke was only a by-product of the process. Two years later the firm began construction on a block of 24 coke ovens that were brought into production in 1918 after the firm's name had

*Officers of Chattanooga Coke & Chemicals Co., Inc. are (from left to right) R. Bruce McClelland, president; Dale Heidt, vice-president; and Robert Gillow, treasurer.*

been changed to the Chattanooga Coke & Gas Company to reflect its new emphasis on coke production.

The coke firm was purchased in 1926 by the Tennessee Products Corporation, headquartered in Nashville. For the next 38 years the company made furnace coke, a coke used in blast furnaces to produce iron for the steel industry, from coal mined in Whitwell on lands leased from U.S. Steel. The company struggled through the hard times of the 1930s by the sale of its gases when it had no markets for its coke. In 1940 Tennessee Products purchased a blast furnace at Rockwood that gave the Chattanooga company a regular customer.

Just prior to World War II the federal government financed a second block of 20 ovens under a Defense Plan Corporation contract, bringing the total ovens in operation to 44. Those 44 ovens remain in operation today. In 1955 Merritt, Chapman & Scott, an early New York City conglomerate, bought Tennessee Products. Nine years later, in 1964, Woodward Iron Company bought Chattanooga Coke from Merritt, Chapman & Scott. Woodward merged with the Mead Corporation, a Dayton, Ohio, paper company. That firm was more in-

terested in Woodward's other assets and in 1974 sold the coke plant to two former Woodward employees who continued to operate it making foundry coke.

During that period, Bruce McClelland and Dale Heidt were selling coke from Chattanooga Coke & Chemicals in Michigan and the Midwest. When the plant was offered for sale, Robert Gillow joined with them and purchased Chattanooga Coke in 1975. Since then they have installed over $5 million worth of pollution control equipment and have substantially modernized the plant. At capacity Chattanooga Coke & Chemicals manufactures 400 tons of coke daily for shipment to customers scattered over 30 states, Canada, Mexico, and Central America. The firm employs 170 people coking coals from several states principally for use in casting parts for automobiles, and selling its by-products to businesses as diverse as the insulation, fertilizer, and petroleum industries.

The only coke company in Tennessee prospers in the last quarter of the 20th century by continuing to manufacture a product vital to the nation's economy.

*Chattanooga Coke & Chemicals Co., Inc. is headquartered at 4800 Central Avenue, Chattanooga.*

# CHATTANOOGA CORPORATION

Chattanooga Corporation is a locally owned and managed company that has set a lofty goal for itself—to become the leading physical medicine firm in domestic and world markets. It is already well on its way toward that end, developing, manufacturing, and selling equipment and other products for treating patients.

Incorporated in 1947 as the Chattanooga Pharmacal Company, the name it retained until 1979, the firm first produced the HYDROCOLLATOR STEAM PACK, used as a moist heat compress. The company also developed heating units for hospitals and clinics to keep the steam packs at a constant temperature. Over the past 30 years the steam pack has been the most commonly used product in physical medicine. Later the firm designed the COLPAC, a plastic envelope containing a gel filler that holds low temperatures well, and chilling units to keep the COLPACs readily available for use.

In the early 1950s Jack Walker bought the company from its founder, Lee Jensen, and developed its reputation for producing a high-quality useful product. Approaching retirement in 1976, Walker sold his company to his friend John Maley. Intrigued by the challenge of building up his own firm, Maley and a co-investor determined to make it a broad-line supplier of physical medicine products.

Emphasizing customer service and a willingness to adapt technology to the needs of physical medicine professionals, the company expanded its product

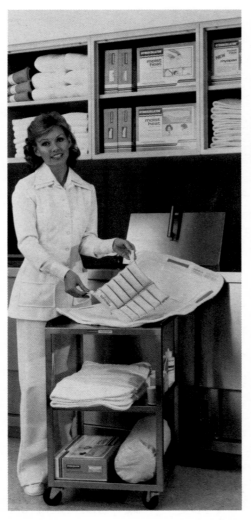

*Hydrocollator products are widely used in physical medicine throughout the world.*

line quickly. The firm's marketing strategy has been the essence of simplicity: the concern has remained in the field of physical medicine where it was already well-known, has developed products with clear performance advantages so that it can win a significant percentage of that market, and has emphasized international sales, currently about 20 percent of its business.

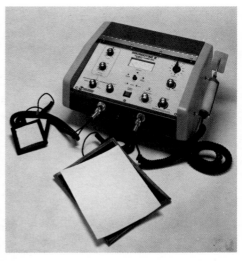

*Intelect 500 high-voltage muscle stimulator—an example of the company's move into high technology.*

In rapid procession, starting in 1977, it introduced TX traction equipment for treatment of various spinal conditions; ADAPTA adjustable treatment tables designed and built for physical therapists; CRYOMATIC and COLSTIM cold-therapy devices for humans and horses respectively—Seattle Slew was the most famous denizen of the track treated successfully with the firm's product; INTELECT high-voltage muscle stimulation equipment; and TRITON traction equipment and tables. More new products are in development.

Chattanooga Corporation's headquarters and manufacturing facilities are located at 101 Memorial Drive in Red Bank. Employing about 170 employees working in a 65,000-square-foot building, the firm has grown so quickly that it has started work on another facility of the same size located on Adams Road in Hixon. Optimistic about the prospects for future growth, the company has purchased additional adjacent land to allow for further expansion.

# CHATTANOOGA TIMES

Adolph S. Ochs, owner and publisher of both the *Chattanooga Times* and the *New York Times*, was a quintessential Horatio Alger character—with one striking exception; Alger's heroes enjoyed only modest successes while Ochs

*The cramped quarters of the* Chattanooga Times *in 1878, when it was purchased by Mr. Ochs.*

left his indelible imprint and enduring legacy in both metropolitan areas.

Born in Cincinnati and reared in Knoxville, Ochs migrated to Chattanooga in 1877 to work on a new newspaper. When it closed its doors after only a few months, Ochs remained to pay off the paper's debts and to seek other employment. In 1878 at age 20, he borrowed money and bought a 50 percent interest in the struggling *Chattanooga Times* for $250. With five employees, who could barely raise $3 in cash among themselves, he boldly brought out his first issue on July 2 of that year. Though a yellow fever epidemic left Chattanooga virtually a ghost town, the *Times* survived. Through Ochs's exceptionally close attention, the business prospered and within four years he was able to purchase the other half of the property, by then deemed to be worth $5,500.

In 1892, Ochs moved the *Times* into what was then the South's most modern newspaper plant which he built at the

*East 8th Street, Chattanooga, looking toward the Times Building around the turn of the century.*

corner of 8th Street and Georgia Avenue. It was the paper's home for half a century and remains a downtown landmark. Ochs had made unfortunate investments in real estate, and in 1896 he went to New York City to seek another outlet for his journalistic efforts. He bought a majority control of the faltering *New York Times*, which he built into one of the world's most respected newspapers, and moved his permanent residence to New York City. He continued as publisher of the *Chattanooga Times* until his death in 1935.

The *Chattanooga Times* has always maintained his tradition of advocating progressive reforms in the city and the region. The *Times* has championed an impressive array of civic improvements: better water and sanitation systems, modernization of city government, pension reforms, bridges, better roads, airports, railroad and river improvements, urban renewal, pollution control, and annexation, among others. The paper long fought the baleful effects of racism and was the first newspaper in the South to support editorially the 1954 Supreme Court ruling on school desegregation, a position that cost it dearly.

In 1942, the *Times* entered into a joint agreement with the *Chattanooga News-Free Press* under an arrangement which pooled production costs but maintained editorial and news independence. That arrangement was terminated in 1966 but renewed essentially in the same form in 1980. The *Times* as a newspaper has remained under the ownership and control of the Ochs family since its purchase in 1878. Its present publisher is Ruth Sulzberger Holmberg, a granddaughter of Mr. Ochs. One of her sons, Michael Golden, is a vice-president of the company.

# JOSEPH DECOSIMO AND COMPANY CERTIFIED PUBLIC ACCOUNTANTS

Since 1952, when Joseph F. Decosimo began practicing accounting in Chattanooga, identification of the Decosimo name with public accounting has become prominent. Three sons, Nick, Fred, and Tom, all CPAs with the firm of which their father is senior partner, have helped establish a Decosimo dynasty in the profession.

In a decade of existence, Joseph Decosimo and Company, Certified Public Accountants, has enjoyed success and growth in size and reputation; the firm now ranks among the top 100 certified public accounting firms in the United States.

The firm was founded in 1971 to incorporate into public accounting affirmative support to clients while maintaining an independent and objective attitude. From its inception, in addition to traditional accounting, auditing, and tax services, the Decosimo firm has provided guidance in personal financial planning, mergers and acquisitions, structuring of transactions, evaluation of tax ramifications, and other financial matters.

Jerry V. Adams, who with Joseph F. Decosimo and Marion G. Fryar founded the firm, is managing partner. Other partners include Barry L. Hoffman, Paul E. Cheney, L. Bernard Stone, Lyman W. Hodge, Carl W. Henderson, and Jack E. Segers. The company began its 10th year with about 40 CPAs and a total staff of more than 75 people.

Active in professional organizations, the firm and all its CPAs are members of the American Institute of Certified Public Accountants and other recognized accounting organizations, partners having served as presidents of the Tennessee State Board of Accountancy and other professional societies.

Chattanooga will continue to be the home of the CPA firm while serving clients throughout the eastern United States. Unlike most larger firms with multiple offices, Decosimo has centralized its strengths here in a community attractive to highly qualified professionals. Promoting Chattanooga with the slogan "Take it from a CPA . . . , Chattanooga is a great city," the firm is contributing to recognition of the city's advantages for industry and its central southern location.

God willing, the firm will continue to offer seasoned judgement from an independent viewpoint to help its clients make key financial decisions.

*Joseph F. Decosimo (left) is senior partner and Jerry V. Adams is managing partner of Joseph Decosimo and Company, Certified Public Accountants.*

*R. Fred, J. Thomas, and J. Nick Decosimo (left to right) are CPAs working for Joseph Decosimo and Company, Certified Public Accountants. Their father, Joseph Decosimo (far right) is one of the firm's founders.*

# CHATTEM, INC.

Chattem, Inc., a multimillion-dollar corporation which develops and manufactures health and beauty aids and specialty chemicals sold worldwide, owes its existence to a Union soldier by the name of Zeboim Cartter Patten. Z.C. Patten was wounded in the Battle of Chickamauga and, to the considerable benefit of Chattanooga, chose to remain here and make the city his home. He and four

other local businessmen pooled $25,000 in 1879 and established the Chattanooga Medicine Company, the small forerunner to the widely diversified international enterprise that Chattem, Inc. is today.

The first product was Black-Draught, a laxative to which Patten had purchased the rights and renamed. First-year sales for this product, which is still being produced more than 100 years later, were $35,488. The following year Patten ac-

quired McElree's Wine of Cardui, a menstrual relief preparation, and these two products provided the cornerstone for the firm for nearly 50 years.

Consumer loyalty was the key to success in the world of patent medicine at that time, and the company developed an ambitious advertising program in its early years. The firm recruited an energetic sales force to promote its products. In addition, women were hired to solicit endorsements. They were often sent on horseback up into the hills seeking genuine and persuasive testimonials. The company also relied heavily on mail advertising and printed tens of millions of Cardui wall calendars and "Ladies' Birthday Almanacs" on its own press, the fastest in existence at that time. The Medicine Company's volume of mail was so heavy that the government established a post office in the plant.

Z.C. Patten guided the fledgling enterprise through two fires at its headquarters, a drought, a yellow fever epidemic, and several infringements of its patent rights. Sales continued to grow and surpassed one million dollars in 1903. Patten also was involved at one time or another with *The Chattanooga Times*, T.H. Payne, Stone Fort Land Company, and Volunteer Life Insurance Company, all of which are still prospering today. Because of other interests, he turned active management of the firm over to his nephew, John A. Patten, in 1906.

John A. Patten understood marketing methods as few others did at that time, and he quickly led the Chattanooga Medicine Company to new levels of prosperity. He expanded and modernized the sales force and pioneered successful new techniques in billboard and print advertising. He also began exporting to Central and South America long before others realized the potential of foreign markets. He died tragically at the age of 48, however, in the midst of a widely publicized and successful libel suit against the *Journal of the American Medical Association*. At that time, the Medicine Company had seemed on the verge of becoming a giant in the drug industry.

The ensuing decades were not the company's brightest. Earnings, which peaked in 1920, leveled off for 40 years. The Medicine Company was handling seven products on the eve of the Depression. Z. Charles Patten, John A.'s brother, managed to cope with the difficulties of that grim decade. He kept his employees working, although with pay reductions, maintained the firm's marginal profitability, paid dividends, and instituted one of the nation's first pension and life insurance programs for his employees. In 1938 he passed the company's presidency to his nephew, Lupton Patten, and became chairman of the board.

Patten, only 32, soon faced a host of problems brought on by the war. Almost overnight he turned the firm into the country's largest wartime producer of K rations, preparing more than 34 millions of these vital packets. As a result of wartime shortages, particularly that of sugar, the medicines had to be reformulated without lowering quality or alienating loyal customers. Including government contracts, company sales topped $5 million in 1943.

After the war Lupton Patten made efforts to modernize the company. He started a research program which gained nationwide attention when Dr. Irvine Grote developed Soltice, a patented analgesic balm, as well as the active antacid ingredient used in Rolaids. Dr. John Krantz brought to the firm the buffering agent used in Bufferin. Patten upgraded the manufacturing facilities and also began to diversify by entering the fine chemical and prescription drug fields. By the mid-1950s, the product line included 26 food and drug products.

Lupton Patten died in 1958, one year after sales first passed $5 million during peacetime. He was succeeded by his nephew, Alex Guerry, who still holds that office but presides over a far different enterprise. Guerry realized that the privately held company had an insufficient financial base to support its desired growth. Four years later he was responsible for making stock available to employees. In 1967 some was sold to outsiders, and finally in 1969 it was offered to the public. In 1974 the company secured a $6.5-million loan to finance acquisitions. In order to professionally manage the growing concern, Guerry recruited more than 20 executives from *Fortune 500* or similar companies who wanted the opportunity to help run a smaller, more responsive organization.

These changes have led to the firm's explosive expansion; in the past decade it has acquired or developed nearly a dozen nationally known product lines, including PAMPRIN, SHY, SUN-IN, CORN SILK, and MUDD, which now account for two-thirds of its sales volume. The company also purchased Petrochemicals, Inc. in Fort Worth, Texas, and recently acquired Love's BABY SOFT line of fragrances for young girls. Sales have risen accordingly, from $15 million in 1969 to nearly $90 million at present.

In 1968 the name of the firm was changed to Chattem, Inc. to reflect its broader scope. Although Black-Draught and Cardui are still produced and a descendant of the founder is at the helm, the modern, professionally managed corporation of today bears little outward resemblance to its predecessor. Yet the basic characteristics of the company remain the same as they have throughout the years—integrity, fair dealing with customers, support of all worthwhile causes in the community with time and money, and loyalty to and from employees.

# ERLANGER MEDICAL CENTER

The Baroness Erlanger Hospital was born of a set of fortuitous circumstances that included a beautiful daughter of the Confederacy, Chattanooga's rapid industrial expansion, an English railway magnate, local public-spirited citizens, and a goodly amount of distilled spirits. Legend relates that Baron Emile Erlanger, married to Confederate diplomat John Slidell's daughter, and a large stockholder in numerous southern railroads, visited Chattanooga in the fall of 1890. At the end of a long banquet after many toasts had been exchanged, an expansive Baron generously offered to subscribe $5,000 for each of his railroads that entered the city if local citizens would raise $50,000 to build a public hospital. The west wing of the hospital was constructed the following year and named in honor of the baroness.

Operated with patient fees and appropriations from the city and Hamilton County, the hospital's east wing was opened in 1896, the two connected with a central section in 1917, and a nurses' home built in 1924. The rapidly growing population in Chattanooga and its increased demands for better health care soon overtaxed the hospital's facilities; with a PWA loan in 1937 a $1.3-million extension was added, bringing its capacity up to 500 beds. In 1952 Erlanger merged with the T.C. Thompson Children's Hosptial, located three miles away in East Chattanooga. Because of the inconvenience and declining physical facilities at the Children's Hospital, a new $5.2-million structure was built in 1975

*Baron Emile Erlanger*

*Baroness Erlanger*

on the Erlanger grounds which contains some of the most sophisticated pediatric equipment found in the Southeast.

By the early 1970s Erlanger was serving almost .75 million people with a physical plant essentially built before World War II. The situation demanded vigorous measures. In 1976 Hamilton County voters approved a transfer of hospital ownership from the city and county to an 11-member Chattanooga-Hamilton County Hospital Authority Board. The board drew up a new master plan for updating facilities and had constructed the area's most elaborate emergency unit, its only intensive care system for distressed newborns, its only burn center, and expanded program for the care of cancer patients, and in 1979 opened the Willie D. Miller Eye Center, a specialty hospital providing sophisticated eye procedures. The following year the center sold a $77-million bond issue to finance construction of a comprehensive cancer center, a new utilities system, a central energy and laundry facility, a 5-story addition above Children's Hospital to bring the center's licensed capacity to 780 beds, and a

*The original Erlanger Hospital building, completed in 1891.*

1,200-car parking garage. A 13-story professional office building, financed from the center's operating budget, is also under construction. If the baron could return to raise yet another toast with the medical center's 2,600 employees, he would be pleased.

# FIRST TENNESSEE BANK N.A. CHATTANOOGA

When one of the ancestors of First Tennessee Bank opened its doors in 1889 at the corner of Market and Main streets in Chattanooga, the bank's cashier deemed the rush of depositors, who put a little over $1,000 in the new institution that day, "very gratifying." From that inauspicious beginning, the little bank has developed into the second largest bank in the state's largest banking system, the First Tennessee National Corporation, with total assets of almost $3 billion.

Few of the charter members of the South Chattanooga Savings Bank dared dream of such riches back on that September day in 1889. But after surviving the 1893 depression that swept hundreds of such institutions across the nation into bankruptcy, its directors changed the bank's name to the Hamilton Trust and Savings Bank in 1903.

Just two years later, many of the principals of the bank, led by its president, T.R. Preston, chartered the Hamilton National Bank, a separate institution with a capitalization of $.25 million. Preston became president of the new institution, and in 1913 it became the first bank in Chattanooga to join the Federal Reserve System. The new bank prospered during World War I; in fact, when a finance officer from nearby Fort Oglethorpe came into the bank to cash a $3.5-million check, the bank covered it.

On the eve of the stock market crash, Hamilton National and the Hamilton Trust and Savings Bank were merged. Undaunted by the Great Depression, Preston and his colleagues chartered Hamilton National Associates in 1930 as a bank holding company which owned stock in 17 banks from Johnson City to north Georgia. The Chattanooga bank, largest in the chain, had resources in 1950 of over $120 million and in the early 1970s, almost three times that amount. In 1976, certain of the bank's assets were purchased by First Tennessee National Corporation.

As First Tennessee Bank N.A. Chattanooga, the institution has been an innovative leader in banking services. It is one of only five Small Business Administration certified lenders in the state, it has combated high interest rates by offering lower rates to smaller businesses, and it has pioneered interest-bearing checking accounts.

The acquisition of the Chattanooga bank gives First Tennessee National Corporation two "anchor" banks—First Tennessee Bank N.A. Memphis and First Tennessee Bank N.A. Chattanooga. The corporation operates a total of 13 banks throughout the state.

With assets of $430 million, First Tennessee Bank N.A. Chattanooga proudly looks back on its "very gratifying" past—and confidently looks forward to many more years in Chattanooga.

*Headquarters of First Tennessee Bank, 7th and Market streets, circa 1911.*

*Main office of First Tennessee Bank N.A. Chattanooga, 1981.*

# FLETCHER BRIGHT COMPANY

The photographs covering Fletcher Bright's office wall attesting to his talents on the violin and his ability to outsmart some very large bass belie the fact that he operates a well-established, traditional, and conservative full-line real estate company in Chattanooga.

The firm's origins date back to 1927 when J.A. Glascock, who was already in the local real estate business, joined with Gardner Bright, a salesman who was handling Queensware pottery, to form Glascock-Bright to sell residential properties. The two men formed such a close partnership that they were known locally, probably behind their backs, as the "gold dust twins." Located in what was the Hamilton Bank Building, where it still covers most of the 15th floor of the renamed First Tennessee Building, their company survived the depressed market of the 1930s and continued to emphasize residential sales right up until 1952 when the two men ended their partnership and Gardner became the sole proprietor of the firm.

Fletcher Bright joined the business in 1953 upon his graduation from Davidson College, and upon the death of his father in 1960 assumed control and acquired a Tennessee state charter for the company in 1969. Until the early 1960s the firm maintained its position in the local real estate market by specializing in properties on Lookout Mountain. Early in that decade, John M. Martin joined the firm, became its executive vice-president, and spearheaded what remains the firm's largest residential development,

*In 1927 Gardner Bright (above) and J.A. Glascock founded Glascock-Bright, predecessor of today's Fletcher Bright Company.*

the creation of the Elder Mountain area. Started in the mid-1960s, it involved building a whole new community even to a road up the mountain to reach the property. Its success can be seen in the fact that property values have continued to rise in the development and resales move quickly.

A few years later the firm acquired its first shopping center in Cleveland, Tennessee, and since then, both as joint ventures and on its own, has developed and purchased commercial properties throughout the Southeast. In the process it has opened branch offices in Atlanta and Orlando to serve more effectively the large number of shopping centers it manages in the region. The company is also a mortgage correspondent for several major life insurance companies, including Provident Life in Chattanooga, negotiating commercial loans for other real estate developers and servicing those accounts once the transactions are completed.

The company and its 32 employees are well-positioned to weather the periodic fluctuations in interest rates; when the financial markets are unfavorable they just concentrate harder on working out complicated 2-, 3-, and 4-party real estate transactions to cope with the changing times. Even so, there is also time for fiddling and fishing.

# THE GILMAN COMPANY, INC.

*Originally located in his cellar, William Gilman's paint and varnish company soon moved to more spacious quarters in Alton Park.*

In its first eight years the Gilman Paint & Varnish Company survived a fire that burned its first plant to the ground, a flood that washed it out of its second location, and the rigors and constraints of World War I. After those disasters Gilman found enduring the rest of the wars and depressions of this century easy.

Gilman was a business built quite literally from the ground up. Begun by William Gilman, Jr. in his cellar where he produced varnish on a coal stove, the firm grew slowly to become a leading paint company in the Southeast. Gilman

*The Gilman Company's research and development laboratory is located on Riverfront Parkway.*

at first delivered his varnish in a rented horse and wagon to his customers; later he moved his operations to Alton Park where he sold and delivered orders as he walked the five miles between there and his home on Missionary Ridge.

After Gilman was burned out in 1915, he moved his business into a former saloon at 416 Market Street in time to be flooded out by the great 1917 inundation. He then divided his operations and moved a part of them to their present location on Riverfront Parkway. After its rocky start the company matured and prospered in the 1920s, developing a talented management team that included Murray Raney, who was internationally known for his development of Raney Nickel, a widely used chemical catalyst.

The solid foundations laid in the 1920s enabled Gilman to weather the next decade's financial downturn. In fact the company grew and diversified, adding wallcovering products to its paint and varnish lines that actually helped to increase the firm's profit margins throughout the Depression and the ensuing war years. When Gilman died in 1951 the company was a nationally known paint

manufacturer.

The firm expanded its operations and introduced efficiencies during the next two decades. The management team Gilman had attracted, together with his son William III and E.L. Gott, opened new wallcovering warehouses in New Orleans, Atlanta, and Memphis, built a new lacquer plant in Chattanooga, and installed improved grinding equipment to produce higher quality and more diversified paints.

The younger Gilman was president only one year before his death in 1968. Ray Adams, who succeeded him, served in that office until 1976 when the company was purchased by the Tennessee Dallas Corporation, a holding company established for that purpose. With new ownership the firm under its next two presidents, C.F. Farrell and William D. Wellbrock, has increased sales and production, introduced improved accounting and data processing methods, and updated the company's retail outlets. From its disaster-prone start, the Gilman Company has grown into a Chattanooga firm that employs 300 people, counts its annual sales in millions of dollars, and produces millions of gallons of paint yearly.

# HAZLETT, LEWIS AND BIETER

Since 1943 clients ranging from manufacturers, universities, and bankers, to cemeteries and even a catfish farm, have sought the accounting services of Hazlett, Lewis and Bieter, Certified Public Accountants. The firm's reputation for providing quality financial and business advice and the partners' interest in helping to develop businesses from their infancy has long attracted clients. Many of the clients Hazlett, Lewis and Bieter served when it opened its door in 1943 are still with the firm today.

In the middle of World War II, Roy D. Hazlett formed Roy D. Hazlett & Associates with only six employees. Thomas S. Lewis, Jr. joined the company in 1946 and three years later Joseph G. Bieter was admitted to the partnership. In 1951 the partnership changed its name to its modern form to reflect the firm's growth. When Mr. Hazlett died in 1963 the organization had grown to about 20 employees. The growth process saw the partnership move from its original offices in the old Hamilton Bank Building to the Maclellan Building and in 1979, at which time the firm had grown to an organization in excess of 50 people, it purchased its present offices, the former Krystal Building at the corner of 7th and Cherry streets.

Hazlett, Lewis and Bieter is a local firm with a branch office in Dayton, Tennessee, and provides services to clients who operate on a regional and national scale. The firm is the only Tennessee CPA firm that is a member of the Associated Regional Accounting Firms, an organization of accounting firms that provides training seminars, management services, and review panels.

The Chattanooga-based accounting firm provides auditing, accounting, and tax services that range from audited financial statements to bank director exams; personal to corporate tax returns and tax planning; and a wide variety of management advisory services. The firm has its own computer center where it performs tax computations and provides bookkeeping services for some clients. It even develops and tests system software for clients.

The partners, associates, and employees in the company have long been active professionally and socially. Several of the firm members have served as officers in local, state, and national accounting organizations, on the State Board of Accountancy, and in various capacities for numerous charitable organizations and church activities. Behind the formal lettering on the entrance to the offices is a personable group of people demonstrating that accounting is much more than just working with numbers.

*In 1979 Hazlett, Lewis and Bieter purchased its present offices, the former Krystal Building at the corner of 7th and Cherry streets.*

# LLOYD E. JONES COMPANY

A DEW-Line station on the Greenland icecap featured in the February 1981 issue of *Smithsonian* shares a common heritage with the downtown Chattanooga Bicentennial Library; the structural steel underpinnings for both were fabricated locally by the Lloyd E. Jones Company and shipped to the sites.

Lloyd Jones had long been a boilermaker with the Walsh-Wiedner foundry, which later became part of Combustion Engineering. When the foundry ran out of orders in 1933 Jones decided that was the signal for him to go out and establish his own business. By securing TVA and Army Corps of Engineers orders, Jones survived the hard times and by decade's end was prosperous enough to move his operations from Central Avenue out to an 8-acre tract on Manufacturer's Road where he built a 9,600-square-foot fabricating shop in which his six employees fabricated both plate and structural steel designs.

That same year Lloyd's son, Don, joined the business just in time to help meet the rush of wartime orders. During the conflict the firm built 1,040 prefabricated bridges for the army, some of which are still giving service on civilian projects in the United States, and components for LSMs under navy contract.

*Lloyd E. Jones*
*Founder*
*1888–1970*

Three times during the war the Jones Company won the coveted "E" award for excellence.

With the return of peace, the steel company enjoyed the fruits of the postwar construction boom by fabricating components for public and private projects all over the nation and overseas. Locally, its handiwork is hidden in Red Food Stores, the First Centenary Methodist Church, the addition to the old Hamilton National Bank Building, Covenant College, and several textile plants. In the 1970s the Jones Company responded to the demand for environmental controls by fabricating precipitators and bag houses for locations as diverse as the Widow's Creek Steam Plant and an oil refinery in Venezuela. Demonstrating its diversity, the firm has also constructed a 50-foot solar dish located in Huntsville, Alabama, that uses a computer to track the sun to provide a constant high-temperature heat source.

The company has expanded its facilities to 75,000 square feet and now employs 50 people fabricating orders of virtually any size, limited only by transport restrictions. Most of the firm's steel is brought to its plant by rail and its finished products shipped out on trucks, although large items are shipped by barge since the company's property runs all the way back to the Tennessee River. The firm is a member of the American Institute of Steel Construction in which Don Jones serves on the board of directors. He is also the past president of the Southern Association of Steel Fabricators. His son, Fort Jones, joined the business as vice-president in 1975, and both men anticipate a bright future for the closely held firm. To that end, they have added another five bays to their fabricating shop.

# KAYO OIL COMPANY

Over 40 years ago Frank P. Kendall, Sr. began an independent service station business, the Kendall Oil Company, "with some real fine fellows, seven stations, and little money but good credit." Kendall was an old hand in the business; the native of Eau Claire, Wisconsin, had spent his entire life in the oil industry in Minnesota, Memphis, and upper East Tennessee before he settled in Chattanooga.

The year 1940, however, was not an auspicious one to start such a new enterprise. Due to wartime restrictions it was very difficult for the company to add to its services for six years. But as soon as the war ended, Kendall brought his son Paul into the business and they aggressively expanded throughout the Southeast. By 1952 they were operating 40 stations, successfully competing with the giants of the industry by offering lower gasoline prices, staying open 24 hours a day, offering limited service, and attracting customers with trading stamps, premium merchandise, and promotional gifts. Throughout the 1950s, the Kendalls continued to lease or purchase stations until by 1959 they operated 171 outlets located in 11 states.

By 1959, as the senior Kendall later explained, "our capacity for expansion outran our money and we felt it more prudent to sell out than to borrow." He had no trouble finding an eager buyer. Back in the 1930s he had been a jobber for Marland Refining Company which, while Kendall was handling its products, merged with a Utah firm, the Continental Oil Company, later to become Conoco. Conoco by the late 1950s was expanding into the East and needed distribution facilities, making the Kendall Oil Company a natural acquisition. Kendall sold his firm in 1959 but stayed on as president until August of 1961, when he was succeeded by his son Paul.

With Conoco's financial and technical backing, Kayo had a steady growth rate during the 1960s, opening 502 stations and closing 144. Bold expansion plans for 1971 brought about the construction and opening of 129 new outlets. But the oil shortage and new government regulations brought expansion almost to a standstill thereafter. In 1977 the company began converting its Kayo, Jet, and Fasgas stations to a new image in order to optimize the sale of non-petroleum merchandise. The program—completed in 1980—included new colors, building modifications, and electronic self-serve dispensing equipment.

Kayo has traveled a long way since 1940. Headquartered in Chattanooga, the company now operates about 680 retail outlets stretching across 27 states, and employs 3,000 people.

*This typical rural Kayo service station in the mid-1950s stayed open around the clock.*

*Kayo's new gasoline-convenience marts are designed to meet the needs of today's customers.*

# THE KRYSTAL COMPANY

The ancient Greeks considered the circle to be the perfect figure. The Krystal Company thinks otherwise; it lives by and in the square. Its first restaurant was square, and the hamburger upon which it made its reputation is still square.

The firm was founded by Rody Davenport, Jr., a vice-president of the family's hosiery mills, and J. Glenn Sherrill, a vice-president of a local bank, at the nadir of the Depression in October 1932. Its first unit was opened in Chattanooga that same month and featured counter service selling everything for a nickel. The company's first sale was for six Krystals and a cup of coffee—total bill, 35 cents. The idea of offering fast service with low-cost, quality food in clean surroundings, still the company's aim, caught on even in the hard times and the two founders expanded until by World War II they were operating 33 units. Always an innovator, the firm opened its first air-conditioned restaurant the day before Pearl Harbor was attacked.

Krystal survived the wartime restrictions and entered the postwar years determined to continue its expansion. In the decades of the 1950s and 1960s the company built new units in the rapidly growing suburbs to attract the family trade, provided curb and take-out service, expanded counter service, and extended its food offerings with take-out breakfasts and fried chicken.

By the end of the 1960s, Krystal was dominant in the Southeast but faced challenges in its territory from a number of well-known restaurant chains. After numerous surveys analyzing its opera-

tions and markets, the organization embarked on an expansion program in the 1970s designed to double the number of its units by decade's end. It redesigned its units; abandoned its traditional black and white decor; created a new logo, the

*The first Krystal Restaurant opened in 1932. Note the NRA Blue Eagle in the window.*

polka-dotted K, began advertising on television; created three costumed animal figures, the Krystal Kritters; reorganized its operations; and began construction of a new headquarters building.

The careful planning paid off; the largest privately held restaurant chain in the nation—Rody Davenport III is chairman of the board and Gordon L. Davenport is president—enjoys annual sales of around $200 million. It still sells about 120 million of the little square Krystals each year. The company has also diversified; it owns three Loft Restaurants, two Buck's Pit Barbeque outlets, a substantial minority interest in a Mexican ice cream chain, Krystal Aviation, and under an affiliate company, DavCo Foods, the franchise for Wendy's Hamburgers in several areas of the country. Maybe the Greeks were wrong.

*New Krystal units are designed to harmonize with their surroundings.*

# McKEE BAKING COMPANY

O.D. McKee and his wife Ruth have built a giant out of dough. From selling someone else's cookies early during the Depression, they have built up their own company to become the leading independent producer of "snak cakes." Adhering to Andrew Carnegie's old maxim, they put all their eggs in one basket and watched it carefully.

Using the family's 1928 Whippet, McKee began selling nickel cookies in Chattanooga for Becker's Bakery. Soon he added a line of cookies from another bakery and in 1934 decided to buy that business. To raise the necessary funds he pawned his panel truck; three weeks later he was able to redeem his truck and within four months he added another shift. O.D. and Ruth divided responsibilities; she ran the plant and purchased supplies while he built routes and promoted sales.

In 1937 the McKees turned their business over to Ruth's father, S.D. King, and moved to Charlotte, North Carolina, to start a new bakery. Fourteen years later they returned to Chattanooga and repurchased King's Bakery from Cecil King, Ruth's brother. King's made layer cakes and large pies for the Chattanooga market. The McKees soon phased out the pie operation to concentrate on layer cakes and small cakes.

The business grew so rapidly that by 1957 they had outgrown the Chattanooga facilities. That year, Southern Missionary College invited them to lease a building in Collegedale, Tennessee. What was originally viewed as a very large building had to be expanded 13 times during the next eight years.

The breakthrough for the McKees came in 1960 when they pioneered a new marketing concept for snack cakes, the "Little Debbie Family Pack," a carton of 12 individually wrapped nickel cakes selling for 49 cents. National bakers took over a dozen years to catch on to the concept. Sales grew rapidly, at least in part because the company did not raise prices until 1973 when its costs for major ingredients suddenly doubled and tripled. To keep pace with sales the firm broke ground in 1967 for an all-new plant embodying the latest and most efficient manufacturing equipment, much of which was designed and built by the firm's employees. Less than a decade later the new facilities had to be enlarged by over 100 percent.

The privately owned business is the nation's largest independent snack cake manufacturer, doing business in 39 states east of the Rockies and producing millions of "Little Debbie Snak Cakes" every day. The McKees are still very much involved in the business. But O.D. has not forgotten his roots; he recently purchased and restored another 1928 Whippet.

*(Top) This recent photograph of Anna Ruth and O.D. McKee shows them posing proudly in front of McKee Baking Company with their restored 1928 Whippet.*

*(Above) This photograph taken in 1940 shows King's Bakery, located at 3500 Dodds Avenue in Chattanooga.*

# JOHN MARTIN COMPANY, INC.

Evidence of the craftsmanship of John Martin and his son, John Jr., is found throughout the city of Chattanooga and its environs. Their construction company has tackled projects costing from a few thousand dollars to those of more than $5 million for over 50 years; in fact, the company has the oldest general contractors' license in the city.

The firm started in a modest way after John Martin, who hailed from Hartsville, Tennessee, moved to Chattanooga and became a brick mason. In 1914 he formed a partnership with Lee Warlick to form a masonry contracting company that secured contracts all over the South. By 1923 the partners had gained enough experience and financial backing to be-

*John Martin Company, Inc. has constructed many Chattanooga buildings over the past 50 years, among them the Maclellan Building in the late 1940s (below) and the Quaker Oats Company facility in 1951 (below right).*

come general contractors and soon were involved in projects as large as a steam plant at Hales Bar complete with employees' homes.

Not limited to school or church work, the company has been heavily involved in industrial construction throughout the city for firms such as Du Pont, Armour, Quaker Oats, Central Soya, Provident Life Insurance, American National Bank, and for retail stores such as Pickett's and Fowler Brothers. The firm also does renovation and remodeling work; it has one employee who for over 20 years has done nothing but remodel the Provident and Maclellan buildings.

Over its more than 50 years of operation the firm has had remarkably few management changes. In 1963 John Martin became chairman of the board and John Martin, Jr. assumed the duties of the presidency. After his father died in 1966, John Jr. assumed that title as well. Four third-generation Martins work for the firm, assuring that in the coming years the John Martin Company will have ample opportunities to make even more of a mark on the area.

After the stock market panic, the partnership was dissolved and in 1931

Martin incorporated the John Martin Company and continued in the general contracting business. Construction was slow, but as soon as the Depression lifted and the pent-up demand for new building was unleashed, the company had all the business it could handle. In the succeeding years Martin and his son, who joined the firm after graduating from the Citadel in 1942 and serving four years in the army, constructed many local buildings that helped to reshape the city's skyline.

The Martins built schools in East Lake, East Chattanooga, on Baylor School's campus, and several in the Sequatchie Valley. Howard High School complex was their largest project and in many respects their most difficult because they had to deal with material shortages resulting from World War II. The Martins were busy at the University of Chattanooga as well, where they built Pfeiffer, Brock, and Grote halls and the Vine Street side of the football stadium. Their talents extend to churches, such as East Lake Baptist, the Cumberland Presbyterian, and additions to Northside Presbyterian and Our Lady of Perpetual Help.

# MILLS & LUPTON SUPPLY COMPANY

During World War II a Mexican farmer with a desperate need for equipment to irrigate his fields, but lacking electricity, somehow located a Mills & Lupton supply catalog. He submitted an order for several windmills and despite wartime restrictions, the Chattanooga industrial supplier promptly filled it. For almost all of the 20th century Mills & Lupton has supplied industrial needs, ranging from donkey engines for mines to solid-state circuitry for industrial controls, but normally only in a 100-mile trade area surrounding Chattanooga.

Such diversity was far from the minds of Walter E. Mills and James Lupton

back in 1910 when they incorporated a firm to sell mill supplies. When they opened their doors with three employees, including John Crimmins and shortly thereafter Frank T. Delaney, who along with their descendants continued to operate the company, their total assets were a horse and wagon and a knowledge of the industrial supply business. Six years later the concern was purchased by the Southern Company, a holding company that controlled numerous utilities properties throughout the South. In the 1920s the rapidly growing firm moved to 1152 Market Street and added electrical, plumbing, heating, and building supply departments.

The Great Depression dealt a severe blow to the speculative utility interests across the country. Through a series of transactions, Central Public Service Corporation in Chicago purchased an interest in Mills & Lupton and held

notes against the Chattanooga supplier. In 1932 the Chicago company wanted to liquidate Mills & Lupton, but the parent Southern Company would not agree to the transaction. At that juncture, Crimmins, Delaney, E.C. Mahoney, Archie M. Day, L.D. Sies, and Miss Sarah Stoner offered to buy Mills & Lupton. They raised one half of the purchase price from their own resources and the remainder from successful operation of the business and paid for the firm in 30 days.

Crimmins became president and Delaney vice-president of the new firm, positions they held until 1963 when Crimmins became chairman and Delaney vice-chairman of the board and Mahoney assumed the duties of the presidency. Five years later, John B. Crimmins, Jr. became president, a position he still holds. Under the leadership of these men Mills & Lupton became a full-line industrial supplier, serving the industrial, construction, and utilities industries. They guided the firm through the worst of the Depression and in the late 1930s began to enjoy the first fruits of their labors. Since then the company has been involved in all of the projects and programs that have helped to enhance the Tennessee Valley. Business expanded so rapidly in the postwar years that Mills & Lupton built new facilities at 749 East 12th Street in 1957; opened a display center at 750 East 11th Street in 1961; a branch in Cleveland, Tennessee, in 1969; and another branch in Dalton, Georgia, in 1972. The firm now employs 110 people and carries an inventory of thousands of items. It no longer carries windmills, but this versatile family concern could probably secure one or nearly anything else for a customer in need.

*In the '20s the rapidly growing firm moved to 1152 Market Street, adding electrical, plumbing, heating, and building departments.*

*This photograph of Mills & Lupton Supply Company employees was taken during the 1920s.*

# MOORE AND KING, INC.

*In 1919 J. Gilbert King (above) and E. Fenton Moore purchased Chattanooga's oldest pharmacy, known today as Moore and King, Inc.*

Compound a firm belief that pharmacies exist to serve their patrons' medical needs, a family tradition of doing just that for over a century, a dash of firmly held principles governing the conduct of men, and the resultant product, Chattanooga's oldest pharmacy, Moore and King, will more than likely be able to heal what ails one.

The firm's history stretches back to 1878 when John D. Eastman opened his store at the corner of 9th and Market streets. After he died in the yellow fever epidemic of that year his business was sold to his nephew, Frank. Eight years later it was purchased by J.F. Voight.

became Voight Brothers, and dispensed relief under that name until 1919 when E. Fenton Moore and former employee J. Gilbert King bought the firm.

The new owners were tough-minded; when they moved their store to the east side of the street they took out the soda fountain and food counter and ended the long-standing tradition of offering doctors free lunches. The two men built up their business over the next 30 years by offering quality prescription services dispensed with a neighborly touch at all hours of the day and night. In 1946 Joseph G. King, fresh from the University of North Carolina College of Pharmacy and a 42-month hitch in the U. S. Navy, joined his father in the concern.

The next decade witnessed vast changes in the firm's operations. In 1953 the company emphasized its commitment to service by instituting citywide prescription deliveries with its Pill Wagon and introduced an ophthalmic laboratory and a conveyor prescription counter that helped double its prescription capacity. Later in the decade the firm added to its line wheelchairs, hearing aids, and a full range of hospital equipment for sale or rent.

The pace of Moore and King's innovations quickened during the next 20 years. Out on Brainerd Road the company constructed the city's first drive-in prescription service in 1961 and a year later began to keep family records for its patrons, instituted internal management changes, began direct mail and later television advertising, opened new outlets, and added an Ostomy Center. Joe King, the firm's president, served as president of the American College of Apothecaries which has recognized his national contributions with its most

*Moore and King, Inc.'s original location was at the east corner of 9th and Market streets.*

prestigious honor, the Lascoff Award. In 1975 Mr. King founded King Medical Equipment, Inc. to carry a separate line of hospital equipment and oxygen supplies. Experts were quickly brought into this affiliate concern, making it one of the community's finest resources for rehabilitation equipment.

Moore and King's rapid changes have been grounded on certain underlying principles; the firm has consistently emphasized the professional rather than the commercial side of its business and has continued to accent service rather than price. At its core, the company remains committed to what it was established to do: meet the health needs of its customers.

# C-E POWER SYSTEMS

Combustion Engineering, Inc. was officially formed in New York City in 1912, but the firm's manufacturing roots were planted right here in Chattanooga when two small boiler manufacturers opened for business in the late 1880s. In 1888, Ohioans Mike Weidner and Patrick Walsh founded the Walsh & Weidner Company; one year later, fellow Buckeyes James Casey and Mertland Hedges purchased the Union Iron Works to form the Casey & Hedges Company. Both enterprises flourished during the industrializing period of the early 1900s, and after merging in 1928, New York-based C-E purchased the stock of the newly formed company. As it turned out, the acquisition was a fortuitous and farsighted one, for C-E's Chattanooga facilities have evolved into one of the corporation's largest manufacturing centers—and Chattanooga's largest private employer.

In their earliest years, both Walsh & Weidner and Casey & Hedges manufactured boilers and associated equipment such as tanks, kilns, stacks, and sheet-iron products. Casey & Hedges added a cast-iron soil pipe foundry in 1900, which also made ornamental cast-iron posts for gas lighting Chattanooga streets. Walsh & Weidner manufactured digesters, autoclaves, and pressure vessels for the chemical and oil-processing industries—a line that would presage C-E's important contributions to the energy field.

As U.S. technology progressed, some of these lines eventually became obsolete, while others were enlarged and still constitute a large part of C-E's current

This is a completed pressure vessel of exceptional length, requiring multiple rail cars for shipment.

The company's first fusion-welded boiler drum is located in front of Combustion Engineering's metallurgical laboratory in Chattanooga.

Chattanooga production. Meanwhile, the firm's pioneering research into energy and ecology systems has made it an international leader in the design and manufacture of electrical and industrial steam supply systems and related energy systems products and services, with licensee companies throughout the world.

One of the most important technical developments in the manufacture of pressure vessels was fusion-welding, a process pioneered by Hedges-Walsh-Weidner and then by C-E in the late 1920s. On May 2, 1930, C-E successfully tested its first fusion-welded boiler drum. In June 1931 the American Society of Mechanical Engineers (ASME) approved the use of welding for boiler construction. That same month C-E shipped what is believed to be the first commercial drum for a land boiler constructed according to these new rules. Recognition of this achievement was given on May 2, 1980, when ceremonies held at C-E's Chattanooga facilities awarded the C-E fusion-welded test boiler drum the status of an ASME National Historic Mechanical Engineering Landmark.

During the lean Depression years of the 1930s, the boiler business continued to grow, but defense work occupied most of C-E's time in Chattanooga during World War II. Orders for defense plant land boilers were bolstered by orders for maritime and navy ship boilers. During the war years, the United States averaged one Liberty Ship launching per day, and more than half of these were equipped with C-E boilers. At the peak of the effort in 1943, about 100 ships featuring C-E equipment were launched each month. For these efforts, the C-E Chattanooga facilities were awarded the Navy "E" and the Maritime "M" awards for excellence.

During the postwar years, the Chattanooga plants converted back to commercial production of boiler components and also designed and constructed nuclear systems for the navy. In 1956, C-E's Chattanooga facilities shipped the reactor vessel for the first commercial nuclear station, which was installed at the Shippingport Station of the Du-Quesne Power & Light Company in Pennsylvania.

By the early 1950s, C-E was a major international supplier of fossil-fueled steam supply systems to the electric utility industry and to other industries requiring process steam for their manufacturing operations. By the mid-1970s, steam supply systems of C-E design produced over 40 percent of the electricity generated in the free world.

In the 1960s, C-E became a prime contractor for nuclear steam supply systems. During three of the past four years (1977-1980), C-E nuclear systems led the U.S. nuclear industry in reliability, as reported by the Nuclear Regulatory Commission. Simultaneously, the company diversified into other energy-related fields: process equipment for the oil and gas industries, the petroleum and petrochemical industries, architectural engineering and construction, and a

*This 14,000-ton hydraulic pull-down forming press is one of the largest of its type in the world.*

wide range of industrial products. As the search for new energy sources continues in the 1980s, C-E continues to pioneer in the design and construction of equipment for prototype plants, including coal gasification, magnetohydrodynamics, and solar and nonconventional fuel-burning techniques, such as waste-disposal and the fluidized bed-burning of coal.

As part of a worldwide corporation that ranked 121st in the 1980 Fortune 500 list of top corporations, C-E's Chattanooga operations are located on 150 acres between West 9th and West 19th Streets and two other smaller sites. Employing 4,000 workers, with the largest dock facility on the Tennessee River, the firm ships everything from package boilers producing 100,000 pounds of steam per hour to pressure vessel components weighing 700 tons. C-E's local plants have also developed facilities for other markets, such as a tube mill for manufacturing stainless steel tubing and pipe, facilities for producing coated welding electrodes and welding flux, and a wire-drawing mill located in nearby Atlanta.

For almost a century, C-E's Chattanooga operations have been a key industrial factor in the economic growth of the city of Chattanooga and the surrounding region.

*All the primary components for an 1,100-megawatt nuclear plant in Southern California were shipped from Combustion Engineering's Chattanooga facility by oceangoing barge to San Onofre.*

# PROVIDENT LIFE AND ACCIDENT INSURANCE COMPANY

Beginning in a small office on the corner of Chestnut and 8th streets in 1887, Provident Life and Accident Insurance Company has grown into one of the 15 largest stockholder-owned insurance companies in the nation. Licensed to operate as the parent company or subsidiary throughout the United States and Canada, the little firm that started out with an innovative idea for selling accident insurance now markets individual and group life, accident, health, homeowners and auto insurance, and annuity and retirement plans.

The Chattanoogans who started Provident to sell accident insurance probably never envisioned success on such a scale.

*Thomas Maclellan, a Scotsman from St. John, New Brunswick, was a major factor in transforming Provident Insurance from a small local business into a national corporation.*

In creating the first such business in the region, their idea was to sell coal miners and timber workers disability and death benefits on a "pay order" basis, in which premiums were collected by the workers' timekeepers or through payroll deductions. The approach proved popular and within a few years the company was operating throughout the coal districts in East Tennessee and Kentucky.

Two young Scotsmen from Canada, Thomas Maclellan and John McMaster, took over management of the firm in 1892. A restless, outgoing individual, McMaster sold his interest in 1900, having seen the company become well-established, and he moved to West Virginia. Maclellan, who served as Provident's chief operating officer, brought zest and imagination to the enterprise. He traveled extensively, expanded its territory, signed up new companies, solicited insurance applications from new employees, and employed many extremely capable managers, several of whom were to serve the firm into the 1950s.

Under his leadership, Provident greatly expanded its group sickness coverage.

In 1910 Maclellan rechartered the company, changing it from an assessment to a stock company to increase its financial strength. As its sales increased, the number of employees also rose and by 1913 the firm's assets had already grown to $240,000.

Provident became known for just claims paid promptly in strict adherence to the Golden Rule. Maclellan stressed that claims must be paid before salaries, and this emphasis on integrity and service helped Provident grow when other companies foundered.

An auto accident in 1916 cost Maclellan his life, and his son, Robert J. Maclellan, who had joined Provident in 1905, succeeded him as president. The younger Maclellan was also an uncommonly active man, and he was instrumental in attracting to the company talented men whose efforts laid Provident's modern foundations. Three of the most notable personalities joined Provident within a period of one year—J.W.

*Provident occupied quarters in the old Temple Court Building in 1910; Thomas Maclellan is seated behind the desk in the center of the picture.*

*The present home of Provident Life and Accident Insurance Company is located at Fountain Square.*

Kirksey in 1909 and W.C. Cartinhour and L.N. Webb in 1910. Kirksey directed group operations from 1921 until his death in 1937. Cartinhour became secretary in 1916 and served as vice-president and secretary until his retirement in 1951. Webb directed the company's claim services and retired as executive vice-president in 1965. Another individual important in Provident's early growth was J.O. Carter, Jr., who joined the organization as a bookkeeper in 1916, served 38 years and retired as vice-president and treasurer in 1955.

In 1916 the firm established the Railroad Department, which in 1959 was renamed the Franchise Department. In 1917 the Life Department was created. The independence and responsibility enjoyed by each of these four operating departments seems to have been the key to Provident's steady growth. Led by talented individuals, the departments were encouraged to focus on well-defined markets where Provident could offer tailored insurance products and services.

In 1926 the company bought the railway accident and sickness business of the Standard Accident Insurance Company of Detroit, thus becoming the leading firm in that field. Three years later, in 1929, Provident became the first private insurance company to offer hospital-surgical insurance to the public.

The Great Depression slowed the company's expansion not a whit. In 1931 Provident entered into a reinsurance arrangement with the Southern Surety Company that moved Provident into the top 10 companies in the nation in total accident and sickness volume. In its 50th-anniversary year, 1937, the company passed the $100-million milestone of life insurance in force. Proving the old adage that the first hundred million is the hardest, Provident reached the $500-million mark in 1948 and an astounding $1 billion in 1952. In only four more years that figure was doubled, and by 1981 the company had $33 billion of life insurance in force.

To expand the area of service for the rapidly increasing number of policyholders, Maclellan in 1951 chartered a separate subsidiary concern, the Provident Life and Casualty Company. A year later Robert J. Maclellan moved up to chairman of the board. His older son, Robert L. Maclellan, was elected president and his younger son, Hugh O. Maclellan, continued to serve as vice-president and head of investment programs.

In 1956 Provident installed electronic data processing equipment under the guidance of a young actuary, Henry C. Unruh, who subsequently rose to the company's top management position. In 1958 Provident purchased its first computer. With a home office staff that had grown from three to over 800, space was at a premium. In 1958 Provident began work on a new office building located at Fountain Square; only a decade later an addition was begun that expanded this facility and raised its employee capacity to over 1,800. In what has become an almost decadal event, Provident announced in 1980 yet another expansion, adding a 6-story annex with room for 1,300 more employees.

The 1970s were years of management changes and continued growth. Robert L. Maclellan became chairman of the board in 1970 and Unruh was elected president. Upon Maclellan's death the following year, Unruh moved up to chairman and Robert's brother, Hugh O. Maclellan, became president. Upon Hugh Maclellan's retirement from active management six years later, H. Carey Hanlin was elected president.

Provident entered the 1980s well positioned for continued national growth as a diversified major insurance company, whose products, services, and management have been acknowledged as among the industry's leaders. While other key people responsible for the company's remarkable growth are too numerous to describe adequately here, Provident has historically credited its successes to the faithful, diligent service of generations of able employees.

# RED FOOD STORES, INC.

The Red Food Stores, begun in the streetcar era, became Chattanooga's largest food retailing chain. It all started when Frank J. McDonald created the company with a simple idea back in 1908. He reasoned that food stores should be highly accessible to residential areas rather than concentrated in Chattanooga's central business district. He located his Red Stores at the end of the streetcar lines and then extended his idea one step further by establishing Roly Red Wagons to take store merchandise to homes in rural communities. McDonald was so successful that he soon had 25 of his mobile groceries serving the area.

In 1921 he sold his operation to T. Grady Parham and W. Ed Lindsay. Soon thereafter new licensing fees and taxes made the Roly Red Wagons unprofitable and the financial strain of discontinuing the wagon routes prompted Parham and Lindsay to sell their Red Stores to the H.G. Hill Company of Nashville; the two men, however, remained in Chattanooga to manage the renamed Hill-Red stores. Later, the stores were identified as H.G. Hill Stores. Under the H.G. Hill banner the number of stores grew rapidly and the enterprise thrived.

The "Roaring Twenties" and the following decade witnessed profound changes in Americans' living styles and under Parham, the Hill Stores adapted quickly. By 1932 he had introduced the self-service grocery store to Chattanooga and had brought meat markets into his stores. The model T revolutionized the grocery business and Parham phased out the neighborhood corner

store locations in favor of large stores that provided customers with off-street paved parking.

The food stores continued to be successful and in 1942, Parham and others purchased all 34 stores in the Chattanooga Division of H.G. Hill Stores, re-

*On the right of this 1914 photograph is one of the group of original Red Stores. This store was located at the end of the Rossville, Georgia, streetcar line.*

*Red Food Stores' modern, efficient distribution center located on Shallowford Road was recently expanded to 300,000 square feet of floor space.*

turning them to their Red Store identity and adding the word "Food" to more accurately describe them. Consumer purchasing patterns changed again in the postwar years and Parham, anticipating future trends, located a Red Food Store as the anchor unit in the area's first shopping center. In 1965 Donald L. Blevins, who had operated a number of food stores in the Chattanooga area, joined

Parham in the management and further development of the company.

The company has continued to trend toward larger, highly accessible stores with an expanded merchandise offering. All stores are served from a modern, efficient distribution center, comprising 300,000 square feet of floor area, located on Shallowford Road.

Red Food Stores is known for its friendly, well-trained employees. The company has recently expanded its training center facility in order to provide additional trained personnel for the major growth program initiated under William F. Stewart, who became president of Red Food Stores in 1980.

# ROCK-TENN COMPANY

In the 1970s the environmentalist movement and the energy shortage converged to produce a public outcry in the United States calling for recycling products to conserve dwindling raw materials and to alleviate the strain on the nation's energy resources. Out on Compress Street off Manufacturers Road in Chattanooga, the Tennessee Paper Mills has been quietly doing just that by recycling used paper into boxboard for over half a century.

The idea for the company originated with A.M. Tomlinson in Athens, Tennessee, who owned a business that manufactured set-up boxes. To ensure a steady supply of raw materials he decided to build his own mill; after considering Atlanta as a possible site, he settled on Chattanooga because of its plentiful supplies of water and coal. To raise funds, Tomlinson approached Chattanoogan John Stagmaier, a wholesaler of food and paper goods, and to oversee the technical end of the business, the two men brought A.M. Sheperd of Vincennes, Indiana, a well-known boxboard manufacturer, into the firm.

The three men raised over a quarter of a million dollars in capital and hired L.T. Murphy, a mechanical genius, to construct the plant. Despite wartime restrictions, Murphy had the mill in operation in mid-1918 and the fruits of his inventive genius may still be seen in the machinery he designed to remove water from the board through a mechanical process, thereby shortening the manufacturing time and saving a great deal of energy.

Thanks to its conservative family

The headquarters of the Rock-Tenn Company is located at 701 Manufacturers Road in Chattanooga.

Standing in front of the Tennessee Paper Mills' number one paper machine, this crew during the 1940s stacks and bundles heavy paperboard for shipment to box and carton manufacturers.

management and secure financial position, the company prospered during the 1920s and showed a profit throughout the Depression. With the advent of World War II the mill operated seven days a week, manufacturing recycled ammunition container board used to package shells for transportation. Today its 200 employees produce about 90,000 tons of board a year which is principally fabricated into clothing boxes, carry-out trays for food outlets, and pizza boxes.

Controlling interest in the company slowly shifted into the hands of the Stagmaier family and the descendants of C.E. Finley, the firm's first office manager. In 1973 the Tennessee Paper Mills merged with its largest customer, the Rock City Packaging Company of Norcross, Georgia, also a privately held concern. W. Max Finley, son of C.E. Finley, was named senior chairman of the board of the newly named Rock-Tenn Company.

In the same quiet way the company has contributed to Chattanooga's industrial prosperity, principals in the firm have contributed their time, expertise, and money to various Chattanooga institutions. Stagmaier Dormitory and Fletcher Hall, the latter named for Tennessee Paper Mills attorney John S. Fletcher, at the University of Tennessee at Chattanooga, for example, attest to those families' interest in recycling their profits to educate the next generation of Chattanooga's leaders.

# SELOX, INC.

All of us are surrounded in our everyday lives by gases; we inhale and exhale them, they help produce the metals in our appliances and autos, put us to sleep before surgery, and even make us laugh in the dentist's chair. Nature, however, played a cruel trick on man by compounding useful gases so that sophisticated equipment such as that owned by Selox is necessary to isolate those that are useful.

Founded in 1938 as the Welding Gas Products Company, the name it retained until 1968, by Marvin E. White, a native Chattanoogan who had been a welding supply salesman, and two friends, Clarence Miller and E.J. Lowrey, the firm has been a successful enterprise from the start. The men built their original oxygen plant at 821 East 11th Street where Selox's headquarters are still located.

Over the ensuing years White bought out his partners and his son, Robert E. White, joined the firm in 1959 and became president in 1963. With his accession to that office, the company rapidly expanded its product lines and marketing territory until it owned four manufacturing plants and six sales locations across the Southeast. Its first expansion was the construction of an air separation plant in 1967 on Access Road designed to produce gaseous nitrogen for the

*Robert E. White (left), president of the Chattanooga-based Selox, Inc., is pictured here with fellow members of his company's management team in front of the firm's newest plant. From right are Dr. Tom Cullen, vice-president manufacturing; Bill J. Hillis, vice-president marketing; and H. W. Feagans, secretary-treasurer.*

nearby Du Pont plant, selling the balance of the production to other customers. Seven years later another plant was constructed at the same location and in 1977 yet another. The three plants manufacture liquid oxygen, nitrogen, and argon, all of which are tested in the laboratory on the premises for purity. Some of the production is put into cylinders at the plant's filling station while the remainder is shipped in liquid form to be stored in cooled vacuum tanks with from 300- to 11,000-gallon capacity located on the customers' grounds.

In 1979 the firm opened another air separation plant at 3510 St. Elmo Avenue, which doubled the company's capacity. Gaseous oxygen is supplied to nearby large customers through a pipeline network connected to the plant. Selox also has an acetylene plant near Ringgold, Georgia, and another facility at Enka, North Carolina. Moreover, the company serves as a distributor for some gases such as nitrous oxide and carbon dioxide it does not manufacture.

With sales locations in Chattanooga, Knoxville, Nashville, Gainesville, Tennessee; Atlanta, Georgia; and Greenville, South Carolina, Selox employs 175 people with 100 of them located in Chattanooga. The company serves all manner of industrial concerns, particularly the metals industry, the frozen food business, and hospitals, and is one of the nation's largest distributors of Hobart and Westinghouse welding equipment. Its sales have more than kept pace with its expansion; they have risen from $5 million in 1972 to $24 million a year in the early 1980s, making Selox the largest privately owned gas manufacturer in the United States. Robert White, now president and chairman of the board, intends to keep it that way.

# SOUTHERN MISSIONARY COLLEGE

Southern Missionary College, an incorporated suburb of Chattanooga, was founded in 1892 in Graysville, Tennessee, as a private elementary school enrolling 32 students in a classroom atop the Clouse General Store. The school quickly grew to a high school known as Graysville Academy. From 1904 to 1916 the institution was known as Southern Training School with academic offerings that included farming, dairy husbandry, and mechanics along with traditional academic subjects.

Rather than rebuild a women's dormitory which burned in 1915, a move that would give permanency to a campus of only 10 acres, the board voted to look for a much larger site and rebuild the school.

A search committee recommended the Thatcher Plantation as a 300-acre location for the newly reorganized campus near Ooltewah. The move was made in time for the opening of the fall term in 1916 under the new name of Southern Junior College. The Yellow Mansion, the James Thatcher family residence, became business offices, cafeteria, classrooms, and women's dormitory. The men lived in tents, while the faculty lived in tents and cabins. Leo Thiel was the first president of the fledgling junior college and served for two separate terms, from 1916 to 1918 and from 1922 to 1925.

From 1914 to 1922 the college built the administration building, men's and women's residence halls, and farm buildings. These buildings formed the nucleus for the college program for almost five

*Wright Hall, Administration Building, Southern Missionary College.*

decades until it became necessary to rebuild the campus, almost entirely because of increased enrollment.

Southern Junior College became Southern Missionary College in 1946 and was accredited by the Southern Association of Colleges and Schools. The expanded curriculum included baccalaureate degrees in 17 areas with special emphasis upon liberal arts and religion.

The enrollment of 400 in the 1950s doubled during the 1960s. In the later 1960s the introduction of a two-year associate degree nursing program attracted many students, and the nursing division was accredited with the state of Tennessee as well as the National League of Nursing. During this time the college was also accredited with the National

Council of Teacher Education. The college as a whole was reaccredited by the Southern Association in 1962 and 1972.

Presently the college owns approximately 1,150 acres and has a valuation of about $25 million with a yearly budget of $17 million. The academic program is organized into 11 divisions which aggregately offer 34 baccalaureate majors and a number of associate and certificate emphases. The college owns several commercial enterprises which provide student labor as well as college income.

Southern Missionary College is owned and operated by the Seventh-day Adventist Church. Approximately 60 percent of the students come from the southeastern United States; the rest come from most of the other states and about 30 foreign countries. The teaching staff of 135 is supported by an additional service staff of about 300.

# STONE FORT LAND COMPANY

The origins of the Stone Fort Land Company are solidly based on a 4-story-high limestone outcropping once located in downtown Chattanooga. That quarry, used by the Confederate and Union armies as a munitions depot, provided the company with its unusual name. Started in 1886 by a group of Cincinnati businessmen to build housing for immigrants in the city, the firm over the years has had a perfect record of never having built a single house. Instead, the Stone Fort Land Company's owners became interested in the commercial development of its land—an emphasis the company's officers have continued until today.

In 1901 J.T. Lupton, a young Chattanooga lawyer, and his wife purchased a controlling interest in the concern. They proceeded to develop a parcel of land stretching from 10th and Lindsay streets to where the Chattanooga City Hall now stands. The company constructed about 15 five-story buildings and the Patten Hotel, sold the land for city hall, and donated a lot to the federal government which eventually became

*The Stone Fort Land Company is headquartered in the Krystal Building, which was completed in June 1978.*

the location of TVA's original computer center.

During the Depression construction projects came to a standstill and tenants fell behind in their payments—at one time a majority of the firm's lessees were delinquent in their rent—but the Stone Fort Land Company carried as many as possible rather than allow them to slide into bankruptcy. And in 1933 J.T. Lupton died, leaving active management of the business to T.A. Lupton. During World War II the federal government leased warehouse space from the company to store the last shipments of Singapore raw rubber, which, despite the wartime shortage, reposed in the buildings swollen from the summer heat.

When Mrs. J.T. Lupton died in 1941 she passed on a two-thirds share in the company to T.A. Lupton. When he died unexpectedly only six years later, management of the firm fell to his wife Louise Lupton, who pointed the company in new directions by negotiating major building leases with TVA. In 1957 Mrs. Lupton turned the reins of the firm over to her son, T.A. Lupton, Jr., who introduced the concept of industrial park development to Chattanooga. Affiliating with a major landholder in the Amnicola Highway area they developed, leased, and sold buildings and land all along the Tennessee River, cre-

ating a new industrial center in Chattanooga. At the same time, continuing its investment in downtown Chattanooga, the firm constructed a major new office center, and, in partnership with the L&N railroad, developed its old passenger station property. The Bicentennial Library, the Tennessee-American Water Company, and the Krystal Building have been built on the site and a huge TVA complex is to be erected there as well.

The Stone Fort Land Company has developed more land for industrial and warehouse use in Chattanooga than all other local companies combined. The firm now owns about 40 major pieces of real estate, 4.5 million square feet of warehouse space, and several hundred thousand square feet of office space which it leases to major corporations such as Sears, Roebuck and Co., General Motors, Coca-Cola, South Central Bell, TVA, Du Pont, and Krystal. The officers of the Stone Fort Land Company remain committed to projects that will enhance the beauty of the city and, like the great Stone Fort quarry limestone blocks still seen in buildings and walls throughout Chattanooga, be something enduring.

*The Du Pont and Sears, Roebuck and Company's warehouses, built and owned by the Stone Fort Land Company, are located in the Amnicola Industrial Park, Chattanooga.*

# TENNESSEE CREDIT UNION LEAGUE

Miss Elizabeth Lynch, the Tennessee Credit Union League's first managing director and its first paid employee, used the public writing table near the league's post office box as her desk during her tenure from 1946 to 1950. Not only did she lack an office, but she spent the majority of her time on trains traveling from one credit union to another all over Tennessee and Virginia.

Lynch's accommodations accurately reflected the league's origins. Born in the hard Depression days of 1934, when 34 representatives of Tennessee credit unions met to organize a state coordinating association, the league for its first 12 years could not afford to pay an employee. During that period, the work of organizing the state's credit unions was carried on by the Credit Union National Association in Madison, Wisconsin, and by local volunteers.

Initially, the Tennessee Credit Union League served 30 credit unions; the number has grown to 550 today and the variety of services it offers its members has grown accordingly. The league holds training sessions for credit union officers, organizes conferences and workshops, provides technical assistance and data processing, and counsels members on their daily operations. It writes, prints, and distributes training materials, furnishes advertising and marketing aids, runs management surveys for members, and maintains a forecasting service that plots future economic trends. The league also writes forms used in Tennessee credit unions to ensure that

*The league's modern headquarters was constructed in 1979.*

*Chattanooga Mayor Robert K. Walker (seated) is flanked by C.E. Arnold (left), former president of the league, and Arthur Davis (right), former director of the league, as he signs the proclamation of International Credit Union Week in this photograph taken in October 1971.*

they meet all the requirements of changing laws.

The league represents Tennessee credit unions at meetings of the Tennessee legislature and occasionally at the U.S. Congress. In 1976 the league was instrumental in having share-draft legislation passed in Tennessee, one of the first such bills in the nation, which allowed credit unions to provide their customers with interest-bearing checking accounts. On the national level, the league lobbied Congress to pass legislation making such accounts available to all consumers, an act that took effect January 1, 1981.

The league has also been instrumental in establishing a separate organization, the State Credit Union Share Insurance Corporation, which protects consumers' credit union accounts up to $100,000, and the Tennessee Credit Union League Service Corporation, a taxpaying entity, which provides fee-supported services for member credit unions.

Miss Lynch built better than she realized; the league has stayed in Chattanooga and now has 38 employees and branch offices in Knoxville, the Tricities, Nashville, and Memphis. Despite its growth, the Tennessee Credit Union League has maintained its consumer orientation, its nonprofit status, and its interest in community involvement.

# TENNESSEE-AMERICAN WATER COMPANY

The history of most American water companies is a progression from investor ownership to municipal control. Tennessee-American is different. Its early facilities were built by the federal government and then sold to private investors after the federal occupation of the city during the Civil War.

Chattanooga's water system actually began in 1850 when local residents began to lay pipes from artesian wells to their homes. On the eve of the Civil War, however, the system was still a makeshift affair that often ran dry in the long, hot summer months.

The Civil War brought great changes to the city's water system. It was simply inadequate to provide enough water to satisfy the needs and provide fire protection to the growing city. General U.S. Grant ordered the army to take control of the existing system and to expand its capacity. Union forces erected wooden storage tanks on the slopes of Cameron Hill and at the foot of Pine Street near the present location of Ross's Landing the troops built a steam boiler and tank to draw water from the river and pump it up to the storage tanks from where it flowed into the city by gravity.

When the war was over the federal government found itself in the municipal water service business, a politically distasteful role, and sold the facilities at auction to a civic-minded group of local investors. On March 11, 1868, they secured a charter creating the Chattanooga Water Company. A few years

*Water company employees lay a 12-inch main along Market Street in this photograph taken in 1935.*

later it was sold to Colonel George H. Hazelhurst, who renamed the firm the Lookout Water Company. The new firm's published schedule of tariffs for 1872 stipulated a charge of $12 a year for a family of three or fewer persons, plus an extra $2 a year for the family cow; public bathhouses paid $18 yearly per tub; "second-class" grocery stores were charged $18 per annum; and eating and drinking saloons had to pay $72

*The City Water Company of Chattanooga's water filtering plant at Citico Creek is seen here in this 1890 photograph.*

yearly for their water.

The Lookout Water Company made numerous improvements to its system, building a new million-gallon storage tank on Cameron Hill, installing water mains in the city, and affording its residents their first fire protection. A major problem developed, however, when Chattanooga began running its raw sewage into the river just above Lookout's water intakes. The currents in the river at that location are such that the effluents cling to its south bank and thus were drawn into the water company's pipes. Because the firm lacked the resources to move its intakes, the company was offered for sale in 1887 and was purchased by the American Water Works and Guarantee Company, the forerunner of the present American Water Works Company, Inc. At the same time the company also bought and consolidated two other local firms and named the new venture City Water Company of Chattanooga.

Immediately the company moved the intakes upriver to the mouth of Citico Creek, where the firm constructed a modern filtration process, pumping station, and improved distribution facilities capable of carrying three million gallons of water daily to thirsty Chattanoogans.

When completed in 1892, Chattanooga became the second city in the South to enjoy filtered water.

The unlimited source of excellent raw water available in the Tennessee River proved an important natural resource for the growing city. It attracted industries to the area which in turn put a strain on the capacities of the water company. In 1913 the City Water Company added another settling basin and four filters at Citico to bring its capacity up to eight million gallons a day. The city was expanding so rapidly, however, that in only four years the firm had to add another four filters to increase its capacity to 19 million gallons each day. The ongoing demand forced the water company to make major expansions in its service three times in the years between the wars that brought its capacity in 1941 up to 52 million gallons a day—quite enough, everyone reasoned, to meet all future requirements. At the same time, the company pushed its distribution system into the outlying portions of the city by laying more mains, building storage tanks, and erecting pumping stations.

For 25 years the water company's capacity was sufficient. In the mid-1960s, the firm launched a major expansion program which, when completed in 1971, raised its capacity to 72 million gallons a day. Just two years later the local company finally dealt with the long-standing confusion caused by its name; many Chattanoogans thought their water company was municipally owned so its name was changed to Tennessee-American Water Company. It remains a subsidiary of the American Water Works Company, Inc., which owns firms all over the nation providing water service to nearly five million Americans in 575 communities in 20 states.

*These are water storage tanks built by federal troops during the Civil War.*

*Tennessee-American Water Company's new headquarters is located on Broad Street in Chattanooga.*

In the 1970s the firm reaped some of the benefits of its earlier large capital investments. When the first federally mandated Safe Drinking Water Act took effect in June 1977, Tennessee-American was already in compliance. Nevertheless, a year later it launched a $1.3-million program to improve its water-treatment facilities, making Chattanooga the first city in the Southeast to enjoy the benefits of carbon-treated water. The new treatment process also enables the company to handle more effectively accidental or intentional discharges of contaminants on the water-

shed. Tennessee-American now has 1,070 miles of underground mains serving 61,000 customers with about 45 million gallons of water each day. The firm's 157 employees do everything from performing 328 tests each day on the water to painting and repairing 3,200 fire hydrants. Tennessee-American Water Company is proud of its service to the Chattanooga metropolitan area and is committed to continuing its legacy of private ownership in providing "the best possible service at the lowest possible price consistent with a fair return to its stockholders."

# THE UNIVERSITY OF TENNESSEE AT CHATTANOOGA

The University of Tennessee at Chattanooga, a unique blending of private support with a public institution, will observe its centennial anniversary during the academic year 1986-87. The institution was a private undergraduate university with a strong liberal arts orientation until 1969, when it became one of the four primary, multidisciplined campuses within The University of Tennessee.

*"Old Main" was one of the original University of Chattanooga buildings on campus later razed for newer construction.*

Following several years of planning, Chattanooga University was granted its charter in July 1886, and opened its doors to some 100 students on September 15. The charter was vested in the Methodist Episcopal Church, whose Freedman's Aid Society was principally responsible for the college's establishment. The church granted a new charter three years later which combined Chattanooga University with Grant Memorial in Athens; the new institution operated under the name of U.S. Grant University. In 1907 the charter was amended to change the name to the University of Chattanooga, the name it retained until 1969.

The early years of the university were often difficult and full of controversy. There was a continuous rivalry from the outset between Chattanooga and Athens for the honor of having the chief campus. In 1892 the College of Liberal Arts was moved to Athens while the Chattanooga campus was limited for several years to the professional schools of theology, law, and medicine. In 1904, however, the undergraduate college was reopened in Chattanooga, and six years later the professional schools were discontinued to concentrate fully on undergraduate education.

The cluster of buildings on the main quadrangle (including Founders Hall, Race Hall, Hooper Hall, and Patten Chapel), which still forms the administrative center of the campus, was erected in the second decade of this century. By the prudent management of its leadership, the university survived two world wars and the Great Depression as well as social and economic disturbances. It finally abrogated its legal ties with the Methodist Church in 1935, but there remained a cordial relationship between the Church and the University of Chattanooga.

In 1969 the University of Chattanooga and Chattanooga City College merged with The University of Tennessee to become The University of Tennessee at Chattanooga. This was the first state institution of higher education in Chattanooga, the only large metropolitan area in the state that lacked such an institution. In the year of discussion which preceded the merger, the trustees and staffs of the respective institutions took great care to see that the new campus retained an element of the emphasis and flavor of its constituent parts; this enabled the transition from private to public university to take place with a minimum of difficulty.

Since the merger, the university has opened educational opportunities for

A new-found pride on The University of Tennessee at Chattanooga campus is the recently constructed fine arts center with its Henry Moore sculpture before the main entrance.

An aerial view of The University of Tennessee at Chattanooga campus.

many individuals who previously had not been able to afford a private education. Enrollment has more than tripled since the establishment of UTC to just under 8,000 in 1980-81. The university is basically a commuter institution with over 75 percent of its students living within a 50-mile radius of the campus, but dormitory housing for another 200 students will bring its capacity up to 1,100 students. As a result of state financial support, the number of departments and majors has been greatly increased, offering students a wider choice in their educational development. The administrative structure has been expanded to reflect this growth; in addition to the College of Arts and Sciences, there are also schools of Business, Education, Nursing, Engineering, and Human Services. The faculty has grown to over 280 with over 70 percent holding the doctoral or terminal degree. The institution has enjoyed substantial growth in its graduate offerings with 11 graduate programs; approximately 20 percent of the institution's students are enrolled in graduate studies.

The state of Tennessee has been most supportive of the needs of The University of Tennessee at Chattanooga, providing funds to construct eight buildings since the merger at a cost of approximately $50 million. Physical facilities now include 22 major buildings on its 79-acre campus. Most notable are the new library, currently containing 700,000 volumes; a university student center, a fine arts center housing outstanding music, art, and drama facilities; and the physical education and sports arena, now under construction, which will seat over 12,000 spectators. The Academic Computing Center has one of the nation's leading computer training programs, offering students the opportunity to learn with sophisticated equipment that includes over 75 terminals located across the campus. Since 1969, the state appropriations for UTC have grown from $2.95 million to $12.1 million in 1980.

A unique feature of the merger agreement was the creation of the University of Chattanooga Foundation Inc., which manages the endowment once held by the private institution. Income from the endowment provides scholarships, distinguished professorships, and special programs not normally available in a state-supported institution. These funds have contributed significantly to the quality and excellence of the university's offerings. As a result of the "Tennessee Tomorrow" campaign, a major fundraising effort throughout The University of Tennessee system, the UC Foundation Inc. endowment now stands at over $14 million.

In its first century of existence, the university has been an increasingly vital part of Chattanooga life and the surrounding region, maintaining a close and cordial cooperative relationship between town and gown. When UTC celebrates its centennial in 1986-87, it will not only be recounting with gratitude the accomplishments of the first 100 years, but it will be looking forward confidently to greater achievements and wider service in the years to come.

# UNITED STATES PIPE AND FOUNDRY COMPANY

Valves, fittings, and soil pipe are not intrinsically exciting until one walks into a valve large enough to turn around in—then they become awe-inspiring. In addition to casting pipe, U.S. Pipe manufactures, machines, finishes, and installs valve assemblies in such castings ranging up to 54-inch giants.

The firm originated right after the Civil War when David Giles, an iron molder, opened the first Southern pipe foundry in Nashville in 1867. Ten years later Giles came to Chattanooga and built another pipe plant on Whiteside Street to manufacture pit-cast pipe. The plant produced pipe using a technology developed in the 1850s in which 12-foot sections of cast-iron pipe were cast in vertical pits. In 1896 Giles again expanded locally and established a pipe plant on Chestnut Street. Within a decade the two plants had earned a reputation as the best pit-cast foundries in the nation.

In the great consolidation movement of the late 1890s, Giles merged all his properties into a new corporation, the United States Cast Iron Pipe and Foundry Company. Giles became president of the new firm and remained in that post until his death in 1910. The company name was changed to United States Pipe and Foundry Company in 1929. In 1936 the Whiteside and Chestnut Street plants were consolidated at the Chestnut Street location; with reorganization the Chestnut Street plant was made responsible

*Modern aerial view of U.S Pipe and Foundry's Chattanooga Valves and Fittings Plant.*

for the production of most of U.S. Pipe's fittings.

The Chestnut Street operation concentrated solely on the fittings business until the early 1960s, when U.S. Pipe purchased a New Jersey firm, the A.P. Smith Manufacturing Company. That concern, which manufactured fire hydrants and gate valves, was moved to Chattanooga in 1971. In mid-decade, U.S. Pipe also entered the general castings market, manufacturing products such as axle spindles, transmission casings, wheel hubs, support trunnions, and

*United States Pipe and Foundry's plant, circa 1930. Lookout Mountain is in the left background.*

brake drums for J.E. Case, Caterpillar Tractor, Clark Equipment, and other companies.

The 1960s was a busy decade for U.S. Pipe. In November 1961 the company purchased the soil pipe plant at 1000 West 19th Street from Combustion Engineering. This manufacturing facility, the former Casey-Hedges Company, later bought by Combustion Engineering, was built on that site in 1955. At one time it produced everything from cast-iron bird baths to boilers, but now manufactures cast-iron pipe and fittings up to 15 inches in diameter and some gray and ductile iron. In 1969 Jim Walter Corporation of Tampa, Florida, bought the firm, which now operates as a division of the parent company.

The two Chattanooga facilities employ about 1,550 people casting about 350 "good" tons a day. Its valves and fittings are shipped to water companies as far away as Saudi Arabia while its pipe is found in houses, factories, and many municipal sewer systems. In the past five years the company has invested over $5 million to comply with new environmental standards and plans to remain an important component of Chattanooga's industrial economy for the foreseeable future.

*This old steam crane took the place of mules in the 1930s.*

# VOLUNTEER STATE LIFE INSURANCE COMPANY

Columbus Day, October 12, 1903, was an auspicious date for a group of Chattanoogans to found a new life insurance company. As avid supporters of a "new" South more in tune with the industrial and financial ideas in the rest of the country, the men led by Zeboim Cartter Patten, E.B. Craig, J.T. Lupton, and T.R. Preston organized Volunteer State Life with the avowed intention of keeping in the South some of the $50 million a year southerners paid in insurance premiums.

A week later the company's incorporators met and elected Patten (who had served in the Union Army in Chattanooga) president. Volunteer sold its first policy in November, carrying a benefit of $5,000, to the state's governor, J.B. Frazier. When the firm closed its books at the end of the first year, it had $2.8 million of insurance in force, a spectacular rate of growth for a new insurance company in any section of the country.

To fulfill its self-proclaimed mandate, Volunteer agents spread across the South selling individual life insurance. When World War I erupted, the company had $21.5 million of insurance in force and in that year paid its first dividend. To accommodate its growing staff, officers began to talk about building a corporate headquarters. They purchased property at the corner of Georgia Avenue and 9th Street that was occupied by L.J. Sharp and Company, livery stable and undertaker; in 1917 Volunteer moved into its new modern 12-story building that was

*Current headquarters of Volunteer, this 12-story facility was built in 1917.*

so well-constructed it serves as corporate headquarters to this day.

Volunteer's assets more than tripled during the 1920s, and even in the ensuing depression-ridden decade they increased by over 50 percent. In early 1939 the company was reorganized by a group of local businessmen, and Cecil Woods joined Volunteer as president, serving in that capacity until 1963. During this time the firm expanded its operations

*Zeboim Cartter Patten, a leader in founding Volunteer, was elected its first president.*

into 42 states and the District of Columbia and entered the credit insurance business. The first one billion dollars of insurance in force was reached in 1951. Joseph H. Davenport, Jr., who became associated with the organization in 1959, was elected president in 1963; and under his direction Volunteer became an affiliate of the Monumental Corporation, a holding company based in Baltimore, Maryland. Volunteer retained its separate identity and has remained a good corporate citizen in Chattanooga. In 1980 William A. Simpson, CLU, was elected president with Davenport remaining chairman of the board.

Today, with close to $3 billion of life insurance in force, over 250 underwriters in the field, and assets approaching the $300-million mark, Volunteer has done more than simply keep southern money at home; it has also drawn money from the North, East, and West into the South.

# THE WALTER A. WOOD SUPPLY COMPANY, INC.

When the phone rings at The Walter A. Wood Supply Company its president, J.F. Gardner, Jr., is likely to be the man to answer it to take a customer's order. Recently a customer called for a 3-foot piece of pipe threaded at both ends but explained that he could not get to the supply house before its closing time. Gardner solved the problem easily; he offered to see that the pipe was cut and threaded and promised to leave it on the back "porch" or loading dock, when he closed up. Now, that is service.

And service is what the company has emphasized since Walter A. Wood opened his doors on April Fools' Day in 1913. Wood previously had worked for 17 years for General A.P. Stewart who was in charge of laying out Chickamauga Park and had made wide acquaintants among the farmers he had employed from Catoosa and Walker counties. When a local banker encouraged Wood with a $1,000 loan to open a supply business, Wood capitalized on the goodwill he had engendered and his firm prospered from the first. He started his store with two employees and a wagon in the 4900 block of Rossville Boulevard, then a dirt road out past 28th Street which turned into a quagmire every time it rained. He stayed at that location only a short time before moving to the 4500 block where the business is still located.

Wood was killed in a truck accident in 1936 and Rossville banker J.F. Gardner assumed a controlling interest in the company. He, with the help of Walter

*Walter A. Wood founded the Chattanooga Supply Company that bears his name on April 1, 1913.*

A. Wood's son-in-law, Vaughn G. Dyer, and Charles B. Clements acting as president, left his son and his son-in-law, J. Leon Henry, a well-established trade with no debts. Gardner Jr. and Henry greatly expanded their firm's lines in the

1970s without resorting to the public lending markets. They have built a combination industrial supply house—most of their sales are to industrial firms—and a full-line general hardware store. They have maintained their company's tradition of offering a tremendous variety of merchandise; until a few years ago they still had harness parts and just recently a customer called asking for a buggy axle. They do, however, stock just about anything anybody could want in the line of pipes, valves, fittings, fasteners, hoses, and electrical equipment.

The closely held business employs 49 people who work in a building with 80,000 square feet of floor space sprawling over two city blocks and deliver to customers in a 100-mile radius. Gardner and Henry so far have resisted acquiring a computer for their business, arguing that the machine would come between them and their customers. They believe the relative inefficiency of doing everything by hand allows them to retain a bit of the old-fashioned flavor of a country supply store while still offering what they think is the largest variety of supplies in Chattanooga—and, of course, service.

*The firm's headquarters, located at 4509 Rossville Boulevard, has over 80,000 square feet of floor space.*

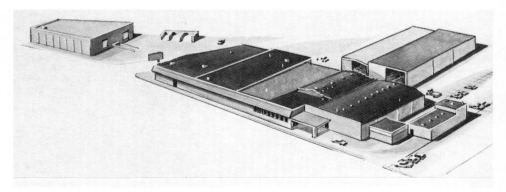

# Partners in Progress Index

# Selected Bibliography

Abshire, David M. *The South Rejects a Prophet: The Life of Senator D.M. Key, 1824–1900*. New York: Praeger, 1967.

Armstrong, Zella. *History of Hamilton County and Chattanooga Tennessee*. 2 vols. Chattanooga: Lookout Publishing Co., 1931–40.

Brown, John P. *Old Frontiers: The Story of the Cherokee Indians from Earliest Times to the Date of Their Removal to the West*. Kingsport, Tenn.: Southern Publishers, 1938. (Reprint by Arno Press, 1971.)

Callahan, North. *Bridge over Troubled Waters*. S. Brunswick, N.J.: A.S. Barnes, 1980.

Campbell, Thomas J. *The Upper Tennessee*. Chattanooga: author, 1932.

Chattanooga Area Historical Association. *Walk with History*. Chattanooga: author, 1976.

Davidson, Donald. *The Tennessee The Old River: Frontier to Secession*. New York: Rinehart & Co., 1946. (Reprint edition by University of Tennessee Press, 1978.)

Flanigan, George J. *The Centenary of St. Peter & St. Paul's Parish*. Chattanooga: Sts. Peter and Paul's Parish, 1952.

Foreman, Grant. *Sequoyah*. Norman: University of Oklahoma Press, 1938, 1959.

Gaston, Kay. *The Story of the W Road*. Chattanooga: author, 1980.

Govan, G.E., and Livingood, J.W. *The Chattanooga Country: From Tomahawks to TVA 1540–1976*. Knoxville: University of Tennessee Press, 1977 (3rd ed.).

_____ . *The University of Chattanooga: Sixty Years*. Chattanooga: University of Chattanooga, 1947.

Hudson, Charles. *The Southeastern Indians*. Knoxville: The University of Tennessee Press, 1976.

Johnson, Gerald W. *An Honorable Titan: A Biographical Study of Adolph S. Ochs*. New York: Harper & Bros., 1946.

Johnson, Leland R. *Engineers on the Twin Rivers*. Nashville: U.S. Army Engineers District, 1978.

Lewis, T.M.N., and Kneberg, Madeline. *Tribes that Slumber: Indians of the Tennessee Region*. Knoxville: University of Tennessee Press, 1958.

Lindsey, Edwin S. *St. Paul's Episcopal Church . . . 1853–1953*. Chattanooga: Vestry, 1953.

_____ . *Achievements of the Chattanooga Opera Association*. Chattanooga: Starkey, 1978.

Mooney, James. "Myths of the Cherokees," 19th Annual Report, U.S. Bureau of American Ethnology. Washington: GPO, 1900. (Reprint edition by Johnson Reprint Corp., 1970.)

Moulton, Gary E. *John Ross: Cherokee Chief*. Athens, Ga.: University of Georgia Press, 1978.

Patten, Cartter. *Signal Mountain and Walden's Ridge*. Chattanooga: author, 1961.

Patten, Elizabeth. *History of Summertown, Walden's Ridge, Tenn*. Chattanooga: author 1956.

Peacock, Mary Thomas. *The Circuit Rider and Those Who Followed: Sketches of Methodist Churches Organized before 1860 in the Chattanooga Area. . . .* Chattanooga: Hudson, 1957.

Pound, Jerome. *Memoirs*. Chattanooga: author, 1949.

Reed, Ishmael. *Chattanooga*. New York: Random House, 1966.

Steinberg, David. *And to Think It Only Cost a Nickel! The Development of Public Transportation in the Chattanooga Area*. Chattanooga: author, 1975.

Sullivan, James R. *Chickamauga and Chattanooga Battlefield*. Washington, D.C.: National Park Service Historical Handbook, Series No. 25, 1956.

Terral, Rufus. *Newell Sanders: A Biography*. Kingsport, Tenn.: author, 1935.

Tucker, Glen. *Chickamauga: Bloody Battle in the West*. Indianapolis: Bobbs-Merrill, 1961.

Wade, Elizabeth K. *History of Chattanooga High School*. Chattanooga: Adams, 1974.

Walker, Robert Sparks. *Lookout: The Story of a Mountain*. Kingsport, Tenn.: Southern Publishers, 1941.

_____ . *Torchlights to the Cherokee: The Brainerd Mission*. New York: Macmillan, 1931.

White, Bliss J., comp. *Biography and Achievements of the Colored Citizens of Chattanooga*. n.p.: 1904.

Wilson, John. *Lookout: the Story of an Amazing Mountain*. Chattanooga: News-Free Press, 1977.

_____ . *The Chattanooga Story*. Chattanooga: News-Free Press, 1980.

Wilson, R.L. *Building Stones*. 1979.

# Acknowledgments

In ancient times Clio, the muse of history, lent her assistance to those who properly petitioned. It is said that Homer, among many others, requested aid from Clio and her sister goddesses, for they knew everything and Man did not. In the preparation of this volume the author humbly sought the blessing of the same Clio; he also requests the forgiveness of fellow mortals who may find this narrative rambling and its omissions annoying.

Throughout the research and writing, I have leaned heavily on others. Simple acknowledgment of this debt seems woefully inadequate. To the officers and members of the Chattanooga Area Historical Association I must first say thanks for their aid and continuing encouragement. Among this company I wish to express special gratitude to John Popham, Spencer McCallie, Joan Franks, Albert Bowman, Elizabeth Wade, and Moira Tingle. Secondly, I wish to acknowledge the splendid, efficient, and professional service rendered by the staff of the Historical Division of the Chattanooga Hamilton County Bicentennial Library, with special kudos to Clara Swann. Most helpful, also, has been the professional staff associated with the Chickamauga Chattanooga National Military Park: Ann Belkov, superintendent, and historians Edward Tinney and Woody Harrell.

In the quest for pictures numerous organizations have been very helpful: the Chattanooga Convention and Visitors Bureau, the Tennessee Valley Authority, the Greater Chattanooga Chamber of Commerce, the Chattanooga Hamilton County Bicentennial Library, which provided a great many of the illustrations in this book (CHCBL), the University of Tennessee Press, the National Archives, the Library of Congress, the Chattanooga Hamilton County Regional Planning Commission, the Woolaroc Museum of Bartlesville, Oklahoma, the Department of the Army, Nashville District of the Corps of Engineers, the Thomas Gilcrease Institute of American History and Art, Tulsa, Oklahoma.

Individuals who have contributed to the undertaking or who have lent their special talents include: Victor P. Hood, Kay Gaston, Michael Crawford, Dorothy Brammer, Terry C. Henson, Robert Elmore, John Payne, Joseph Jackson, James Hunt, David Brown, Charles H. Coolidge, Roy Noel, and Willy King.

James A. Ward, Professor of History, UTC, researched and wrote the business biographies for the section entitled "Partners in Progress," which makes a very significant contribution to the local story.

Members of the editorial staff of Windsor Publications who assisted in compiling this volume include Barbara Marinacci, editor-in-chief; Judith Zauner, picture editor; Phyllis Rifkin, copy editor; Katherine Cooper, editorial coordinator; Karen Story, editor, business biographies; and Angelika Muller, director, business biographies.

To Alma L. Livingood, who typed, edited, proofread, and lived through the time-consuming business of research and writing, I give very special thanks.

James W. Livingood

THIS BOOK WAS SET IN
LUBALIN AND TIMES ROMAN TYPES,
PRINTED ON
70 LB. WARRENFLO
AND BOUND BY
WALSWORTH PUBLISHING COMPANY.
COVER AND TEXT DESIGNED BY
ALEX D'ANCA
LAYOUT BY
PATRICIA BRUCE